GOD'S HEALTH PLAN –
THE AUDACIOUS JOURNEY TO A BETTER LIFE

A Principle Approach® Study of Food, Health Care, and Environmental Issues

Ricki Pepin

God's Health Plan – The Audacious Journey to a Better Life
by Ricki Pepin

Printed in the United States of America

ISBN 978-1-60266-698-6

www.xulonpress.com

DISCLAIMER

This book is not intended to take the place of medical advice and treatment from your personal physician. Readers are advised to consult their own doctor or other qualified health professional regarding the treatment of their medical problems. Before beginning any new dietary supplementation program, always inform your personal physician, understanding that they may or may not have training in the nutritional needs of your body. It's your health; it's your choice; choose wisely. Neither the publisher nor the author takes any responsibility for any possible consequences from any treatment, action, or application of medicine, supplement, vitamin, mineral, essential oil, or herbal preparation to any person reading or following the information in this book.

ENDORSEMENTS

"*God's Health Plan – The Audacious Journey to a Better Life* is a compelling study of biblical principles which under-gird good stewardship of our minds and bodies. Ricki Pepin provides a basis to evaluate the conflicting voices clamoring for our attention and money in the world today. Those of us who 'think we eat pretty good' will be challenged to look again at what we allow in our minds as well as what we put in our mouths. Read this book because you love yourself and want to live to the fullest and die healthy."

Dr. Chester Kylstra and Betsy Kylstra
Founders of Restoring the Foundations Ministry

****

"… I was extremely impressed with the breadth of your study and the biblical basis upon which you have presented your ideas. This book would be a valuable reference to anyone who wants to understand God's principles of health. I trust that you will receive a wide hearing for it."

Bill Gothard, President
Institute in Basic Life Principles

****

"This book candidly reveals a simple but healthful dietary fact: if God made it, it's healthy; if not, it's suspect. In this book you will learn to better understand your God-designed body and how to care for it."

William Sears, M.D. (widely known as "America's Pediatrician")
Author of *The Healthiest Kid in the Neighborhood* and 30 other books
Guest on television shows such as *Oprah, Good Morning America*
Regular monthly columns in *Baby Talk* and *Parenting*

****

"Engaging. Fascinating. Convicting. Ricki has done an incredible study into Bible truth regarding God's plan for health. Through solid biblical research and clinical studies, she has debunked the 'mystery' of modern illness and urges us to return to God's design for health-filled lives. It is a design that is unfortunately at odds with popular culture, including many in the church. As a lone Christian in the world of alternative medicine for a long time, I wish this book had been available twenty years ago. First, to hand out to my unsaved colleagues and, secondly, to give to Christians who saw me as a heretic."

Janel Messenger, N.D.
Naturopathic Doctor and Principle Approach Homeschooler

****

"The Word of God – the Bread of Life – speaks to and sustains every big and minuscule aspect of created life. In the Christian search for wholeness and health, the first access must needs be the Word of God. In *God's Health Plan – The Audacious Journey to a Better Life,* Ricki Pepin takes on the all-encompassing subject of the human habitat and allows the Scripture to speak. In a friendly, upbeat spirit, the troublesome habits and areas of omission or commission in our daily regimens become opportunities for increasing the quality of our service before the Lord and the joy of life. Ricki has taken complex and often contradictory ideas and made them simple and even appealing. It's a great starting place on the road to abundant living!"

Carole Adams, President
Foundation for American Christian Education
www.face.net www.principleapproach.org
757-488-6601

****

"Ricki Pepin has done an outstanding job in *God's Health Plan*. It is a thorough and organized presentation that held my attention throughout. I especially appreciated the links provided between good health and sound biblical principles. There is so much information available in the health industry that it is often hard to decipher what is true and what is mere hype. This book makes it much easier to discern the real truth.

"The foundations developed in Part One laid the groundwork for the logical conclusion of the overall thesis that 'good health is not an accident' but is God's intended provision for His creation. I feel her material is balanced in the presentation of competing views of how to attain and maintain vitality, and yet clear on the importance of understanding and applying biblical principles of good health. Mention of the value of specific foods for maintaining well being was both useful and enlightening and an excellent reference for future use.

"Finally, I am impressed with the 'how to' nature of the book. I discovered many new principles of good health that can easily be put into practice. I truly enjoyed this book and I offer it my highest endorsement."

Rev. Dr. James L. Van Zile

****

"Ricki Pepin has done a service to the body of Christ by providing a comprehensive manual for addressing the health crisis among evangelical believers. The Bible declares that our body is the temple of the Holy Spirit and we must not do anything to harm it. However, we often live as if divine health were a mystical answer to a faith-filled prayer that has nothing to do with the stewardship of our diet or our attitudes toward one another. The truth of the matter is that we are reaping what we have sown, and the physical state of today's believer reveals much of what is going on in our hearts. I urge believers, parents, young people, and pastors to study her research and consider her conclusions."

Dr. Paul Jehle, author, historian, and pastor
Plymouth, Massachusetts

****

"A very balanced and comprehensive approach to health and nutrition from a biblical perspective; written with a conversational approach that I find refreshing."

Janet Roberto, M.D., Family Physician

****

"I thoroughly enjoyed reading this book, and I must confess it has made me think even more about my eating habits. I can happily endorse your book with the following statement:

"In *God's Health Plan*, Ricki Pepin weaves a tapestry of spirit, Scripture, and science. She has created an interesting, informative, and easy to understand book highlighting the connection of our spiritual and physical being. The Holy Bible is her main reference, but there are many others. There is a plethora of websites that are of great interest as well as many references in other books. All of this is the result of her journey dealing with a major health problem in her family. Her thoughtful approach will be controversial in some areas, but I recommend this book to anyone who is interested in seeking and applying biblical principles to what we eat and the world in which we live."

Fred E. Aurbach, DDS, FAGD, FACD, FICD

ACKNOWLEDGMENTS

I would like to express my heartfelt gratitude to my family and friends for accompanying me on this journey—in search of health—with very little complaint. During the time of radically changing our diets, they rarely complained about the "new" foods put before them (except for the "Tapioca Meatloaf"....ugh).

To my dear husband, Michael, who continually financed and endured all of my learning experiences (aka failures), and never rebuked me for my foolishness, but continued trusting my judgment as I moved to the next trial: You were then and still are the love of my life, and I am so grateful for your companionship, patience, and love. Life's trials nearly split us apart, but God's mercy and love held us together instead. I am so glad. I couldn't imagine life without you.

A second "thank you" to Michael and also to Dorothy Slaga, a dear friend and sister in the Lord, both of whom spent many, many hours poring over these pages and giving their suggestions. Their wisdom and insights were priceless and very appreciated and needed.

To my daughter, Jenny, who received much less attention than she deserved, due to a sick sibling who often was at the forefront of my focus: Thank you for being the one who so often "put things back together" and made life a little easier for all of us. I love you bunches and am enormously thankful for the relationship we are building today, now that you are a grown, mature woman.

To my son, David, my "guinea pig" in so many trials and experiments as we searched for the answer to your mysterious, ongoing, and ever worsening illnesses: I cannot recall (and hope you can't either) how many different medical tests you endured, herbal and vitamin supplements you swallowed, natural tonics you drank, and "alternative" methods of treatment you withstood. (I believe the "ear candle" probably ranks near the top of the "You want me to do what!?!?" list.): You have my greatest love, respect, and gratitude for bearing up under twelve years of trials and tribulations, with very little protest, until we found the solution!

Finally, the largest part of my gratitude goes to my Lord and Savior, Jesus Christ. He promises to never leave or forsake us (Hebrews 13:5), and I experienced His amazing and comforting presence amidst the battles of continual sickness through to the victory of health. The trials we endure are most often a future vehicle we are to use to bless others when we come out the other end in triumph. That is the true purpose of this book. I pray that you, the reader, will be truly blessed as you begin (or continue) your own re-education process about your personal health and diet using God's Word as your primary source. But even more, I pray that this discovery will deepen or perhaps introduce you to a personal relationship with the sovereign God of the universe, who cares about every aspect of your life, including what you eat.

TABLE OF CONTENTS

PART ONE

RE-ESTABLISHING THE FOUNDATION

Psalm 11:3 – If the foundations be destroyed, what can the righteous do?

Chapter 1

From Desperation to Inspiration

A Mother's Cry for Help

David lay sick in bed again. His joints ached painfully, his head throbbed, his breathing was difficult. Any movement was agony. He had spent the last twelve of his nineteen years in varying degrees of this condition. At age seven the symptoms had begun and shortly thereafter the long odyssey of trip after trip to the doctor, test after test at laboratories, all searching for a diagnosis and cure. All to no avail.

Doctors wrote prescriptions and David took them. Antibiotics helped for a couple of weeks only to have the same aches and pains return with a little more severity each time. Over the years stronger and stronger antibiotics had to be used as his body built up a resistance to each of the previous ones. When antibiotics were no longer of any effect the physicians switched to steroids. Same result: seemingly well for two to three weeks, but then the inevitable return of the same hurts slowly escalating until "normal" life of school, friends, and play ended and his bed became a poor replacement for his daily routine.

At age 19, David was 6 feet tall and weighed only 118 pounds. He was pale and gaunt and I could see the pain in his eyes on a daily basis. My own health began failing through these years as we searched for an answer to David's dilemma, and now I needed answers for mine as well. We had exhausted every test and pill the allopathic medical world had to offer, and no relief was in sight.

My heart was broken as I realized David had no positive future for education, work, marriage, and family. He couldn't complete a semester of college before he would be flat on his back again, unable to take the finals. What hope did he have of being successful in life or starting and supporting a family of his own?

End of the line. Bottom of the pit. No open doors. These were the phrases that filled my mind as I cried out to God in desperation, *"Where do we go from here, Lord? How can I help my son?"* The answer came, unwittingly, from a new acquaintance who phoned as I was drowning in these hopeless thoughts of a hopeless future. Her words opened an entirely new world to me that propelled me into eight years of research, study, and application. Within the first two months David had a new life and was well on the road to health. Today, he is healthy and strong, has a wonderful wife and two daughters, and works hard at a great job to support them. Life is good!

As I shared this wonderful story of restoration I was occasionally asked to lecture on the principles I had learned. After each lecture I was further asked if I had written these principles down so they could read the book and learn them for themselves. I was hearing the heart-cry of others who wanted and needed to study and learn what I had learned about food, health, and environment. This book was "born."

Looking for Health in all the Wrong Places?

Who holds the key to your health? You do! After twelve years of praying, searching, and crying out for answers, I learned that I had the key the whole time. The key was not the doctor. The key was not the latest prescription. The key was not the latest book published on health. The key was God and His Word and finding His health plan for my life and my family's life within those pages.

And yet, while the key was God's Word, opening it was like stepping into a gold mine. Even though I was entering the richest gold mine in the universe, few nuggets were lying openly on the floor waiting to be picked up. The riches were located in the many tunnels within the mine and more often than not buried deeply within the walls of those tunnels. How could I get at them? How could I even know where to start digging?

I didn't need another book or another expert on health. The "experts" contradict one another. One declares the benefits of butter, the next says to never touch it. One book says eggs are the perfect protein, while another says to avoid them because of their cholesterol content. What makes one author's opinion more valuable or accurate than another's? In the ageless question of a frustrated Pilate asking Jesus "What is truth?" I needed a way to find the answers to my personal health challenges – physical, but also spiritual and emotional.

The Principle Approach® to education provided the answer for me and is the key for anyone willing to seriously use this method to search out their solutions.[1] But be prepared to have your presuppositions challenged and your thinking altered about some of the most basic principles. What is health? What is sickness? What is food? What isn't food? These may seem like simple or even foolish questions, but searching out the surprising answers through the Principle Approach® proved to be the building blocks that restored my health and my son's.

In my life as a military wife, I have been exposed to many different environments, people, and situations. We have lived in rural areas and suburban areas, from Southern California to northern Massachusetts, in the Heartland, the South, and three times near our nation's capital, Washington, D.C. I have been exposed to and personally involved in all kinds of education—the government/public school system, the private and Christian school system, and even spent four years home educating my children.

It was during the four years of home education that I first encountered the Principle Approach®, the method of education used by our Founding Fathers which teaches the learner *how* to think, not *what* to think. Modern education is made up of "facts" (or authors' opinions) poured into students' heads for memorization and later regurgitation on tests. These facts are usually forgotten soon after as the student had no mental "investment" in the learning or investigative process. This is the bleak result of being told *what to think*.

In the case of health, the "facts" (*what to think*) from one book often contradict the "facts" in the next, plunging the reader into deeper confusion, and perhaps even causing them to give up the idea of reforming their lifestyle habits, since no one can agree on what is really good or bad for you anyway! Using the Principle Approach® helps individuals to search out truth for themselves, learning *how to think* and reason logically for themselves, based not upon different authors' opinions, but upon a solid foundation of truths from God's Word that they must personally study.

In the Principle Approach® the Bible is a resource book, indeed the *foundation*, for every subject studied, including health. Individuals using this method learn how to measure and evaluate everything that is presented to them through God's Word. Leading ideas and questions, word studies, and seven foundational principles are also used. *The American Dictionary of the_English Language*, more commonly known as "Noah Webster's 1828 Dictionary,"[2] is the dictionary of choice for this study.

THE PRINCIPLE APPROACH®

Noah Webster's 1828 Dictionary

While the Bible was my primary and premier text in research, the second resource book I used was *Webster's 1828 Dictionary*, a totally unique reference work of great worth for any in-depth study. Noah Webster, one of our Founding Fathers and a master of twenty-seven languages, dedicated years of his life to compiling the first *American* dictionary. Webster also held very strong Christian convictions, and wherever possible or applicable he used biblical applications, verses, or principles in his definitions.

Noah's mastery of language and strong Christian underpinnings are two main purposes for using this specific dictionary over a newer one. But there is a third even stronger reason. As many are aware, there is a movement in the field of education today to rewrite history, what is known as "revisionist history." But as far fewer are aware, "revisionist dictionaries" have also been written. There's an old saying: "He who defines the terms wins the debate." In other words, if you can rewrite the meaning of words, you can declare that black is white and not be proved wrong. Modern "educrats" (combination of educators and bureaucrats) have rewritten many key definitions, replacing God's immutable standard of truth with relativistic, wavering humanistic standards. Allow me to give you two definition examples to illustrate the magnitude and consequences of such revisionism:

Right - conformity to standards or prevailing conditions - *Harcourt Brace Intermediate Dictionary* (New York: Harcourt, Brace & World, 1968), 631

In this modern definition, "standards and prevailing conditions" are the measurement of right and wrong. Since standards and prevailing conditions are constantly changing, there can be no absolute measurement of what is right. For example, today abortion would be "right" since the Supreme Court has ruled it to be legal in its infamous *Roe v. Wade* decision.

Now let's look at *Webster's 1828 Dictionary* and see what he had to say:

Right - according to the will of God - *Webster's 1828*

According to Webster, "right" does not change with man's prevailing and fluctuating standards, but rather is determined by an absolute, immutable God. Let's look at one other:

Truth - a theory that is accepted as fact – Harcourt, Brace, 796

This is a very subjective definition as theories constantly change, which would mean that *truth changes as theories change*. Evolution is an accepted theory by some scientists, so it must be truth. Therefore, you not only came from a monkey but pond scum somewhere before that. But wait! I believe in the theory of creationism, as do many others. Therefore, that must also be truth. This brings about an even bigger problem: *There is no absolute truth. Truth is whatever anyone believes.* (Are you confused yet?) Let's see what Webster's 1828 says about truth:

Truth - conformity to fact or reality; exact accordance with that which is, or has been or shall be. Jesus Christ is called the truth. - *Webster's 1828*

My confusion just left. This dictionary "takes no prisoners." It speaks *truth* with no apologies. These two words that I have chosen – right and truth - are but two examples of many other revisions (re-definitions) such as sin, marriage, Satan, and God, all of which have been rewritten to develop a secular, value-free worldview in the one using it. A recent Barna poll found that, among Christians, only 9 percent expressed a belief in absolute truth.[3] You can now better understand why there is so much confusion in many areas today, including health and nutrition. When we stop using the Bible and an *accurate* dictionary to learn, we fall prey to the lie that there is no absolute truth to be learned.

The Four R's

The process of the Principle Approach® is known as the "Four R's: Research - Reason – Relate – Record."

Research begins in God's Word to identify basic principles which govern the "what and how" of life and living. Definitions from *Webster's 1828 Dictionary* play a key role here as well.

Reasoning then assists the learner in identifying these principles as they specifically relate to food, health, and environment, areas few of us have used the Bible for studying in the past. Here is where you can truly begin to understand not only what you should and should not eat, but *why*.

Relating is the process by which we see these principles as they would apply to us in forming our own Christian character, self-government, or stewardship of God's gifts to us. Now that I know the truth, what will I eat and drink? Will I exercise and develop healthy habits? How and what will I teach my children?

Recording is the actual writing—in a personal journal, letter to a friend, letter to the editor, etc.—of the principles and noting the way they are being applied to your life and living. This final step truly makes the material you have learned "yours"—you will remember it!—as you go through the exercise of putting the principles and your thoughts into your own words on paper.

The Seven Principles

There are dozens of principles that can be found throughout Scripture, but this adaptation of the Principle Approach® focuses on seven:

1. God's Sovereignty – *"supreme power; the possession of the highest power. Absolute sovereignty belongs to God only"* *(Webster's 1828)*. God is God. Not the State, not a king, not a man, not self, only God is God. He is the sovereign ruler of the universe and there is none other. Our allegiance and obedience are always due to God first, including what we eat and the care of our body. Only when the principle of sovereignty is firmly established can we move to the other six principles.

2. Individuality – *"separate or distinct existence; a state of oneness" (Webster's 1828)*. Just as there is only one God, there is only one *you*. God created you as a totally unique, different, and distinct individual with certain attributes, characteristics, talents, and purposes that belong to you *alone*. God has a destiny in mind for every person He creates, and there is no one else in the universe who has ever existed who can do what God has planned for you to do, and there will never be another individual who will exist that has been given your attributes, characteristics, and talents, or who can perform the job God has purposed for you to perform. You matter and your health matters to God!

3. Government – *"control, regulate or restrain" (Webster's 1828)*. This principle is incredibly broad in scope, beginning internally with the individual in the form of *self*-government, then moving outward to *family* government, *church* government, and finally to *civil* government. The main thrust of this book will be on *self*-government since we are talking about personal health choices. However, there will be places in this text where civil government's involvement is seen to *hinder*

our self-government in food and medical choices (Food & Drug Administration, American Medical Association, etc. Details later).

4. Property (Stewardship) – *"the exclusive right of possession, enjoying and disposition of a thing; ownership. In the beginning of the world, the Creator gave to man dominion over the earth (Genesis 1:26-30), and over every living thing. This is the foundation of man's property in the earth and in all its productions" (Webster's 1828).* We all own property, for each individual has a property in himself, in his unalienable rights and his conscience. James Madison said, "Conscience is our most sacred property." Your body belongs to God but was given to you by God, who expects you to exercise good stewardship over it so you can perform the destiny He planned for you.

5. Christian Character – *"a mark made by cutting or engraving, stamping or impressing. The peculiar qualities, impressed by nature or habit on a person, which distinguish him from others" (Webster's 1828).* A person's character is formed over time through proper education and experience, and it determines all their thoughts, words, and actions. Character should be the first concern of education, *even before scholarship*, which is why it is so important that parents be the primary teachers of their own children. Genius without character will still make wrong choices. If you don't control your habits, your habits will control you. Good character comes as a result of right thinking.

6. Sowing and Reaping (Education) – *"Sow – to spread, to originate, to propagate. Reap – to obtain the fruit of labor or works in a good or bad sense" (Webster's 1828).* This principle is evident and simple as it relates to health. Think, live, and eat right – reap "ease." Think, live, and eat wrong – reap "dis"-ease. Whatever crop we reap is a reflection of the seed we sowed. Education is needed to learn what to plant (sow) and what not to plant. Education - *"all that series of instruction and discipline intended to enlighten understanding, correct the temper and form the manners and habits of youth, and fit them*

for usefulness in their future stations" (Webster's 1828).

7. Unity and Union – "*Unity – the state of being one; oneness. Union – concord, agreement of mind, will, affections and interests" (Webster's 1828).* An internal unity of ideas brings about external union of actions. As we internally learn through our own search of principles in Scripture, and then agree with God's principles of health, we enter into the blessings of the union of our mind, will, affections, and interests with His. Within this blessing is the power to *do* what is right.

You can now see why I have chosen to use the Bible, *Webster's 1828 Dictionary,* and the Principle Approach® method in this study on food, health, and environment. God has a lot to say about these subjects, and who could possibly better instruct us on how to feed and care for our bodies than the One who created them? Any study that is started on any foundation apart from scriptural truth is built on shifting sand, and my desire is for you to *build your own* nutritional understanding on the solid Rock.

Additional Disclaimer

I make no claims to be an accredited expert on the subject of health. I am not qualified to give medical advice and want no part of this teaching to be so construed. Severe personal and family health problems literally catapulted me into a search where I logged hundreds (thousands?) of hours of study and experimentation. This book is the culmination of that study, and it has received enthusiastic endorsements from several health care professionals, educators, and pastors.

This book is presented to the reader as a *study* on health, where the foundational principles will be laid down, and some of them spelled out. The specific applications, however, are up to the individual reader. While there is one source of truth, the application of that truth is as varied as individuals' unique needs (an illustration of the principle of individuality!). I have taken this time to explain the basis of this book (Bible, principles, and original, accurate definitions) because its purpose is to give you a foundation from which *you* can begin your own personal study on your own personal health concerns. You don't need my opinion on what to eat and how to care for your family; you need truth. I hope to arm you with enough basic information to excite, stimulate, and motivate you to further study and to make lifestyle and dietary changes that will put you on a path to better health, higher energy, and longer life – to help you fulfill your individual, God-ordained destiny and to do it with vigor and victory, health and wellness.

My best attempts were made with any other materials I have used as secondary sources in this study to be certain they lined up with biblical principles before accepting their content. However, I am a "work in progress" and am still learning to discern. I reserve the right to amend any statements contained within this text as new revelation or understanding comes my way. *My word is not the last word*. Pray and reason through as you read.

May God richly bless you in your search, keep your mind clear and your heart pure, and strengthen your convictions and your health as you begin to apply what you learn!

END NOTES

1. The Foundation for American Christian Education (F.A.C.E.) is the organization responsible for resurrecting the Principle Approach® to education, the method used by our Founding Fathers that resulted in a 95% literacy rate during the founding era – the highest ever known! This method of education emphasizes Providential History, Christian scholarship and *character* formation. The superior scholarship is evidenced by SAT scores averaging 20% higher than all other Christian or public schools. Providential History teaching brings about an understanding of our limited, Constitutional form of government. Character training forges young people who will become involved in their churches *and* government to the betterment of both. *I highly recommend everyone investigate this organization and see what part you could play in spreading this Godly method of teaching and learning.* (800-352-3223 or www.face.net)

2. The <u>American Dictionary of the English Language</u> (Webster's 1828 Dictionary) has been reprinted by F.A.C.E. It is possibly one of the most important reprints of the 20th century and can be purchased through them, for those who would like to add it to their home libraries. Call 800-352-3223 or 757-488-6601 for information. (Be sure to ask about group discounts!)
3. Del Tackett, "What's in a Worldview Anyway?" *Focus on the Family*, July/August 2004, p. 7-8

Chapter 2

God's Most Precious Jewel

In 1999, when my daughter became engaged to be married, memories flooded back to me as she excitedly showed us her beautiful, shimmering diamond ring. The most precious jewel I ever owned was the diamond ring my husband-to-be gave me more than thirty years ago, upon our engagement. It was truly a precious jewel and my special treasure. My future husband, Michael, had to work hard and save long to be able to buy that diamond for me. I had never owned anything so valuable and did all I could to keep it beautiful, carefully following the special instructions given by the jeweler for its care and upkeep. I was to take it off when I showered to avoid soap scum, take it off when I put on hand lotion to avert grease that would cloud its luster. I was never to actually touch the diamond, because the oil from my hands would also dull it. There was a special cleaner to soak it in weekly to revive its sparkle. And if there was ever a really dirty job to do, off came the ring until the job was done and the hands washed.

In the months prior to the wedding, and for the first year or two after, I was careful to follow all the instructions the jeweler provided. But over the course of time, the details of life overshadowed the care of my precious jewel—working, starting a new household, having babies, PTA meetings—and I began to forget to take it off every time I showered. I rationalized that hand lotion would come off the next time I washed my hands, so it wasn't really that important to take it off. When the special cleaner was gone, I didn't order anymore.

Ten years went by. One day, while weeding my flowerbeds, I realized I had forgotten to remove my ring. It seemed a waste of precious time to take off my muddy shoes, go into the house, take off my ring, and put it on the jewelry box, then put back on the muddy shoes, etc. Time was precious, after all, and I could save several minutes by just keeping the ring on my finger, and the dirt would wash off later. So I continued the task of weeding. But as I worked, I noticed that my hands were getting exceptionally grubby, and so was my diamond. Feeling remotely guilty about not caring for it like I should, I slipped it off and put it on the edge of the porch so I wouldn't get anymore mud on it. I reasoned that it would be safe there, as our back yard was fenced and nobody but me was there.

An hour or so later, I heard the kids come home from school, so I stopped weeding and got up to go inside, stopping by the porch on the way to pick up my ring. It wasn't there. The only other living creature in the yard with me was our dog, Gypsy, who sat there smiling and wagging her tail at me. Horrified, I could only assume she had either buried or eaten my diamond! Gypsy was a "Beagadore" (half Beagle and half Labrador) who had a reputation for eating or carrying off anything and everything she could wrap her mouth around. In one careless moment, and one lazy decision, my precious jewel was gone. There was no way to recover it.

But what about God? What does He value most? He is the Creator of all things, from majestic mountains to minuscule molecules, from dirt to precious gems and jewels. In man's eyes, some of the more valuable treasures of God's creation would surely be the jewels and precious stones mentioned in Revelation 21:19-21 as the materials making up the walls and foundations of the New Jerusalem: jasper, sapphire, chalcedony, emerald, sardonyx, sardius, chrysolite, beryl, topaz, chrysoprase, jacinth, and amethyst. The Bible also speaks of pearls of great price. Solomon possessed literally tons of pure gold, much of which was used in building the temple and its implements. Wow! What a place! Who could begin to put a dollar amount on that magnificent edifice and its furnishings! But which is the most precious treasure to God? Which does He consider to be of the greatest value?

In Exodus 19:5, God is speaking to all the Israelites after He has miraculously saved them from the Egyptians by parting the Red Sea so they could walk through the middle unharmed, and then bringing it back together to kill the Egyptian soldiers when they tried to pass through. This is one of the greatest demonstrations of God's power and love for His people in the entire Old Testament. Now, as they stand safe on the other side, He is speaking to them and says,

> Now, therefore, if you will indeed obey My voice and keep My covenant, then you shall be a **special treasure** to Me above all people; for all the earth is mine.
>
> Exodus 19:5 NKJV

Strong's Concordance says this phrase – special treasure - means "precious jewel." God considers His people—you—to be His most precious jewel. Amazing. The Bible says your body was created by God, in His image and likeness; that you are fearfully and wonderfully made...a precious jewel. So how are you taking care of God's most precious jewel?

Much like the jeweler who sold the beautiful diamond ring to my future husband, and provided instructions for its care, God has given us an "instruction manual" for how we are to care for His most precious jewel. The Bible is full of God's commandments, statutes, and ordinances (instructions). Some tell us how we are to worship Him. Others emphasize the importance of aligning our thoughts with His. Still more are civil laws regarding murder, theft, assault, and other crimes. But tucked away in these many ordinances are also specific health instructions regarding relationships, cleanliness, and diet, some specifically stating what we are to eat and not eat. As the perfect Father, God's instructions in every area, including nutrition, are always for our good, *to bring us health and life*. Let's see how we're doing:

According to a 1998 study by the National Center for Health Statistics, heart disease was responsible for 50 percent of disease-related deaths and cancer takes another 33 percent. These numbers indicate more than *four out of five* people who die from disease are killed by one of these two maladies! This means entire families are dying from these diseases! But even more shocking is the fact that both of these diseases are *diet and lifestyle related!* We are not dying from contagious diseases. Germs are no longer our biggest enemy in fighting disease. We are. We are killing ourselves with our attitudes and forks! (Or at least what we are putting on our forks!)

God's precious jewels are disappearing at an alarming rate. We are not caring for them properly. We are not following the instructions He has given us so carefully and precisely.

My people are destroyed for lack of knowledge.

Hosea 4:6 NKJV

One of *Strong's* definitions for the word *destroyed* is "to die needlessly." God says, "My people are *dying needlessly* for a lack of knowledge." Surely, one way of dying needlessly is when our eating brings about death rather than life. Let's dig a little deeper: *Webster's 1828 Dictionary* defines:

Knowledge – a clear and certain perception of truth

Science has shown the irrefutable relationship between diet and disease. Statistics (to be cited later) consistently show that more than 80 percent of us are dying from diet-related diseases.[1] We are killing ourselves with our forks! If this is true, surely we must lack a "clear and certain perception of truth" about what to eat and what not to eat. This lack of knowledge is at least in part due to all the contradictory information presented to us about food through television, print media, and the Internet. We are either too confused to understand how to feed ourselves properly or too stubborn and rebellious to practice what we have learned. It is my hope that this book will address both of these concerns: to align our thinking with God's thinking by teaching those who are confused the basic principles of diet and health maintenance, and to motivate both groups to obey God's revealed dietary and health principles.

Let's begin!

END NOTES

1. Though the main thrust of this book is health through proper
    nutrition and lifestyle habits, my studies have led me also
    to the inescapable connection between incurable or debili-
    tating diseases and unresolved spiritual issues. The spiritual
    aspect of healing is far too often overlooked and deserves
    our serious attention. This will be covered in more detail in
    Chapters 6 and 14. In addition, I *strongly recommend* two
    resources in this regard:

The first is Henry W. Wright's book, A More Excellent Way –
Be In Health – Spiritual Roots of Disease – Pathways to Wholeness.
Henry Wright's understanding of this subject is deep and profoundly
life-changing. Call 800-453-5775 or go to www.pleasantvalley-
church.net for more information. This teaching is mainly group-
centered with some individual ministry time.

A similar ministry of Chester and Betsy Kylstra, known as
Restoring the Foundations, incorporates an individualized program
with follow-up, personal ministry sessions, all searching for the
root of emotional and spiritual hindrances to our health and healing.
They have written an accompanying book entitled, An Integrated
Approach to Biblical Healing Ministry. They can be reached at 888-
324-6466 or online and www.rtftrainingcenter.org.

PART TWO

HISTORY AND DEFINITIONS

Exodus 15:25-26 – God made a statute and an ordinance for them. "If you diligently heed the voice of the Lord your God and do what is right in His sight, give ear to His commandments and keep all His statutes, I will put none of the diseases on you which I have brought on the Egyptians. For I am the Lord who heals you."

Chapter 3

Does What We Eat Really Matter to God?

There are many who would question taking the time to do a lengthy Bible study on food, or what we are to eat every day. After all, does what we eat really matter to God? Time is precious and there are other issues, especially for Christians, of much more significance that need our attention. It is true that the *most* important message the church has to offer is that of salvation: that *everyone has sinned* [see Romans 3:23], *that the wages for that sin is death/ separation from God* [Romans 6:23], *but God sent his son, Jesus, to save everyone who confesses their sin and believes in Him* [John 3:16 and Romans 10:9-10]. But once we are saved, most of us will be around a long time before we leave this earth, and our biggest job then becomes transforming our thinking to God's way of thinking and finding our God-ordained destiny. This is one of the biggest reasons we should read and study the B.I.B.L.E. (Basic Instructions Before Leaving Earth) every day and for every subject – to find God's plan for our lives.

God created each of us in His image and likeness.
The principle of individuality is illustrated by the fact that
He also has a unique plan, a destiny, for each and every
one of us on this earth, in this life.

We are all *individuals,* called to do specific jobs: evangelize, preach, teach, minister, serve in various capacities. And regardless of your calling and gifting from God, if you are sick to a large or small degree, the working out of your daily life or doing that which the Lord has called you to perform is anywhere from difficult to impossible. Time is not only priceless but an irreplaceable commodity. A day spent on a sickbed cannot be recovered, nor can the opportunities we miss because of it.

For several years I suffered from continual and severe migraine headaches, causing me to "lose" three to ten days every month. The pain was often so bad that I couldn't even sit up in bed or I would be sick to my stomach. Thus bedridden for up to ten days every month, I couldn't even concentrate to pray properly. If I was able to get up, I couldn't see straight enough to drive a car, cooking smells made me physically ill, movement of any type nauseated me, and bright light was like a sword piercing the side of my head. Needless to say, whatever was supposed to be done that day didn't get done. Whatever sickness you may be fighting, or have fought in the past, it probably slows you down or stops you from your daily, God-ordained mission.

The connection between disease and diet is not even arguable today among the scientific community, including physicians. Cooperation between traditional MDs and practitioners of "alternative" or "complementary" medicine is growing, and one of the most promising aspects of this new *detente* has been the stimulation of interest in nutrition. Dr. Isadore Rosenfeld, member of The Practicing Physicians Advisory Council for the Secretary of Health and Human Services, said in a recent interview, "Almost every medical condition is either caused by or affected in some way by what we eat." [1]

Based upon this understanding of the health/diet connection, I readily declare that the issue of health and nutrition is, therefore, second only to salvation, because no one can operate fully in the gift God has given them or in the calling God has placed on them when they are sick. This includes *spiritual and mental health – right thinking!*

Food has been a "hot button" with God and His people from the beginning. As you read this quote, ponder each point carefully:

There is much confusion in many believers' minds about the relationship of body and spirit. Few people recognize that the problem of *eating better is an issue of spiritual warfare* [emphasis mine]. Here are some reasons why we know this to be true. Physical food was God's first gift to mankind. He involved food's use in His test of man's obedience. Satan used food as an enticement for man's rebellion against Him. The Israelites' rebellion against God in the wilderness concerned food. Jesus' first temptation by the devil in the wilderness was a food temptation. The first contention that arose in the early church was over a matter of food distribution. The expression of the most important spiritual truth in all time – that Jesus Christ died on the cross for sins – is represented by the food symbols of bread and wine, established by Jesus Christ Himself.[2]

Today, wrong thinking, wrong eating, and wrong lifestyle habits bring about degenerative diseases. Those which are the most disabling and even cause premature death manifest as we grow older. As Christians age, we are supposed to be maturing in Christ - growing in wisdom, not in sickness. In Titus chapter 2, God underscores the importance of the older generation giving godly instruction to the younger generation, telling the older women to teach the younger women, and the older men to give wise counsel to the younger men. Assisting the pastor, the middle-aged and senior Christians are expected to be supplemental contributors to the spiritual growth and development of the church.

From Scripture as well as other ancient manuscripts, we can ascertain that God intended for man to live beyond 100 years. Old writings containing the last wills and testaments of Israel's 12 patriarchs (Reuben, Simeon, Levi, Judah, Issachar, Zebulun, Dan, Naphtali, Gad, Asher, Joseph, and Benjamin) give their dying ages from 110-137, and only 2 of the 12 were sick at the time. The other 10 were sound in health, lived to a good old age, and died in peace. God's intent is for all our years to be healthy and productive, including our time as senior citizens! The word *retirement* is not found in Scripture, and I personally believe our latter years were intended to be the most productive ones for Christ, not the ones spent in nursing homes and assisted living facilities because of ill health.

Today, degenerative diseases not only kill us off at younger and younger ages, but even if we manage to make it to maturity, we are variously disabled either in body or mind or both and cannot offer the godly guidance and/or physical assistance we are supposed to give to the younger generation. Mentoring and wisdom are desperately needed in the body of Christ, and bad thinking, bad eating, and bad lifestyle habits are robbing the church of these resources.

Health Is Part of the Salvation Message

The ultimate argument in the Bible supporting the importance of studying nutrition is its direct link to salvation. Salvation is an interesting word. It comes from the Greek word *sozo*. When you look it up in a Bible concordance you find that it has four meanings. The first meaning is, indeed, to be saved from our sins, but few Christians know that it also means to be healed, to be made whole (in body, mind, and spirit!), and to be delivered. Knowing this, however, brings up a very uncomfortable question: If our salvation includes being healed, made whole, and delivered, why is the church full of people who are sick, some with minor colds or viruses, and others with chronic, crippling, and even life-threatening, terminal diseases? Let's look in God's Word for answers.

There are many passages in Scripture where God makes promises or bold statements about the health and well-being of His people, especially in the Old Testament. For foundational purposes, you need to understand that if you are a born-again believer today, you are one of God's people just as surely as the Israelites were, and you can read and accept the promises in the Old Testament as literally and personally as the Israelites did. Let's look at a scriptural example of a promise regarding health. Listen to God speak to His people:

...I will put none of the diseases on you which I have brought
on the Egyptians....

Exodus 15:26 NKJV

What diseases did God bring on the Egyptians? Recent autopsies performed on hundreds of Egyptian mummies revealed they died from many of the diseases that plague us today – cancer, heart disease, stroke. Pick up any current periodical, and you will see that today's people (including Christians) are dying from cancer, heart attacks, and strokes. But this passage is clear! God said He would not put these diseases on us. Did God lie?

...God, who cannot lie...

Titus 1:2 NKJV

No. That rules out that possibility. God is the Truth. When He makes a promise, He keeps it. When He makes a statement, it is true. So what's going on here?

I believe the answer to this question of so much sickness in the church is many faceted. One aspect is that of sin entering the world, accompanied by the curse and all kinds of sickness and diseases. But this promise was given well *after* the curse began. So I believe this second aspect to be the much more likely answer: The major part of our sickness and disease is self-inflicted, sometimes by personal choices (which have both physical and spiritual consequences), and other times by the corporate fouling of our environment (air and water) and not taking proper dominion as instructed by God. *In other words: God did not put the diseases upon us; we put them upon ourselves!*

God has given us over 600 laws, statutes and commandments. Approximately one-third of these precepts have to do with health, nutrition, hygiene, sanitation and diet. These rules were provided to greatly enhance our well being, and help us to stay healthy, *if we learn them and live by them.*

The principle is sowing and reaping:
If we abide in God and by His dietary, health, lifestyle,

and environmental statutes, we will experience health.
If we don't abide, we will suffer the consequences
– ranging from a lack of well-being and poor health up to
and including degenerative diseases and premature death.

The Scriptures clearly teach how to deal with the spread of contagious diseases by isolation, how to bury excrement, the necessity of hand washing, and many other principles of health – all written down 3,500 years ago for everyone's benefit. Yet in the Middle Ages buckets of filth and contagious excrement were dumped into the streets from second-story windows. Fifteen hundred years after Christ, plagues ravished society and destroyed lives by the millions. Was this God's judgment being worked out? Was this the devil at work? I don't think so! Rather it was man reaping the direct results of his own ignorance, stubbornness, and rebellion.

Do not be deceived; God is not mocked, for whatever a man sows, that he will also reap.

Galatians 6:7 NKJV

The Exodus passage cited previously is a great example of this principle. It is a promise, but it is a *conditional* promise. To understand this promise in its proper context we have to look at the previous verse. Verse 25 indicates that God is actually setting before His people an *unchangeable law*, an ordinance or statute, not just a promise. Let's read it:

…[God] made a statute and an **ordinance** [law] for them……
If you diligently heed the voice of the Lord your God and do what is right in His sight, give ear to His commandments and keep all His statutes, **[then]** I will put none of the diseases on you which I have brought on the Egyptians. For I am the Lord who heals you.

Exodus 15:25-26 NKJV

Promises with Conditions

Some of God's promises come with conditions. Do you see it in the Exodus passage above? This is a *law with a conditional promise.* That is a promise with a provision, a statute and ordinance which must *first* be obeyed by us, and *then* we can receive the promise. We have God's promise that He will not put any of these diseases on us, but He does not promise to keep back the consequences – *disease and premature death -* if we disobey or disregard His statutes and ordinances. Health comes as we build a relationship with God and work with Him (*learn* and *obey* His Word) in accordance with His commandments and ordinances regarding thinking, diet, health, and cleanliness.

Let me give you an illustration (Jesus taught with parables, and I love them too): There's the story of Pastor Britton who was working in his garden one bright summer day, when along came a parishioner who commented, "My, my, Pastor, doesn't God make a nice garden?" To which the pastor replied, "Yes, He does, but you should have seen it before I got here."

The point is, God does His work, but we are expected to do ours as well. The seeds you plant in a garden will produce plants because God will make plants grow from those seeds. You can't make that happen. He does. But to a large measure you determine how healthy those plants will be based on how much weeding, watering, and fertilizing *you* do. The same principle applies to our health. God will do His part if we do *our* part. Our part, according to this Exodus passage, is to diligently heed the voice of God, do what is right in His sight, give ear to His commandments, and keep *all* His statutes.

But to keep all His commandments, statutes, and ordinances about health and diet, we first have to *know* them. As we begin to look at these laws, I want you to keep a primary principle about God's character in the front of your brain. God did not give us all these regulations because He is a control freak who likes to be in charge and boss everybody around, making rules about every little thing. God gave us His commandments because He's our loving Father, our Shield and Protector. He wants a relationship with you that a loving dad has with his children. He wants what is best for us, and He knows what will help us and what will hurt us.

The principle of God's sovereignty is wrapped around all of His character traits. One of these traits - His fatherly love – wants what is best for us in all things, including diet and lifestyle choices.

If we disregard any of God's laws, dietary included, we do so at our own peril. This is not legalism but common sense, for there are always negative consequences to any act of ignorance, rebellion, or disobedience. The consequences of eating what God says not to eat can range from a lack of well-being to overt sickness and even untimely death. Our weakened or compromised immune systems result in a weak gene pool, which can then be passed on to our children, making the consequences multi-generational. All of God's laws are placed in Scripture for our *good*. Which brings us to a fundamental dietary principle:

The principle is God's sovereignty.
Just because something tastes good does not mean God meant for us to eat it. God's Word is the final authority on food, not our taste buds!

My people are destroyed [die needlessly!] for a lack of knowledge.

Hosea 4:6 NKJV

When more than 90 percent of us in this nation are dying from diseases directly related to dietary choices (a listing and footnote of this statistic is located in chapter 3), we are truly dying needlessly. What a waste of life! What a tragedy not to fulfill the whole destiny God has planned for us, not finishing our life's course in victory, but rather succumbing to an early demise in large part because we are slaves to the fleshly desires of our taste buds! We truly must seek out and find the truth in God's Word about proper health and eating.

You shall know the truth, and the truth shall make you free.

John 8:32 NKJV

Only the truth you know can make you free. So the first step is to search out the Word for these dietary principles. Truth you don't know cannot make you free. But let's take that one step further: Just knowing the truth is not enough to make you free. You must also *apply* that truth to your life personally, and then you will be free indeed. Knowledge without application merely puffs up our ego or sends us into rebellion. ("I know that's not good for me, but I like it and I'm going to eat it anyway!") Application of knowledge, on the other hand, *changing your thinking to match God's thinking,* is almost always a humbling experience. It is hard work because it involves personal change and saying no to our flesh, sometimes to lifelong habits. But changing ourselves into compliance with God's standards is always a good change and will always carry a great reward.

Most adults already have knowledge that disease is often directly related to diet and lifestyle. But, strangely, their thinking does not connect that fact to their personal habits. We are much like the teenager who doesn't wear a seatbelt, drives too fast, or drinks and drives, but never thinks they could become the next statistic in vehicular deaths due to their own irresponsibility.

Similarly, when adults are asked about what they eat, most will tell you their diet is basically healthy. As you will learn in the coming chapters, God's plan was for us to be eating mainly roots and fruits, seeds and weeds, greens and beans. Don't panic! I'm not telling anyone they have to be a vegetarian. However, most of those claiming a "basically healthy diet" eat far too many meats and sweets, pies and fries, cakes and shakes, chips and dips. This reality is clearly reflected in a greater than 90 percent death rate from diet-related disease. These people who think they are eating "basically healthy" are only deceiving themselves. They are not only wrong, they will soon be *dead wrong.* I hope this 90 percent death-rate statistic will open your mind to change your thinking – to receive God's Word on food and also provide you with ample motivation to begin to make changes in your own diet. What you eat is, indeed, a matter of life and death.

God Doesn't Have to Tell Us "Why"

When God created the world, He created a masterpiece of beauty and design. But it was not merely beauty for beauty's sake. Everything has a purpose, a function, a job to do, a reason for being. And much if not all of it is governed by scientific, unchangeable laws. God is immutable, and His creation reflects His beauty and His immutability. Particularly when we examine God's creation of man, we are struck by His attention to details and His care and love for us. God gives many, many commandments throughout Scripture, and as we learn more about ourselves, we learn that every one of these commandments was for our benefit, our health, our prosperity, our safety. It is noteworthy that God seldom explains *why* He gives certain commandments regarding eating, but without exception, as we learn more about how certain body systems operate, it becomes clear again and again that obedience will bring rewards of health and safety to us—God's blessings, in other words.

Obedience to God's commandments, statutes, and ordinances is for our benefit, not for God's, and God does expect us to obey even when we don't understand *why*. For example, He gave cleanliness rules to the Israelites on separating themselves from the camp when they had a discharge. He told them what to wash and how to wash it and when it was safe to return to the group. What is a discharge? A runny nose, an oozing infection. Today we know these discharges are filled with germs and that proper laundering, washing our hands, and separating ourselves will keep those germs from spreading and infecting others. The Israelites didn't know what a germ was, but when they followed God's commandments regarding cleanliness, the individual benefited by recovering from the disease, their family was spared the infection, and even the entire nation of Israel profited because the disease was kept in check and not allowed to spread.

What is the single most-often-asked question by our children? "*Why?*" Do you explain every command you give your children? No. Neither does God. But He still expects us to obey Him, just as we expect our children to obey us. When we obey, we benefit. When our children obey, they benefit. The principle is obvious.

*We know God loves us, just as we love our children,
but it is the knowledge of His sovereignty that should
provide us with ample reason and desire to obey Him,
whether or not we understand the "why" of any particular
command given in Scripture.*

But even though we are to obey God whether or not we understand His reasons, there is nothing wrong with seeking out the "why" of His commandments. God is not offended, and He can stand the scrutiny! It is also important to learn as much as we can about God's creation and how things function. As Christians, learning should be a lifelong pursuit for us because to learn more of creation is to learn more of the Creator. But I believe it is *absolutely imperative* for us to get to know God, His attributes and character, and how He feels about us as individuals. *Getting intimately acquainted with God and seeing ourselves as He sees us should be our primary pursuit in life!*

Now that we have established that God does, indeed, care about what you eat, let's move on to the next step and find out just what "food" is. The answer will probably surprise you.

END NOTES

1. Isadore Rosenfeld., M.D., "Medical Détente," Success Express, (Summer 2001):13
2. Emilie Barnes & Sue Gregg, The 15 Minute Meal Planner – A Realistic Approach to a Healthy Lifestyle, (Eugene, Oregon: Harvest House Publishers), 1994, p. 27

Chapter 4

What Is Food?

Scripture should be consulted to determine the truth in any subject, including food. The other resource I will be relying on heavily, as stated in chapter 1, is *Webster's 1828 Dictionary* (the first American *Christian* dictionary). It will be used for definitions of key words relating to food, health, and diet, followed by a search of God's Word for what it has to say about these subjects. Other sources that are not in agreement with the principles we find in God's Word concerning food should be regarded as man's opinion, not God's truth, and treated as such.

The principle in question is God's sovereignty.
In other words, just because we eat it, or our great-grand-mother ate it, does not make it food. God's Word alone determines truth.
We are looking for the revelation of God's perspective, not the validation of our personal tastes or family traditions.

In the Beginning...

As you start to read the Bible, you notice God doesn't take long to get to the subject of food. Genesis is the book of beginnings, and it is here where we see the first reference to and instruction about food. In the first twenty-seven verses of Scripture, God has created everything (or the raw materials for everything) that exists today! In Genesis 1:27 God produces His masterpiece and the reason for the rest of creation—man. God immediately establishes communication and a relationship with man, including graciously giving *general* instructions regarding this mind-boggling array of creatures and resources He has set before them. To these new beings in their own right, now face-to-face with a brand new world with all new life forms, God simply says:

> ...Be fruitful and multiply, and **replenish** the earth, and **subdue** it; and have **dominion** over the fish of the sea, and over the fowl of the air, and over every living thing that moveth upon the earth.
>
> Genesis 1:28 KJV

That's it. Replenish it, subdue it, have dominion over it. Think of all the details, responsibilities, and applications involved in replenishing, subduing, and taking dominion over *all* that God had just created! Where would they start? What would they do first? How would they do it? Would the animals cooperate? This was an incomprehensible assignment, *a huge job*, yet God did not give any *specific* directions, or even a priority list for the order of operations.

The very next instruction from the mouth of God related to eating, something you would assume to be a much simpler and smaller task, of much less significance, yet unlike His first statement, God did not leave the details of this instruction up to mankind. He told them precisely what they were to eat:

> And God said, "See, I have given you every **herb** that yields seed which is on the face of all the earth, and every tree whose **fruit** yields seed; to you it shall be for **food** [meat]."
>
> Genesis 1:29 NKJV

Defining Our Terms

According to the Bible, these instructions about eating were the second words spoken by God to man. Let's examine them more closely. We'll start our investigation with the most obvious word, food. In the King James Version of the Old Testament, the word *food* is synonymous with "meat." In Hebrew, this word *food/meat* means dry food, flesh, or fruit. So when you read the word "meat" in this version of Scripture, it is not necessarily referring only to animal flesh. *Just this generic word – meat [or food] - is used 351 times in Scripture.* Additionally, there are hundreds of other references to specific foods. Obviously, food is a subject of importance to God. *Webster's 1828 Dictionary* definition of food includes its *purpose*, something we have largely forgotten or ignored today:

> **food** - flesh or vegetables eaten for sustaining human life; whatever is or may be eaten for **nourishment**.

God specifically mentions fruit and also herbs. I always thought of herbs as relatives of spices and flavorings, so at first glance it would seem that God only meant for us to eat spicy fruits. Fortunately, the true definition of herb is much broader:

> **herb** - a plant or **vegetable** with a soft or succulent stalk or stem which dies to the root every year and is thus distinguished from shrubs and trees.

Most of us would consider vegetables to be what we cultivate or grow by choice in a garden. But God planned for us to also eat many other "plant" herbs that grow wild in the field:

> ...you shall eat the herb of the field.
>
> Genesis 3:18 NKJV

A brief study of herbs confirms that not only can many of these "uncultivated" herbs be eaten, but certain ones have specific nutrients found in no other food, and many are used as the basis for medicines and ointments. Herbs are also an excellent example of God's overabundant supply for us and our needs: At this point in time, over *three million* herbs have been identified by man. But beware! When it comes to herbs, caution is necessary. Remember the definition and *purpose* of food? It must sustain human life and be nourishing. Some herbs are inedible and others are even deadly:

And Elisha returned to Gilgal, and there was a famine in the land. Now the sons of the prophets were sitting before him; and he said to his servant, 'Put on the large pot, and boil stew for the sons of the prophets.' So one went out into the field to gather herbs, and found a wild vine and gathered from it a lapful of wild gourds, and came and sliced them into the pot of stew, though they did not know what they were. Then they served it to the men to eat. Now it happened, as they were eating the stew, that they cried out and said, 'Man of God, there is death in the pot!' And they could not eat it.

2 Kings 4:38-40 NKJV

Personally, I believe that God's original intent for us was to be able to eat all the herbs because Genesis says that everything He created was "good." But when Adam sinned and the curse came upon the earth, some of the herbs became poisonous for man. My Uncle Ronald in Massachusetts, an experienced woodsman and camper, informed me that in most cases, wherever a poisonous plant is located in a field, its antidote is almost always growing within a few feet. (What an example of God's mercy!) My advice: *Don't eat an unknown herb of the field unless you're prepared to eat every-thing within a few feet radius around it!*

We can derive another basic principle about food and God's plan for it from Genesis:

...you shall eat **bread**...

Genesis 3:19 NKJV

You can't plant bread seeds to grow muffins, buns or pastries. They don't grow wild in a field somewhere. Bread's most basic ingredient is flour, which comes from whole grain seeds, a dry food that Adam was instructed to eat. However, this grain seed (most commonly wheat) must be milled into flour which must be mixed with other ingredients, and then baked, to make bread. The obvious conclusion is that while God gave us the raw, whole foods to be eaten as they come from the plant or bush, he also knew that man would create recipes from those raw materials, and that was acceptable to Him. As we dig deeper into His Word, we will also learn that there are ordinances which govern these recipes, their ingredients and their preparation.

> *The overriding principle for whatever we eat is contained in the basic definition of food: flesh or vegetables eaten for sustaining human life [food must sustain life, not diminish it]; whatever is or may be eaten for nourishment.*

Nourishment is the next key and our next definition. Again, Webster illuminates the three-fold *purpose* of nourishment:

nourishment - nutrition; that which serves to promote the **growth** and **health** and **eliminate** the waste from our bodies.

Even Frank and Ernest found out that "food" has to meet certain requirements in order to be called "food."

By these two first simple definitions – food and nourishment - we have just eliminated about 90 percent of our Standard American Diet (SAD). According to God, in order to be classified as food, or what He designated for us to eat, it must be nourishing and promote the growth and health of our bodies, in addition to helping us eliminate wastes. There is little fast food or restaurant fare that will meet this criteria. Vegetables that are overcooked so all their enzymes are dead and vitamin content gone will not promote health or growth. White bread has little fiber and no bran to help eliminate waste from our bodies and is therefore disqualified as "food." Refined sugar actually leaches calcium from our bones – certainly not an action that "promotes health." Chemicals, additives, artificial colors, and preservatives are all foreign invaders to our bodies, often toxic, and thus could never be classified as "food." Try to find anything on the grocery shelf (including the produce aisle where most fruits and vegetables have been sprayed with toxic chemicals) without additives in one form or another. By now, you are beginning to get a picture of how far we have strayed from God's statutes and ordinances regarding food. Food is not merely something to tickle our taste buds or fill our stomachs. On the contrary, **true food is fuel:** it must meet nourishment regulations set out by God; it must sustain life!

The Necessity of Nourishment

To provide nourishment is an act of nurture, something we provide for those we love.

Then Joseph provided his father, his brothers and all his father's house with bread according to the number in their families.

Genesis 47:12 NKJV

This Hebrew word for bread means "food, fruit, loaf bread, meat, edible sustenance." In other words, Joseph provided his family with all kinds of nourishing food, including bread. If you are familiar with this section of Scripture, you know that Joseph was *thrilled* to have his family near him once again after a long, painful separation, and he was demonstrating his love and affection for them in providing this nourishing food.

God, our Father, tenderly loves us, His children, and provides us with nourishment. In this next passage, He is speaking to the nation of Israel when He says,

...I have nourished and brought up children...

Isaiah 1:2 NKJV

Nourishing is a kind and loving act, supplying food that promotes health particularly to those we love, and even more specifically to our children. Parents, you are responsible for bringing up your children with the right nourishment for their bodies as much as the right nourishment for their minds and spirits. If you are single, or your children are grown and gone, you are responsible for nurturing and being a good steward of your own body which God gave to you. He has a ministry for you to perform. Your destiny can only be worked out *to its fullest* when you are the best you can be for God, including your health.

There are many references in Scripture to nourishing food. In the verse below, Abigail is providing sustenance for David and his men, a way of showing appreciation for the protection from thieves they gave to her sheep shearers. (Observe that this list includes prepared, cooked recipes, meat and raw, and whole foods.)

> Then Abigail made haste and took 200 loaves of bread, two skins of wine, five sheep already dressed, five seahs [measures] of roasted grain, 100 clusters of raisins, and 200 cakes of figs, and loaded them on donkeys.
>
> 1 Samuel 25:18 NKJV

There are twenty-one references in Scripture to God giving the Israelites a "land flowing with milk and honey." Scripture speaks of butter, cheese, olive oil, spices, nuts, almonds, raisin and fig cakes, lamb, beef, fish, and fowl. All of these are mentioned as foods that are good for us to eat, foods that will promote health. God has given us many, many choices from which to partake, enjoy, and be healthy!

We will cover some general principles on food groups in later chapters, as well as specifics on some of the more important and difficult topics. Scripture will be our guide as we search out which foods God promotes and which He says never to touch.

The overarching principle is God's sovereignty.
Just because we think something tastes good does NOT
make it food. God intended for us to eat food that
promotes health and meets nourishment requirements.

Who's in charge? You or God?

Before we get into specific food groups, let's define and study "health," a topic of many misconceptions and misinterpretations. Since the primary definitions of food and nourishment both speak of the "promotion of health," any serious study about food and nutrition must include a clear understanding of what health really is. Similar to most people's misunderstanding of what constitutes food, their perception of a healthy body is a far cry from truth as well. Let's press on!

Chapter 5

Are You Healthy?

Health and healthy eating are front-running topics of the new millennium. You can hardly pick up a newspaper or magazine and not find an article on these subjects. Barna Research Group conducted a random nationwide telephone survey in February 2000, asking people to list their top priorities. Of the 1,002 adults questioned, *9 out of 10 named good health as their highest goal.*[1]

At the turn of the 20th century a health survey was taken of 110 nations. The United States ranked 13th from the top for good health. Recently another survey was taken and the United States *ranked 79th in health out of the 79 nations studied.*[2] We die earlier and spend more time disabled than any other civilized country in the world.

According to Dr. Richard Dubois, chief of Internal Medicine at Atlanta Medical Center, 66 percent of cancer incidents and 90 percent of colon cancer cases could be prevented with good nutrition. In spite of this knowledge, deaths from cancer as a percent of deaths from all causes have greatly *increased* from 1900 to 2000, a time when our health should have been improving along with the new knowledge we were attaining in the fields of medicine and health. The below statistics, shared in a lecture given by Dr. Dubois on April 27, 2002, in Dayton, Ohio, show the stark opposite reality:

- 1900 – 1 out of 30 died from cancer
- 1980 – 1 out of 10 died from cancer
- 2000 – 1 out of 3 died from cancer

What really constitutes "good health"? Are you healthy? Most people, when asked that question, will answer that they are "basically healthy." The statistics listed above refute this belief. In addition, the figures released by the National Center for Health Statistics show that over 90 percent of the 1.9 million deaths in America in 1998 were related to diet or lifestyle choices![3] *This means more than 90 percent of us are dying from disease, nearly all of which is linked to personal choices!* There seems to be a near total disconnect in the average person's brain/thinking in regard to their perception of *their personal health* and this statistic. We can't all be "basically healthy" if this many of us are dying from various diseases!

More Definitions

In our search for knowledge ("a clear and certain perception of *truth*") let's go back to *Webster's 1828 Dictionary*:

> **health** - The state of a living body in which the parts are sound, well organized and in which they all perform freely their **natural functions**. In this state there is *no pain*.
>
> **heal** - to cure of a disease or wound and restore to that state of body in which the **natural functions** are regularly performed. *To purify from corruptions.*

Since the words *natural functions* appear in both these definitions, it is worthwhile to check out this meaning as well:

> **natural** - the **laws** and growth impressed on bodies by divine power; not forced; produced or coming in the ordinary course of things.

Now let's search out and reason through some of these definitions to the correlating principles from Scripture: In the first chapter of Genesis, it is clear that all of God's creation was accomplished in an orderly fashion. As we study certain individual components of this creation—nature, chemistry, human body functions—we discover that His creation is also ordered by scientific, unchanging *laws*. From this definition of "natural," it is evident that there are "laws" involved in the growth and function of our bodies. These are *ordinances* or *statutes* that were put into place by God at the moment of our creation. But what exactly are "natural laws"?

> **natural laws** - the laws of nature have been established by the Creator and are **invariable** [cannot be changed] and predetermine a body to certain motions, changes and relations.

Health and the Principle Approach®

Using the "Four R's" of the Principle Approach®, let's put together the pieces of what we've just learned: We just completed some basic *research* of primary sources by looking through several key definitions and some basic principles from the first chapter of Genesis. Let's *reason* [think] through those definitions and principles and put them together to look at the *whole picture* in order to *relate* them to our study on what God has to say about health and nutrition. (The next paragraph contains the *recording* or writing down of the conclusions.)

To have *health* means our bodies are performing certain *natural functions* automatically and regularly; specifically, functions that will continually purify the body from corruptions. These natural, cleansing functions were put there by God, our Creator, and they fall under the category of *natural law*, which means they are unchangeable. We already saw that putting *nourishing* foods in our bodies will promote health and help "eliminate waste from our bodies" – another way of saying "purify from corruptions."

> *The principle is – sowing nourishing foods in our body is an important part of what will bring about (reap) health.*

This is part of God's plan and His unchangeable, natural law. Everything He made in creation He declared to be "good" (Genesis 1:31). We can, therefore, assume He did not create unhealthy, nonnourishing foods for us to eat—which brings about the next logical and inescapable principle:

Anything edible that is non-nourishing (does not promote growth, health, and elimination of waste from our bodies) was not intended by God for man to eat!

OUCH! That statement hits everyone in an uncomfortable place! However, this principle is the very reason why God could promise the Israelites, long before salvation and healing through Christ, that they would be healthy, *if* they followed His health and dietary statutes. God also addresses this principle of sowing and reaping in the New Testament, along with the fact that there are consequences to sowing and reaping improperly:

Do not be deceived. God is not mocked; for whatever a man sows, that he will also reap.

Galatians 6:7 NKJV

The logical conclusion is simple: To one degree or another, as you sow/eat nutritious, God-ordained foods you will reap health. Conversely, as you sow/eat non-nutritious, or "non-foods," (*junk* foods - anything other than God-ordained) you will reap varying levels of sickness and disease.

Disease and the Principle Approach®

To verify the above assumption, let's use the Principle Approach® and look at some more definitions:

sickness - disease, a morbid state of the body in which the organs do not **naturally** perform their **functions**.

disease - to interrupt or impair any or all of the **natural** and regular **functions** of the organs of the living body.

The phrase "natural functions" appears here again, as it did with the definitions of health and heal, clearly confirming their connection. As in almost all of God's truth, the message is simple and clear: Sickness is not simply the diagnosis or manifestation of a horrible, disabling disease. By definition, sickness is simply when any of your body's organs or natural functions aren't functioning naturally. Pain disqualifies you from being able to claim personal health....*to have a headache is to be sick.* Improper digestion does not promote health...*to have heartburn, gas, or acid reflux is to be diseased. Poor elimination (constipation or hemorrhoids) is a sign of disease.* A key point or truth emerges here:

> **To be healthy is much more than NOT manifesting some terrible disease. To be healthy is to manifest NO pain,**
> **NO bodily dysfunction (minor or major), NO DIS-ease! It is to have ALL of our organs and natural functions operating properly [functioning naturally].**

These definitions clarify the true state of our health (or lack thereof). I challenge you to find a medicine cabinet in North America that doesn't have either aspirin (or other type of pain killer), Tums or Pepto-Bismol (or other indigestion relief products), Ex-Lax and/ or Preparation H (or other constipation remedies). These three are "standard equipment"—over-the-counter drugs found in nearly all American households. But as you can see by the above definitions, *taking any of these on a routine basis disqualifies us from being "basically healthy."* Indeed, we are much more likely to fit into the category of "basically sick" to one degree or another. If you are truly healthy, your medicine cabinet would contain *no* drugs! Much more likely is a bathroom cabinet containing a variety of common over-the-counter treatments, in addition to a few prescription drugs to treat all our minor dis-eases.

Another area of dis-ease may come as a surprise. Our "natural functions can be impaired" when we *think wrong thoughts!* For every thought we have there is a conscious or unconscious "natural function," a chemical hormone or nerve signal that goes forth. Our glands were designed to maintain our chemical balance through neurotransmitters that work together to release proper hormones and chemicals to achieve this balance. Wrong thoughts (e.g., unforgiveness, fear, stress, anxiety) bring about the over-release of adrenaline and other hormones which will bring about serious health issues over time.

In spite of all this *dis*-ease and *non*-health, and much of its proven connection to poor eating habits, there are still many in the church today who argue against following the dietary regulations set out in the Old Testament, claiming these principles regarding eating have been nullified by the New Testament and the promises and provisions of Jesus. They speak of "being under grace, not the law." In further support of this stance, they cite new farming and feeding techniques that render any previous restrictions of clean and unclean obsolete. To these folks, health is largely an issue of faith. If you have enough faith, you can simply pray and be healed. You don't have to eat right.

Then there are others who say miraculous healings are part of church history, limited to Jesus and the first apostles. Not only can we not walk in "divine health," but God occasionally makes us sick to teach us life's lessons, or to keep us humble. When sickness and disease are viewed in this light, adherence to Old Testament health and dietary habits are not only unnecessary, they could actually get in God's way of teaching us what we need to learn.

Lastly, there are those who believe we should adhere to the Old Testament dietary regulations as part of our health plan. These are three distinctly different schools of thought. They can't all be right, can they? Let's explore each of these three concepts next.

END NOTES

1. "Survey Reveals What Americans Want from Life," <u>American Family Association Journal</u>, August 2000.
2. <u>The McAlvany Health Alert</u>, P. O. Box 84904, Phoenix, AZ 85071 (April 2002), quoted in "Internal Cleanliness is Key – Where Did We Go Wrong?" <u>The Cutting Edge Health Digest</u>, P. O. Box 1788, Medford, OR 97501 (Winter-Spring 2003), p. 7.
3. Dangerous Dozen: Leading Causes of Death in the U.S.," <u>Parade</u>, 16 February 2000, p. 8.

Chapter 6

Did God Really Promise Health to His People?

Walking in Divine Health

He Himself [Jesus] took our infirmities and bore our sicknesses.

Matthew 8:17b NKJV

This is the verse that many New Testament believers hang their hats on today. It is the foundation for their expectations (faith) concerning health and healing in any and every situation. They would argue that under the new covenant, if believers get sick or diseased, a simple prayer of faith will remove any disease or infirmity. If your prayer doesn't work, your faith isn't strong enough. "Jesus bore it all, didn't He? Why do we have to be concerned about what we eat? That's legalism. All we need is faith for God to heal us, right? Besides, we're under grace, not the law!"

First of all, Jesus did *not* do away with the law of the Old Testament. In speaking to the multitudes at the Sermon on the Mount, He said:

Do not think that I came to destroy the Law or the Prophets.
I did not come to destroy, but to **fulfill**.

Matthew 5:17 NKJV

fulfill – to perform what is required; to answer a law by **obedience**

If we call ourselves Christians, we are calling ourselves "followers of Christ." Jesus came to *obey* the law, not to do away with it. To truly follow Him, we must do the same.

The principle is individuality:
Individuals count and are accountable.
We often remember we count, but much less often
remember we are also accountable for all our decisions
and actions.

We must also take into consideration that anytime New Testament scriptures tell us to obey the Word, they are referring to the Old Testament, as the New Testament did not exist at the time of their writings! Most importantly, to obey God's statutes and ordinances isn't legalism but a demonstration of our love for God:

This is love—that we walk according to His commandments.
2 John 6 NKJV

Furthermore, Jesus spoke about God's commandments, telling a lawyer what the greatest commandment in the law is:

You shall love the Lord your God with all your heart, and with all your soul, and with all your mind.
Matthew 22:37 NKJV

According to Jesus, establishing a deep, abiding relationship with God the Father is the most important commandment. To do this requires much time spent with God in the Word and prayer. It requires commitment and diligence. This brings a new aspect to searching for "divine" health. It is not so simplistic (or presumptuous?) as to just pray and expect to be delivered/healed from whatever sickness is overpowering us by standing in faith on Matthew 8:17. Did Jesus truly bear our sicknesses and infirmities or not?

Scripture is true, so *yes*, He did bear these on our behalf. But a closer look at the word *divine* will reveal why no one except Jesus walked in "divine" health.

> **Divine** – Godlike; heavenly; excellent in the highest degree; extraordinary; apparently above what is human. (*Webster's 1828*)

From this definition we can see that only Jesus ever walked in "divine" health because only Jesus walked in perfect holiness and/ or perfect relationship with the Father His entire life. We are to be *like* God, imitators of Him, growing in sanctification from glory to glory, but only Christ walked in "excellence in the highest degree" *at all times.*

In reality, I cannot find a scripture where God promises that we will never get sick. He said in Exodus 15:26 that *"...I will put none of these diseases upon you..."* but this does not mean we cannot put the diseases upon ourselves. Another scripture:

> Bless the Lord, O my soul, and forget not all of His bene-fits: Who forgives all your iniquities; who heals all your diseases.
>
> Psalm 103:2-3 NKJV

This word is clear. In God's grace and mercy, just as surely as He forgives *all* our sins, He also heals *all* our diseases! However, to heal all our diseases presupposes we will have diseases from which we need to be healed. So it would appear that while we are not promised "divine health," we are promised that God will heal *all* diseases that come upon us. So the question becomes, How do we appropriate this benefit? Clearly, neither individuals inside nor individuals outside the church are being healed of *all* their diseases.

Webster's 1828 Dictionary comes to the rescue again in shedding some critical light on this subject of healing. Check out this part of the definition:

Heal – In scripture, to forgive, to cure moral disease and restore soundness. (*Webster's 1828*)

What is a "moral disease?" Sounds like sin to me. And this definition even includes *forgiveness* as part of the healing process! To heal is to forgive? To forgive is to heal? If this sounds strange, consider Christ's words to the Pharisees:

> "Which is easier: to say, 'Your sins are forgiven,' or to say, 'Stand up and walk'? But I will prove to you that the Son of Man has authority on earth to forgive sins." So Jesus said to the paralyzed man, "I tell you, stand up, take your mat and go home."
>
> Luke 5:23-24 NCV

In this passage, Jesus clearly and directly linked forgiveness of sin to the healing of disease. But this is not always the case.

> His followers asked [Jesus], "Teacher, whose sin caused this man to be born blind – his own sin or his parents' sin?" Jesus answered, "It is not this man's sin or his parents' sin that made him be blind. This man was born blind so that God's power could be shown in him..."
>
> John 9:2-3 NCV

The bottom line is – We must learn to discern and obey what we learn! God is sovereign and has the power and authority to heal and deliver us from every calamity and malady. *But God's sovereignty and being in control are governmental terms, not manipulative ones.* He is the Governor of the Universe whom we are to choose to obey, not the Great Puppeteer pulling our strings, manipulating us to perform certain deeds, such as eating right or forgiving those who have wronged us. Nor do our prayers "force" God into action on our behalf.

The principle of stewardship relates to the (New Testament revelation of our bodies as the "temple of

the Holy Spirit" which we should care for and feed in a way to promote wellness, spiritually and physically. This includes knowing and obeying God's (Old Testament) commandments regarding diet, cleanliness, and health.

The best daddy in the world isn't the one who gives us everything we want but rather provides everything we need. God's highest desire is for us to know Him *intimately* and His will thoroughly through prayer, reading, and studying. Ask for wisdom as you seek His direction for any healing. His mercies are new every morning, and His compassions never fail (Lamentations 3:22-23). He wants you to learn how to receive the healing for which you pray, whether it is physical or spiritual in nature.

Sickness as God's Teaching Tool

Let's deal with the idea of healing being limited to Jesus and the apostles, or God using illness as an avenue of enlightenment. The first half of this belief is so easy to discount it is difficult to believe anyone could seriously still adhere to it. I can't imagine there is anyone alive today who has not personally witnessed or at least heard of a miraculous healing in one arena or another. Medical reports abound, showing tumors that "mysteriously disappeared" after friends and loved ones prayed. Countless other immediate and spontaneous recoveries have occurred that cannot be explained except by God's people praying in faith. Healing did *not* stop with Jesus and the apostles. I thank God it is a very real part of modern times.

The second idea, however, that God uses sickness as a teaching tool, is a much deeper and more difficult study. I will share my personal thoughts on this subject. It is not my intent to sway your beliefs; rather I recommend you dig deeper and solidify *why* you believe what you believe according to biblical principles, not blindly follow a particular church's or pastor's doctrine or traditions.

I do not believe that God strikes people with an illness to teach them something. That is not in keeping with His character. God "put[ting] the diseases on the Egyptians" would be better understood as saying they "reaped what they sowed" regarding their choices of gods, food, and lifestyle, a consequence of their own actions. However, this does not limit God from using sickness in a variety of ways. There are many times when, rather than immediately begging for healing, we should pray for insight to better understand the health challenge before us. Joni Eareckson Tada, a dynamic lady who was paralyzed at age seventeen in a diving accident, prayed for healing, fully expecting to walk again. What she says she found instead was:

> ...the peace of God which surpasses all understanding...
> Philippians 4:7NKJV

Her physical crippling led to her spiritual unfolding and a life-long ministry. Which one of us would *choose* to be a paraplegic or quadriplegic? Yet who could minister better to those with such disabilities than one who is in the same condition, and has suffered the same pain, frustration, anger, and tribulation? To attribute her absence of "healing" to a lack of faith is an insult to her and God. There is *always* a purpose for our suffering, one of which is that we will be able to comfort others when they suffer similar difficulties. The one who best understands your pain is the one who went through that same pain:

> [Blessed be God] who comforts us in all our tribulation, that we may be able to comfort those who are in any trouble with the comfort with which we ourselves are comforted by God.
> 2 Corinthians 1:4 NKJV

The sickness or infirmity of a beloved family member often provides the motivation for research or experimentation with subsequent discoveries that can often bless more people than we could ever imagine. Alexander Graham Bell used the deafness of his mother and wife as inspiration to invent the telephone by patterning the integral parts of the telephone after a sheep's ear. How many disease cures were found by desperate people searching for remedies because someone they loved was terribly ill? This book and part of my teaching ministry are the direct result of my son's twelve-year debilitating illness that was not cured by drugs or even identified by doctors. It was stress, frustration, and pressure that brought about my search which eventually led to my son's healing.

> In everything give thanks; for this is the will of God in Christ Jesus for you.
>
> 1 Thessalonians 5:18 NKJV

Do not misunderstand. This verse does not imply that it is God's intention for anyone to be sick or crippled, or that He inflicts us with such maladies, but rather that He can *use* our circumstances and suffering to mold our character and shape our destiny. *Tragic things happen because people have free will and can make bad decisions.* But God has a master plan in mind for each of us beyond what we can ever imagine. The Bible says that even Jesus learned obedience through suffering. If God did not spare His only Son from suffering, why do we think He will treat us any differently and save us from all pain?

> *The principle involved is Christian character.*
> *Seldom will one choose the path of pressure and pain,*
> *but a diamond was nothing more than a piece of coal*
> *until it is put under extreme pressure*
> *for a long period of time.*

Character - a mark made by cutting or engraving, stamping or impressing. The peculiar qualities, impressed by nature or habit on a person, which distinguish him from others. (*Webster's 1828*)

This is a painful process when related to human beings: cutting, stamping, impressing! But, remember, in the physical realm muscles do not become strong unless they meet resistance; they stretch, they strain, they *hurt*! They must work, often to the point of *pain*. The same is true of our spiritual being.

...work out your own salvation with fear and trembling.

Philippians 2:12b NKJV

Remember, part of our salvation is healing. Learning the healing process – right thinking, bodily exercise, drinking *lots* of pure water, when to eat, what to eat, how to prepare it, changing our habits accordingly - is *work*. It requires choosing to put our fleshly appetites for wrong foods under Christ's Lordship to make life and food choices that will benefit our bodies. It would be much easier to vegetate in bed or on the couch in front of the TV rather than making yourself do a daily workout and exercise routine. The entire health process is indeed *working out your salvation.*

Health, Old Age, and the Law

The original question of this chapter was "Did God Really Promise Health to His People?" In chapter 3, we saw where God promised His people:

If you **diligently** heed the voice of the Lord your God and do what is right in His sight, and give ear to His Commandments, and keep all His statutes, I will put none of the diseases on you which I have brought on the Egyptians...

Exodus 15:26 NKJV

Here is a great example of how *Webster's 1828 Dictionary* is a wonderful aid in Bible study. The word *diligently* is extremely important here.

diligently – with steady application and care; with industry; not carelessly; not negligently

In regard to our obedience to God's revealed statutes, He does not expect *perfection* from us. He expects steady application and for us not to be negligent or careless. What a relief! We just have to keep on trying and not give up. That is doable.

There is further backup of this promise in Exodus. When the Israelites were wandering the desert without a home, God *again* made the same covenant regarding health, as they were about to enter the Promised Land to settle and make their homes. In Deuteronomy 7, the same chapter where God refers to the Israelites as His "special treasure above all the people on the face of the earth" (verse 6), he repeats this vow:

> Then it shall come to pass because you listen to these judgments and keep and do them....the Lord will take away from you all sickness, and will afflict you with none of the terrible diseases of Egypt which you have known....
>
> Deuteronomy 7:12-15 NKJV

Today, most Americans will die as a result of a degenerative sickness, not because our time to die has come according to God's plan, or because you have finished the work He put you here to do. I previously used an old manuscript and Israel's twelve patriarchs as examples of God's idea of health, strength, longevity, and even the idea of knowing when it is your time to die. We can also look at three individuals in Scripture for these same examples.

Moses and Joshua both lived to a very old age and knew that it was time for them to die because God told them so. They were not fading away from old age, cancer, or heart disease. They had finished their course in this life, and it was time to join God in the next one. They died "healthy."

> Moses was 120 years old when he died. His eyes were not dim nor his natural vigor diminished.
>
> Deuteronomy 34:7 NKJV

Joshua and Caleb were both leading battles of hand-to-hand combat when they were eighty years old! They did not have a special anointing; they simply loved God and obeyed His ordinances, including the dietary and health regulations.

> And now behold, the Lord has kept me alive, and He said, these 45 years, ever since the Lord spoke this word to Moses, while Israel wandered in the wilderness; and now, here I am,

this day 85 years old. And yet, I am as strong this day as on the day that Moses sent me; just as my strength was then, so now is my strength for war, both for going out and coming in.

Joshua 14:10-11 NKJV

Do you know any eighty-five-year-olds who are combat ready? Do you know any eighty-five-year-olds who feel as strong as when they were forty-five? Do you know many eighty-five-year-olds who are still living at all, much less in a healthy state such as Joshua describes?

As stated previously, "the diseases of the Egyptians" are the diseases of modern-day man. Doctors recently performed autopsies on thirty thousand Egyptian mummies. What killed these Egyptians was not germs such as those precipitating the bubonic plague but rather heart disease, calcification of bones (osteoporosis), stopped up arteries (heart attacks, strokes), cancer—*the same diseases that kill nearly 90 percent of us today!* These diseases came upon them the same way they come upon us today. Did you know that the Egyptians were the first people to eat white bread?

The Health and Holiness Connection

We all know that when we become Christians, God expects us to behave differently from the world. It's part of the sanctification process, or being set apart from non-believers, and it usually happens a little bit at a time. We know we are supposed to stop swearing, smoking or drinking to excess; we are to listen to different music, pick different friends, read different books, and most of us will begin working through that process after we are born-again. But from these passages in Exodus and Deuteronomy where God is making distinctions between the Egyptians (the world) and His people (Israelites/Christians), another important principle emerges:

As part of the sanctification, or Christian character-forming process, God commands His people to **eat differently** *from the rest of the world.*

As further verification of this principle, it is interesting to note that *health and holiness are linked in the Hebrew language.* The root word for shalom, *shlm,* has three basic meanings: *shalem* (health), shalom (peace), and *shelem* (relationship with God). Rabbi Eric Braverman, in an article written in *Total Health* (June 1987), said, "The Israelite does not observe the laws on account of their dietetic or sanitary value, but to be holy."

This statement brings us back again to the fact that only Jesus ever walked in "divine" health because only Jesus walked in perfect holiness: a sinless, peaceful, and perfect relationship with God. It also introduces the idea that *holiness is part of health!* With this in mind, I again mention and recommend Pastor Henry Wright's book, *A More Excellent Way – Be in Health,* which traces many diseases to *spiritual roots,* and Chester and Betsy Kylstra's book, *An Integrated Approach to Biblical Healing Ministry,* where you will learn to identify significant spiritual roots and ways to lay an ax to those roots. These are soul-searching books, in the "must read" category, and are at the top of my Recommended Reading list. Diet and exercise are important to "maintain the temple," but the spiritual aspect of health must be investigated in dealing with "incurable" diseases or ongoing maladies. (I'll be covering more details of this important topic in chapter 14 on "Scrutinizing Alternative Practices.")

God's commandments are given for our benefit, our health, indeed, for a *holy* life spent in close relationship to God. He wants to bless us with health, not curse us with disease. But we have to cooperate. We have to follow His directions on how to achieve that health. To the degree we think, live, and eat God's way, we will be blessed with health. To the degree we think, live, and eat the way of the world, we will be cursed with disease. With this understanding it becomes clear that part of a Christian's responsibility is to educate ourselves about God's idea of nourishing foods, and the way He created our bodies to function naturally, and to begin eating what we should, avoiding what we can when we learn it is not part of God's natural plan for our diet.

Bottom Line: God's Way Is Best

But, having said all that, the clear fact remains that our God is a healing God and *does still heal us today*. I have prayed for and seen several miraculous, spontaneous healings through the years. But even more often I have prayed for healing and it has not manifested immediately. When this happens to Christians, it does *not* mean that God is not going to heal you, or that your faith is necessarily too small, but more likely He is using a method other than miracles, or has a greater purpose to accomplish. It can also be that your disease is spiritually rooted and you can receive your healing once you have discerned the cause behind it. I again refer the reader to Henry Wright's remarkable book, *A More Excellent Way*, or Chester Kylstra's book, *An Integrated Approach to Biblical Healing Ministry*, for your personal research in this regard.

Only God, in His wisdom and knowledge of all the facts from here to eternity, can determine what is best for us. We must therefore seek Him continually when dealing with disabling or "incurable" health challenges. We will never learn all there is to know about God, and we also must be certain never to try to "put Him in a box" that matches our presuppositions. (He won't fit anyway!)

In my own circumstances, if God had answered my prayer for healing for my son in the form of a miracle, an instant cure, it would have been temporary because the cause of his sickness was rooted in environmental problems along with wrong food choices. Not knowing this, we would not have made the lifestyle and diet changes necessary to maintain the healing. God knew that, so His answer to my prayer for healing came in the form of education, attaining knowledge regarding the root cause of the sickness, which enabled us to regain health through application of this new information. He showed me so much through those years of struggle and study, and now I am able to pass this learning on to others so they can live longer, healthier lives. A miracle healing would have only been for me and David. The healing that came through education and application of principles has blessed me *and* many, many others.

In summary, health challenges, sickness, and disease occur for many reasons. There are times when these challenges will build our faith as we pray and see God move in an immediate, miracle cure. More often, however, these health problems are the result of "sowing and reaping," the natural consequence of a particular sin or behavior, and should cause us to study, discern, and apply what we learn. God is always desirous for us to learn more about Him and His ways. But in every instance there remains the underlying principle of God's sovereignty regarding sickness, prayer, and healing:

In every sickness or health challenge,
we should seek God's plan, purpose, and method
as we pray for healing.

Several years ago, God placed the ministry of teaching in my life. While meditating on His Word, God "spoke" this passage directly into my heart, making it clear to me that I was to share the knowledge He would give me through these years of study:

So that your trust may be in the Lord; I have instructed you today, even you. Have I not written to you excellent things of counsels and knowledge, that I may make you know the certainty of the words of truth, that you may answer words of truth to those who send to you?

Proverbs 22:19-21 NKJV

I have indeed been "sent for" by several people in several states in recent years, to "answer words of truth" regarding health and nutrition. During my twelve years of "desert experiences"—a pilgrimage of trials, fears, and frustrations encountered because of a child's sicknesses—I never imagined I was walking in the God-ordained path of my destiny which would lead not only to my son's restored health, but to my ultimate ministry and blessing to others.

Chapter 7

My Personal Pilgrimage

My husband, Michael, and I were married in May 1973. As of this writing, we have been married thirty-three years and have two grown children – Jennifer, thirty, and David, twenty-eight. Michael spent a successful thirty-year career in the U.S. Air Force, from which he retired after achieving the rank of colonel. He now works as an engineer in the civilian world. Through the years, I supported the family from the home front, raising our kids, home-schooling them from fifth through ninth grade, and having various small home businesses.

The Doctor's Dilemma

We faced many of the same minor health difficulties and challenges as other families, nothing particularly noteworthy or extraordinary, until 1985, when our son, David, first started showing signs of chronic illness. At age seven he began having mild asthma attacks, allergy symptoms, and often-recurring cold/flu-like aches and pains. As a military family, we moved every two to three years, so continuity in medical care, or a personal physician who knew David and his medical history, was the impossible dream. His health problems became more constant and more severe as the years passed, until he was no longer able to attend "regular" school by the middle of the fifth grade. I began to homeschool so he would not fall behind in his education. By this time, it seemed as though we were constantly either at the doctor's office searching for a diagnosis, a lab of some sort undergoing one more of an unending series of tests, or the pharmacy waiting for newer and stronger drugs to perform the job the previous ones had failed to do.

Doctors were unable to even label David's disease, let alone cure it, and he was unceasingly ill for twelve years, from age seven to nineteen. At age ten, he went into uncontrollable convulsions, and we made a panic-stricken 2 a.m. emergency trip to Children's Hospital in Dayton. After three days of more testing, including *three spinal taps*, the convulsions stopped on their own, the horrific pain dissipated, he was able to keep food down, and we were sent home. Still, no doctor could diagnose his problem, and all the tests through those years came back negative, except to say he had "minor allergies." As the days, weeks, months, and years went by, those "minor allergies" manifested in headaches so severe he could not focus his eyes to read, joint pain so deep and aching that movement was agony, and muscles that either gave out or began trembling uncontrollably when he tried to write.

David's doctors introduced us to more drugs than we ever wanted to meet, beginning with antihistamines. These were of little or no effect, and after about a week the sniffles invariably turned into infection. Now it was time to meet the antibiotic "family." These worked initially but were prescribed so frequently through the years that David's body built up a resistance to them, until the strongest ones were of no effect. Then we became acquainted with steroids. These always worked—for a few days. Several times through those years a new drug would bring temporary relief and new hope. But always, as predictable as tomorrow's sunrise, the same old aches, pains, and tremors returned, bringing a deeper level of frustration and despair than the time before, as yet another avenue of escape from this unknown malady had been cut off.

In those first eleven years of sickness, all we learned about health care was drug experimentation and tests. The drugs temporarily masked the symptoms with various chemical and manmade concoctions and tests, tests, and more tests. EEGs, EKGs, CAT scans, X-rays, MRIs, blood and urine workups, allergy scratch tests, spinal taps – all were of no avail! Through those same years, I developed horrific, disabling migraines, two pre-cancerous conditions, and was under threat of surgery.

It never occurred to me to investigate these maladies myself. I thought taking responsibility for your own health or medical problems meant calling the doctor early enough in the morning so you could get an appointment that same day. I didn't even know there were other credible alternative medical practices involving natural remedies. Then, in the 12th year of sickness, we reached the proverbial "end of the rope." David was 19, we were living in Florida, and his health (mental and physical) bottomed out. He was 6' tall, weighed only 117 pounds, and was as gaunt, pale, and bony as some of the Holocaust victims you see in photographs.

David had started college, but because of his ever-deteriorating health, he just couldn't keep up with his classes. With only one week before finals, he was once again in such pain and so depleted of energy he didn't have the strength to get out of bed. He had to drop out, losing the time and money investment as well as the course credits. David and I had both reached the point of utter despair – in my friend's words, "lower than a snake's belly in Death Valley." We had exhausted all the possibilities the allopathic (drugs and surgery) medical world had to offer and finally concluded there was truly no hope, no prospect of any "real life" for David. He could not get and stay well enough, even on drugs, to function normally in this world for any significant length of time before he was flat on his back again.

I prayed a lot through those years, but now with virtually all known avenues of treatment (forget healing!) closed, I cried out to God in complete desperation to show me what to do to give my son a life. I could not fix his problem with my intellect. I could not take away his pain with my love. My mind was overtaxed and my heart was broken. Fortunately for us, these are the types of circumstances in which God shines.

Light at the End of the Tunnel

In the midst of my prayer and tears, the phone rang. The person calling introduced herself to me, saying a mutual friend had given her my name and explained my situation to her. She began to tell me about alternative medical practices, natural methods and treatments—choices I never knew existed. She said some of these methods encompassed the application of *God's natural laws of healing.* She explained that drugs only masked David's symptoms *temporarily* but ultimately did nothing towards correcting the root cause of his disease. (Important Note: Not every alternative medical practice follows God's created order or His plan, and this will be discussed in chapter 12, along with principles on how to determine which to use and which to avoid.)

Her words touched me to the core. Like brown grass turning green after rain had broken a long drought, hope slowly re-emerged where there had been only despair. We had already tried every route possible, but she was showing me an entirely new map. I knew her words were God's answer for me:

[The Lord has anointed me...] to console those who mourn...
to give them **beauty** for ashes, the oil of **joy** for mourning,
the garment of **praise** for the spirit of heaviness, that they
may be called trees of righteousness, the planting of the
Lord, that He may be glorified.

Isaiah 61:3 NKJV

This verse truly began to manifest in my life. God did not simply take away my mourning, fear, and grief. In that moment and in the days, months, and years to come, He would replace them with the *beauty* of truth as I learned of God's natural methods; the *joy* that came as healing began to slowly manifest; and *praise* to God that was a natural by-product of the joy! As only God can do, He transformed what was formerly frustration into more than just personal satisfaction as healing took place. In the midst of David's and my restoration process, He birthed a new, budding, and fulfilling ministry as my education on health continued, and I was actually able to begin to assist others.

Before the message of alternative medicine and personal health responsibility (prevention!), my "pilgrimage" had been filled with potholes, detours, and dead ends, none of which I would have chosen. I hated it when we had to move to Florida, leaving behind our "dream homestead" in another state. I hated Florida even more when we got there as the heat, humidity, and accompanying mold intensified David's illness. I hated the fact that David was sick all the time. Yet, in the midst of these things I hated, and after twelve years of suffering physical and emotional torment, God began teaching David and me how to *work out our salvation/healing.*

The Principle Approach® to the Rescue!

The Principle Approach® to education—personal edification through definitions and leading ideas—became the tool I used to learn about food, nutrition, and how our bodies operate. Psalm 139:14 says that God created us "fearfully and wonderfully." For example, if you cut your finger, it is nearly impossible to stop it from healing. All by itself, your finger will bleed to cleanse the wound and then begin to seal it as new skin growth is generated—literally self-healing over the course of time. Unless it was a particularly deep cut, you'll not be able to even see where the cut was after a month. That's pretty wonderful! It's part of the *natural function* of our bodies mentioned earlier in the definitions of nutrition, health, and heal.

As I continued to study natural methods of healing and restoration, I discovered God made the inside of our bodies in this same way—to be self-healing through purification and regeneration. Drugs do *not* have healing properties. They mask symptoms or manage disease but do not correct the underlying malfunction. Cold medication does not cure your cold. It simply helps you live with it while your body is repairing itself. On the other hand, assisting your body to "purify itself from internal corruptions" (*part of the definition of heal*) will cause a "basically healthy" body to rid itself of an invading germ or disease naturally, and health will be restored and/or maintained. To be truly "well" or healthy is to need and use no medication!

The principle is stewardship:
One of the keys to purification and health
maintenance is good, whole foods.

Our internal parts cannot continue in their *natural functions* if our body is not properly nourished. The building material needed for those natural functions to take place comes from eating the right foods, foods "alive" with enzymes. Dr. Mitra Ray, a biochemist from Stanford University, was interviewed on "Health Talk America" and said, "Disease is simply a set of cells not working properly. Drugs mask the problem. Nutrients make new cells." This is a simple yet powerful truth. Live foods produce life! Conversely, nutrient-depleted/dead foods (no living enzyme activity) cannot make new cells. Nutrient-depleted foods are a precursor to disease. Ultimately, dead foods produce death.

Simply put, sickness often comes as a result of poor eating, no matter that these choices may have been made in ignorance. No mother would intentionally feed her children substances that would poison them or make them ill. But when we habitually feed them fast food or restaurant foods—French fries fried in carcinogenic oil, meats filled with hormones and antibiotics, sodas with brain-destroying Nutrasweet (or sugar that can suppress the immune system by 92 percent for up to five hours![1])—that is precisely what we are doing: slowly tearing down their immune systems and gradually making their bodies unable to fight off a disease which will eventually kill them. This is the SAD (Standard American Diet) story that kills 90 percent of Americans!

Sowing and reaping is the principle involved in disease, which is often present long before obvious symptoms manifest.

The American Malnutrition and Disease Connection

As stated earlier, most people think they eat a fairly healthy diet, but they are gravely mistaken. If 90 percent of us will **die** from diseases brought on by what we eat, then we are **not** eating healthy, nutritious foods. We have seen through definitions that health is the outcome when we have godly relationships, think right thoughts, and eat foods that nourish us. We can therefore conclude that disease comes when we have poor relationships, think wrong thoughts, and eat foods that do not nourish us. God has clearly told us which ones are which, as we will see when we get into specifics in the coming chapters.

After God made us fearfully and wonderfully, He then furnished us with instructions on how to maintain this fearfully and wonderfully made body. If we do not follow His instructions, knowingly or unknowingly violating His laws of nature regarding food, we will get sick and die too early. You don't have to understand gravity to fall down. If you jump off the top of a ten-story building, you will fall to the ground because gravity is a scientific, unchanging law of the universe. Likewise, you don't have to understand that you are eating poorly to get sick or be in the process of building a degenerative disease. It happens because of God's immutable dietary laws.

God designed our bodies to be incredibly resilient, which sometimes works to our disadvantage. No one dies on the first cigarette inhaled, or the first drunken evening, or the first decade of unhealthy relationships and eating. Here's an oxymoron: 40 percent of Americans are overweight[2], yet they are malnourished.[3] Malnutrition in America is not from a lack of things to eat; it is from eating devitalized foods with insufficient nutrients to properly feed our bodies.

Degenerative diseases such as cancer take time to build, sometimes twenty to thirty years, so we don't realize (or *feel*) what we are doing. Dr. Russell Blaylock, a respected and well-known neurosurgeon, has stated that *clinical, neurological disease, such as Parkinson's, does not present itself with visible symptoms until 80-90 percent of the involved brain cells are dead.* God was right when He warned us of the principle of sowing and reaping:

> Do not be deceived. God is not mocked; for whatever a man sows, that he will also reap.
>
> Galatians 6:7 NKJV

Simply because you are not *manifesting* a disease visibly right now does *not* mean that you are healthy. If you are eating (sowing) non-nourishing foods today, you *are* building (will reap) a degenerative disease later. Most cancers have been growing ten to twenty years before we *see* or *feel* them!

Now we've finished laying the foundation for your understanding through some principles and related definitions of food, nutrition, health, and disease. And we've seen in Scripture that God's blessings or cursings are the result of our own obedience or disobedience to His revealed laws, statutes, and ordinances. We are going to explore those ordinances in more detail later so we will learn what to think, do, and eat to maintain health. But the next step before learning this is clean-up!

Have you ever bought an older home, a "fixer-upper," a "handyman's dream?" You can buy all new light fixtures, tubs, toilets, pick out paint and wallpaper, new tile, carpets, and trim. But if you don't clean up or throw out the old as you put in the new, your investment in the new will largely be wasted. Changing your diet is a similar prospect. You can (and should) begin today to make changes, but you must also take measures to clean up what has been put into your system from past years of bad eating. This process is known as *detoxification.*

To properly understand the importance of detoxification, you first need to learn a few basics of how your body was designed by God, or how it works to maintain health. Then it will be easier to understand *why* you need to take certain steps in cleansing your internal organs, in addition to developing new thinking and eating patterns if you want to achieve maximum health results. *You can help your body in the effort to get and stay healthy* naturally, *and turn to drugs or surgery as a last resort instead of the first option!* First step: detoxification.

END NOTES

1. "What to Do for a Miserable Cold When Mother Is not Around," <u>Young Living Essential News</u>, (November 2001), 1
2. Gordon S. Tessler, <u>The Genesis Diet: The Biblical Foundation for Optimum Nutrition</u>, (Raleigh: Be Well Publications, 1996), 71
3. Patrick Quillin, <u>Healing Secrets from the Bible: God Wants Us to Be Healthy, and the Bible Tells Us How</u>, (Tulsa: The Nutrition Times Press, Inc., 1996), 13

PART THREE

DETOXIFICATION–
A Modern Problem with an Ancient Command

2 Chronicles 29:16 - "Then the priests went into the inner part of the house of the Lord to cleanse it, and brought out all the debris that they found in the temple of the Lord..."

1 Corinthians 3:16 – "Do you not know that you are the temple of God....?"

Chapter 8

Cleansing the Temple – Then and Now

The Old Testament Temple

Before we tackle the subject of detoxification (a clean temple), let's establish the fact that it is a biblical principle and therefore important to God. In the Old Testament book of Exodus we can see God's emphasis on the temple. Moses makes a trip up Mt. Sinai where God speaks to him, giving him the Ten Commandments, but also giving him extremely intricate, precise instructions on how to build His temple. The materials used, how, and by whom they were to be made are all mentioned in minute detail. In fact, it takes God *five chapters* to get in all the particulars (Exodus 35:4 – 40:33).

The Israelites built the temple precisely as God instructed. Running it and keeping it clean through the years was the responsibility of the priests, but the cleanliness was largely determined by the king who happened to be ruling at the time. When an evil king ruled who had little or no regard for the one true God, the priests followed his lead and allowed the temple to degenerate into various stages of disrepair and ruin. The good kings, such as Hezekiah, made maintenance of the temple a priority, commanding the priests to perform their God-ordained functions:

> In the first year of his [Hezekiah's] reign...he opened the doors of the house of the Lord and repaired them. Then

he brought in the priests...and said to them: "Hear me, Levites!...sanctify the house of the Lord...and carry out the rubbish from the holy place..."

2 Chronicles 29:3-5 NKJV

Then the priests went into the inner part of the house of the Lord to cleanse it, and brought out all the debris that they found in the temple of the Lord...

2 Chronicles 29:16 NKJV

Many years and several kings later, the temple was tragically destroyed by Israel's enemies and the Hebrews were taken captive. They were eventually allowed to go back to their homeland and rebuild the temple. Upon their return, they started the building campaign, but construction ceased as their enemies mocked their efforts. The prophet Haggai joined these returned exiles about fifteen years later and delivered God's rebuke to them regarding their stalled building project:

Is it time for you yourselves to dwell in your paneled houses, and this temple to lie in ruins? Now therefore, thus says the Lord of hosts: "Consider your ways! You have sown much and bring in little; you eat, but you do not have enough; you drink, but you are not filled with drink; you clothe yourselves, but no one is warm; and he who earns wages, earns wages to put into a bag with holes...."

Haggai 1:4-11 NKJV

Wow! Not only does God consider it a priority to rebuild and keep the temple clean, but the consequences of not doing so would deplete or shrink their food and water supply, their clothing, and even their income!

The New Testament Temple

Fast forward to the New Testament and we find that the keepers of the temple are still the priests, but today believers comprise the priesthood:

You also…are…a holy priesthood….

1 Peter 2:5 NKJV

We also find in the New Testament that the temple of God is no longer a building constructed with mortar, wood, and gold.

Do you not know that you are the temple of God, and that the Spirit of God dwells in you? If anyone defiles the temple of God, God will destroy him. For the temple of God is holy, which temple you are.

1 Corinthians 3:16-17 NKJV

Or do you not know that your body is the temple of the Holy Spirit who is in you, whom you have from God, and you are not your own? For you were bought at a price; therefore glorify God in your body and in your spirit, which are God's.

1 Corinthians 6:19-20 NKJV

Spiritual Detoxification

In this age, you and I are the temple of God *and* the priests who are responsible to maintain its cleanliness and purity, *physically and spiritually*. Both of these aspects are important to our physical health, although few people would connect spiritual purity with their physical well-being. God, however, made this connection even in the Old Testament:

A merry heart does good like a medicine, but a broken spirit dries the bones.

Proverbs 17:22 NKJV

merry — exhilarated to laughter; pleasant, agreeable, delightful
heart – disposition of mind; utmost degree; seat of the will
good (*Strong's Concordance*) - make well, sound or beautiful.
good (*Webster's 1828*) – The primary sense is strong, fit, firm; a medicine good for disease

These definitions of "good" clearly describe a healthy body – strong, fit, and firm. In this proverb, the "merry heart" or the *disposition of the mind – your thoughts, your soul –* is what brings about this health. A healthy soul – mind, will, and emotions - reflects a healthy spirit. A healthy spirit is a pure spirit, once again reflecting a cleansed (detoxified) heart. Looking at two different translations of Matthew 5:8 further verifies the heart/soul/thinking connection:

> Blessed are the *pure in heart*: for they shall see God.
> Matthew 5:8 KJV

> Those who are *pure in their thinking* are happy, because they will be with God.
> Matthew 5:8 NCV

The second half of Proverbs 17:22 is very sobering to examine ("a broken spirit dries the bones"):

broken – parted by violence; rent asunder; infirm
spirit - the intelligent, immaterial and immortal part of human beings; cheerfulness; fire; courage; elevation or vehemence of mind.

A "broken spirit" is an infirm, sick, or diseased spirit. A broken spirit destroys our fire, our courage, our good thinking (elevation of the mind) and will actually "dry the bones." What part of the bone can get dry? The marrow. What does the marrow have to do with health? It is literally the heart of your immune system! So the first area to be considered in a detoxification or cleansing program is your own spirit and soul—begin right thinking! To overlook this aspect is to possibly overlook the very root of sickness and disease in many instances.

On the other hand, what we put into our fleshly body is of equal importance, both in caring for it and also demonstrating our love and obedience towards God. Rabbi Eric Braverman, author and health practitioner, says, "I tell my patients that every table is an altar, and that all the food eaten is a sacrifice to the Holy Spirit within us. The home and kitchen are scenes of divine service, just as much as the houses of worship and study."[1]

God apparently agrees with Rabbi Braverman as to the importance of what we put into our temples. Note the part of the Corinthians passage above that states "If anyone defiles the temple of God, God will destroy him." It is apparent that God puts even greater emphasis on the upkeep and purity of His temple today than He did in Old Testament times. Detoxification plays a major role in the bodily (temple) purification process.

Detoxification – Individual and Corporate

Most of us are familiar with this term (detoxification) but have usually heard it used to describe alcoholics or drug addicts going through withdrawal programs. It also applies to any form of cleaning toxins from the body. Indeed, the definition is simply –

detoxification - internally purifying the body of toxins.

We are living in the most toxic time the world has ever known. Our ability to get and stay healthy is increasingly determined by our body's ability to detoxify. The task of "internally purifying the body of toxins" cannot be overemphasized, and it involves both areas of personal and corporate responsibility. Consider the following:

- Industrial contamination infects our air and water
- Foods fried with any oil besides canola or olive oil promote carcinogenic activity in the blood
- Devalued foods (90% of what most of us eat) provide no enzymes to aid in digestion and thus produce toxic buildup
- Food from non-organic fields are sprayed with chemicals
- The ground is saturated with chemicals from more than 50 years of toxic sprays; therefore plant roots include these toxins
- Water enters our system not only through drinking but through our skin pores when we bathe

Chemicals we ingest go down into the intestinal tract, cause a weakening of the membrane wall, then leach into the liver. They cause cell mutation which alters our DNA – the beginning of cancer. They change the pH chemistry of the blood from alkaline to acid, effectively creating a body that is a friendly host for disease. After years of such exposure, we "all of a sudden" come down with a degenerative disease such as cancer, diabetes, or heart disease, and we wonder where it came from when we were trying so hard to take good care of ourselves. This is not to depress you but to impress upon you the importance and necessity of personal, bodily detoxification, in addition to making dietary and lifestyle changes, and becoming proactive in positive ways to corporately clean up our environment.

The principle is personal stewardship: God owns your body and expects you to nurture and maintain it properly. Because of all the pollutants in our environment and the fact that our foods are grossly devitalized, detoxification is of equal and perhaps even greater importance than eating right.
The principle is also corporate stewardship: God gave man dominion over the earth and expects us to responsibly care for and manage it in ways to promote health and propagate life.

Cleansing Is a Process, Not an Event

Let me insert two very important qualifications about the material we are going to cover. First, for the reasons just listed about pollutants in our twenty-first century environment, it is impossible for anyone to reach a state of bodily purity in diet or health. This teaching is not meant to put a guilt trip on anyone. It is meant for education and encouragement in the hope that you will begin to learn more on your own and start to make incremental changes in your diet and lifestyle. Don't try to do it all at once! You'll be frustrated and your protesting family will probably make you walk the plank!

Remember, the undergirding principle is obedience to God's revealed commandments for our personal and environmental upkeep.

Do what you can. Some things we can change; some things we can stop; others are beyond our control because of availability, time or cost, government regulations that take time, and persistent effort to change. As we saw in Deuteronomy 28:1-2, God is looking for *diligent* (steady application) obedience, not perfection. He desires to see honest, constant effort, and will reward accordingly. To the degree we are willing to obey and work to make changes (physically and spiritually) is the degree we will begin to see our health restored and our world cleaned up. God's command for us is clear:

> I call heaven and earth as witnesses today against you, that I have set before you life and death, blessing and cursing; therefore, **choose life** that both you and your descendants may live.
>
> Deuteronomy 30:19 NKJV

This is a commandment, *not an option*, and it relates to every aspect of our lives. This is also another proof that God wants you and me and our families to live long and healthy.

The principle is twofold: Christian character formation as we obey God's commandment to "choose life," and stewardship as we work to make changes in our lifestyle to improve our current health condition. The key is to begin!

Guidelines for Learning and Discerning

The second qualification is of equal importance. I have just begun to scratch the surface in this area of cleansing, rebuilding, and natural treatments, and there are new discoveries daily in this realm. I do not have all the answers, nor is it my intent to try to provide them all. However, I have begun the journey. There is a lot of "junk science" or half-truths in any arena, and diet, detoxification, environmental issues, and alternative medicine are no exceptions.

It can be difficult to sift through to find the whole truth. To that end, I offer some guidelines for discernment in any especially difficult areas. First of all, pray and put on your spiritual armor every day, remembering that God has given you "the mind of Christ." Then

"Get out of your box!" Do not openly dismiss something simply because it is new to you, seems strange, or doesn't fit your presuppositions. (I will be outlining some specific questions to ask in later chapters to discern your way through particular foods, medical practices, etc.). Approach every situation as a child, eyes wide open and searching. Pray every step of the way, looking to see if scriptural principles are upheld or violated. God wants you to learn, not to be hurt. He will lead you to truth as you ask. Jesus said,

> For everyone who asks receives, and he who seeks finds, and to him who knocks it will be opened. If a son asks for bread from any father among you, will he give him a stone? Or if he asks for a fish, will he give him a serpent instead of a fish? Of if he asks for an egg, will he offer him a scorpion?
>
> Luke 11:10-12 NKJV

With the understanding that God wants us to ask for, search out, and know truth – let's move on to a biology lesson.

END NOTES

1. Eric Braverman, "The Bible & Health – Is The Bible a Medical Book?" The Cutting Edge Health Digest, Issue #005 (Winter-Spring 2003):8

Chapter 9

Helping Your Body to Detoxify

K nowing some specifics about how our bodies function will help to better understand what is good for us and why we should eat according to God's laws. For example, telling people they should not smoke because it causes lung cancer may cause some people to stop smoking. However, explaining their personal suffering and what happens to their lungs, or showing them pictures of a pink, healthy nonsmoker's lung beside a black, charred smoker's lung that looks like a piece of paved blacktop will motivate more people to make right choices. The more we actually see or understand the details and consequences in our own bodily destruction, the more likely our choices will be for health.

The principle is education – sowing and reaping.
You study to learn how to maintain health and then apply
what you've learned. This knowledge is worth far more
than medication, for good health cannot be purchased. It
must be earned.
You work for it.

God designed our bodies to gather and use necessary nutrients from air, food, and water, but we also assimilate varying amounts of toxic material from those same materials. Fortunately, it was also part of God's design to include in the natural function of our cells the ability to eliminate these leftover toxins. When these toxins can be eliminated from the body there is no problem, no disease. However, we are living in the most toxic time the world has ever known. Our ability to get and stay healthy is increasingly determined by our body's ability to detoxify.

Current environmental factors (and poor dietary choices) push our elimination systems into overload. When one or more of these systems are overloaded or under-active, trouble lies ahead as toxic accumulations create the necessary pre-conditions for disease to develop. As these toxins gather in the tissues of our bodies, increasing degrees of cell destruction take place.

By the time a degenerative disease is recognized and diagnosed, toxic settlements have already taken over parts of the body, slowing or even shutting down some of our body's natural cleansing (puri-fication) functions. Do you recall that part of the definition of *heal* was "*to purify from corruptions*"? These toxins are the corruptions from which we need to be purified in order to be healed. Regular purging/detoxification of these internal toxins helps to maintain health. Occasional purging can assist in the healing or restoration process if disease has already settled in our bodies.

Detoxification is the job your body works at the hardest and longest. On a daily basis, a normal, healthy body's energy is care-fully delegated:

- ❑ 80% detoxifying
- ❑ 5% immune building
- ❑ 10% thinking
- ❑ 5% maintenance of organs[1]

Our bodies have many ways of eliminating toxins. Five areas I will deal with include:

- ❑ **blood** - through cell renewal and cleansing
- ❑ **lungs** - through breathing
- ❑ **skin** - through sweating
- ❑ **liver** – through filtration
- ❑ **intestines** - through kidneys and bowels

Let's take a closer look at each of these.

Blood

The blood is made up of *trillions* of cells which are constantly renewing. These cells are the byproduct of whatever food we are putting into our system. Food is fuel. Living food – fresh fruits and vegetables and whole grains – provide for healthy cell reproduction, which will make healthy blood and a "clean," healthy system. Dead foods – overcooked vegetables, devitalized grains, fat-saturated meats – recreate unhealthy cells that are unable to keep your system clean or maintain health. It's an oversimplification, but Dr. Mitra Ray, a well-known lecturer, author, and biochemist, said, "Disease is simply a set of cells not working properly. Drugs mask the problem. Nutrients make new cells."[2] In other words, cleansing the blood happens on a daily basis if we are eating properly. The best news of all is that each red blood cell is replaced every four months, so we have the continual ability to improve our health and vitality!

Lungs

The lungs are an organ that is very negatively impacted by a bad environment. Our nose, pharynx, larynx, trachea, and lungs make up our respiratory system. Air enters through the nose and travels across the trachea, which branches into the lungs, which in turn receive oxygen. The oxygen then goes to the cells via the capillaries. Lungs also expel toxins – metabolic waste – in the form of carbon dioxide. When our respiratory tract is diseased, it can manifest as wheezing (asthma), inflammation (bronchitis), emphysema, or other illnesses. Lungs use mucous and cilia to help protect against harmful inhalants. When our system can trap these toxins, it is possible to remove them through sneezing and coughing.

Skin

Your skin is comprised of an outer layer, the epidermis, and an inner layer, the dermis. The health of the epidermis determines how easily chemicals can penetrate the skin. The dermis gives skin its elasticity and strength. Sweat glands and hair follicles contained in the dermis help to regulate our internal temperature. "The skin is our largest cleansing organ. It can eliminate more cellular waste than the colon and kidneys combined."[3] It is also the single biggest entry point for toxins (via hair follicles) in the form of everything from skin lotions and antiperspirants to the water we bathe in. (I'll be covering water in some depth in a later chapter.) Detoxification through the skin is one of the simplest and most affordable cleanses anyone can do. I highly recommend Cheryl Townsley's book, *Cleansing Made Simple,* a very basic primer on detoxification. She makes several simple recommendations for detox baths using easy-to-find ingredients such as Epsom salts, apple cider vinegar, soda, and salt. But she also gives the caution: "Should you experience dizziness, headache, exhaustion, fatigue, nausea or weakness at any time during the bath, stop the bath. This is an indication that you are cleansing too quickly, or that your toxic load is too heavy at this time."[4] Her warning makes it clear how necessary and effective this kind of cleanse can be.

Liver

Your liver is truly an unseen and unsung hero. It's about the size of a football, weighs around five pounds, and is the largest and hardest-working organ in your body. It detoxifies in three main ways: filtering your blood, secreting bile, and using a two-step enzyme process. Most livers are terribly overloaded with toxins simply because toxins can come from so many sources, including processing every drug we ever take, whether over-the-counter or prescription. Other sources:

- toxins in our food
- water with too much bacteria, chemicals, heavy metals, and so forth
- digestion problems
- yeast and bacterial overgrowth in the small intestines
- food allergies
- parasites
- toxins in the air
- toxins in the home or workplace

- free radicals produced in the liver from detoxification[5]

Bile eliminates poisonous toxins by becoming the vehicle for flushing them out through your colon. Toxins pass through the bile ducts, which empty into the small intestine and eventually are eliminated through the colon. However, if you are constipated or don't eat enough fiber, these toxins and bile may remain in the intestine too long, and instead of being flushed from your body, they are actually reabsorbed! This can be happening for years without any noticeable symptoms, but eventually diseases and/or chronic pain begin to manifest in such ways as rheumatoid arthritis, lupus, multiple sclerosis, Crohn's disease, chronic fatigue, chronic headaches, psoriasis, acne, food allergies, diabetes, constipation, infections, hypertension, coronary artery disease, etc.[6]

Liver toxins need to be flushed out periodically if we are to experience true health. There are many, many methods to detoxify the liver, and I highly recommend you search until you find a competent medical professional to assist in the process, rather than attempting to purchase aids from your local health food store. You will pay more by seeking professional help, but if you do your homework properly in finding a good one, the money will be very well spent, and the results can be profound.

Another precaution to be offered in this type of cleanse is that it should probably be accompanied or followed by a colon cleanse. This is due to the fact that many toxins are being stirred up and released, but the colon debris needs another avenue of escape. This leads us to the next section.

Intestines

The intestines work hard every day to eliminate leftover toxins from what we eat. Partially digested food enters our small intestine, which is about 20 feet long. From there it enters our large intestine, or colon, which is about 5 feet long and about 2 1/2 inches in diameter. By the time food enters the colon, it is *all* waste material that needs to be *completely* eliminated from our bodies—within 18-24 hours after it was eaten. If, for any reason, this is not accomplished, parts of this toxic waste will stick to the colon wall, while other residue will actually be reabsorbed into our system. This causes "numerous health problems in the areas of digestion, liver and gall bladder, heart, vision, acne, prostate, body odor, arthritis, putrid gas, headaches and chronic illness, to name just a few. A step beyond this, of course, is degenerative disease."[7]

I believe cleansing the colon is an absolute necessity to any serious detoxification program, and not doing so is the root cause of the majority of health problems. I am not alone in this thought. The U.S. Public Health Service has estimated that 90 percent of all Americans have a clogged colon to some degree.[8] "The dominant symptom in more than 90% of all patients first visiting my clinic indicates the colon as the origin."[9] "No other single health condition plays so great a role in the development of disease as does constipation."[10] The average adult has *five to thirty pounds of fecal matter* that is not moving![11] For these reasons, I am going to spend considerably more time and detail on the colon.

Our bodies need 25-50 grams of fiber per day. The average American gets 11 grams. Because our diets do not include the proper amounts of roughage/fiber, the colon cannot get a grip on part of the waste it contains, and some is not eliminated. As the years go by, our colon continually cannot properly clean itself, and the waste that is not reabsorbed into other body parts begins to build up in the colon itself. The pathway of the colon becomes more and more obstructed so fewer and fewer toxins can pass through anymore. Other body organs begin to be affected, and our body's defenses slowly break down, all because of the toxic material trapped in our colon, as well as what "escaped" to other parts of our body. The most frightening thing about this stage of disease is that it is possible to "feel fine" through all this breakdown time.

Colon detoxification was my family's first major step into alternative medical practices, and the results were dramatic. A close friend recommended the procedure, and after close investigation into it we decided to take the plunge. After twelve years of constant sickness and a non-ending stream of new drugs, David and I began the daily drive of almost one hundred miles to the nearest licensed colon massage therapist. (We began on January 10 – David's nineteenth birthday – and we laugh about it today when we talk about "celebrating" his birthday with his first colonic treatment.) A colonic is not just a fancy name for an enema. An enema cleans out the anus, the very end of the colon. A properly performed colonic, accompanied with natural supplements to assist in the procedure, cleans both the large and small intestines from top to bottom.

For an entire month I drove him daily for these hour-long treatments, which included five to six fillings and evacuations of the colon. Some of the nutritional supplements he was taking at the time acted like a scrub brush inside his colon, while others helped to cleanse his blood and rebuild his strength. All these natural agents working together, plus the daily moistening, softening, and removal of years-old fecal matter, not only cleaned his colon but helped other organs begin to detoxify as well. The results were immediate and dramatic.

In a rapid cleansing program such as this, a healing crisis can occur when the detox pathways are flooded with loosened toxins, creating a "dirty traffic jam." We were thoroughly grossed out and amazed at the volume of old, rotten fecal matter that flushed out daily, including gallstones. But after a few days of treatments discharging so many toxins so rapidly, the healing crisis commenced. David began to experience all the symptoms he had through the years—blazing headaches, joint pain, extreme fatigue—as toxins started exiting through any avenue of escape they could find. His lungs began to clean out from previous bouts with asthma and other respiratory ailments, and he began to cough up large amounts of old, rotten infection that had been trapped there for years. Other toxins escaped through multiple mouth sores which appeared and then resolved themselves in a day or two. *Because of the healing crisis factor, it is always advisable and beneficial to work with a qualified health care provider when detoxing rapidly.*

Toward the end of one month of this intense detox regimen, we began to *see* the return of health! Color slowly returned to his cheeks; his complexion was peachy instead of ashy; his strength was restored (he could lift weights again); his lungs were healthy enough for him to run a mile or more; his weight increased (over the next three months) from 118 to 148 pounds. (David is 6' tall.)

Financial constraints forced us to stop after twenty treatments as our insurance did not cover colonics, a source of much frustration since this was the first method of treatment that worked. We weren't "finished," but we had done enough to jumpstart his entire body into self-cleaning mode. As we cleaned out his colon from old, trapped wall material that had become toxic to his system, his other body parts began to self-clean and purify themselves as well, until his entire body was "purified from corruptions" — the true definition of *healing*. Remarkably and ironically, after twelve years and thousands of dollars' worth of drugs and tests, *this healing was accomplished entirely without any medication.*

David's story is not unusual in the non-allopathic medical world. Another book I highly recommend – *Tissue Cleansing Through Bowel Management* - has stories of people with terribly ulcerated feet and hands. Photos were taken when they arrived at a colonic/health clinic and then again on the fourth and seventh day of colonic treatments. Just as in David's case, no medications were given, yet these people's external, terribly ulcerated symptoms began to disappear as their diets were changed and their colons were cleaned for just one week.

> *External symptoms abate and disappear as proper*
> *and efficient internal cleansing takes place.*
> *The body begins to heal itself.*

The Disease and Detox Connection

A true story in the natural world illustrates this phenomenon. Several years ago, there was a garbage worker strike in New York City. When this strike occurred, the people of New York did not stop producing garbage. They still filled up their wastebaskets, emptied them into trashcans, and put them at the curb every week to be picked up and hauled away to the dump. But the trash man did not come. Garbage began to accumulate as the days and weeks went by. It looked terrible, smelled worse, and continued to pile up higher and deeper. The trash that had sat out the longest began to putrefy and produce worms, parasites, germs, and diseases that were picked up by the animal population. Soon sickness and disease began to multiply alarmingly among the people. Fortunately for New Yorkers, the strike ended, the trash was picked up and taken away, the disease problems slowly disappeared, and the whole New York City elimination system was functioning normally once again. Health was restored.

The analogy isn't hard to see. When we engage in harmful eating habits, our waste accumulates—a "strike" has begun in our system in which all the garbage is not being taken away anymore by our elimination system. As it builds up through the months and years, it rots, putrefies, and begins to cause all kinds of disease problems. When we do not change those eating habits, there is no "end to the strike." *The old garbage is never picked up* and diseases begin, varying in intensity from simple colds to terminal cancer.

This process happens slowly over time. I can't tell you how many times I've heard people say, "I've been healthy all my life, and then all of a sudden—BOOM—for no reason at all I got diabetes... heart disease... cancer" (you fill in the blank). This is often followed by the classic question: "Why did God let this happen to me?" God didn't. The harsh reality is that these diseases, by and large, are *self-inflicted*. The laws of nature, God's immutable laws, are in effect.

> *The principle is sowing and reaping. Knowingly or unknowingly, when we continually break God's immutable dietary laws, eating (sowing things into our flesh) what He told us not to eat, we will reap disease sooner or later.*

We are all in need of some form or other of detoxification. We are all building up toxins in our bodies to one degree or another that will bring about some manifestation of disease – some great, some small. Detoxification is necessary for *everyone*, critical for some! Indeed, when the colon is impacted with sugars, hamburgers, French fries, white flour, and processed foods of every nature, the body can never expect to assimilate sufficient nutrients from the good food we occasionally do eat.

There are several ways to detoxify your body. I have a recommended reading list at the end of this book where many of them can be found. (One of my favorites is Don Colbert's *Toxic Relief.*) My best suggestion to the reader is to educate yourself, read about cleansing, and get to know your own body and its needs. Then search out some alternative health professionals, ask lots of questions, pray, and seek God's direction for your cleansing. I'll be giving a few guidelines in Part Four regarding choices in alternative medical practices.

But first we're going to examine some lifestyle changes that will aid in getting and keeping your body (God's temple) cleansed – namely, fasting, daily diet choices, and exercise.

END NOTES

1. Cheryl Townsley, <u>Cleansing Made Simple: What is a Cleanse? Why Cleanse? Who Should Cleanse? How to Cleanse?</u> (Littleton, CO, LFH Publishing, 1997) p. 38
2. Dr. Mitra Ray, "Call Me in the Morning," NSA Promo Plus Item # 1055.
3. Ibid., p. 15
4. Ibid., p. 46
5. Don Colbert, <u>Toxic Relief,</u> (Lake Mary, Florida: Siloam, 2003), p. 105
6. Ibid, p. 106
7. Terri Hawkins, "Death Begins in the Colon," <u>Healthy Living</u>, March 2000, p. 37.
8. V. E. Irons, "How You Can Seem to Reverse the Aging Process," <u>Healthview Newsletter</u>, Issue #1 (July 1983) : 2
9. Cliff H. Robertson, <u>The Health Explosion</u>, (Utica, Kentucky: McDowell Publications, 1983), p. 40
10. Ted Broer, <u>Maximum Energy</u>, (Lake Mary, Florida: Creation House, 1999), p. 39
11. Glenn Kirkwood, Prevention Plus+ Lecture, Dayton, Ohio, 11 January 2003.

Chapter 10

Fasting, Dieting, and Lifestyle Changes

Introducing positive lifestyle changes that bring about new life-long habits should be the goal of anyone who is serious about their health and caring for God's temple (your body). These habits include:

- Spending more time with God in prayer and meditating on His Word to us
- A balance of aerobic and resistance/weight-bearing exercise to get our bodies moving and muscles toned
- Complementary dietary alterations

Surprising to a lot of people, one God-ordained dietary habit we should all add to our lives is that of *not* eating on occasion – fasting!

Fasting

Fasting is a forgotten discipline among the body of Christ, but it is making a slow return. As we read Scripture, it becomes clear that God intended for us to fast:

[Jesus said] – "When you fast...."

Matthew 6:16 NKJV

It is noteworthy first of all that Jesus was speaking to His followers when He said this, and secondly that He did not say *if* you decide to fast, but rather *when* you do! The obvious implication is that fasting is part of the Christian's life. As with all of Jesus' commands, obedience brings with it multiple blessings.

Spiritually, we benefit as we grow closer to God because when we fast we should be spending more time in His Word and in prayer. Since our bodies are not working on digesting food, our minds are much clearer and able to "eat and digest" fresh revelation from God that will enhance our spiritual strength in much the same way good food enhances our physical strength. In the realm of the soul (our mind, will, and emotions), we are strengthened as we discipline and take control over our will to eat, saying *no* to feeding our flesh while saying *yes* to Jesus and feeding our spirit instead. For the purposes of this book, we are going to focus mainly on the health and physical benefits of fasting (intending in no way to diminish the importance of the spiritual side):

> [When you fast] Then your light shall break forth like the morning, your healing shall spring forth speedily.
>
> Isaiah 58:8 NKJV

How is healing related to not eating? In many ways! When we fast, our bodies produce a substance known as human growth hormone at a greater rate than at any other time. This growth hormone is essential to our body's physical health and strong immune system. Fasting is also a way to cleanse your body. Toxins stored in fat cells and organs are rapidly released during a fast. Nothing known to man equals the fast as a means of increasing the elimination of waste from the blood and tissues.

This rapid release of toxins can cause real problems for many individuals. For this reason I strongly recommend anyone desiring to do more than a three day fast to take specific precautions, up to an including conducting your fast under medical supervision. True North Health Education Center specializes in medical fasting. Their website – www.TrueNorthHealth.com – offers great information, articles and case studies on fasting. There is also a listing of other fasting health professionals at www.naturalhygienesociety.org. This organization has published a book by Herbert M. Shelton called, *Fasting Can Save Your Life*, which includes case studies of various health problems that were resolved through fasting.

If you cannot or will not seek medical assistance for a longer fast, there are steps you can take to assist your body in fasting. Complete rest and a supportive environment are major players. In addition, I personally believe anyone who fasts for more than three days should take some form of supplementation to aid their body in ridding itself of the loosened toxins. Bowel function normally stops when you stop eating, and your colon will need help to keep moving out old waste matter that your fast will be stirring up and loosening. I have fasted for as long as twelve days and during that time took supplements that brought about one to three bowel movements *daily*. Logic says this has to be old waste material as there is no new food being sent down during a fast! As disgusting as it is to acknowledge this, it is equally health restoring to get rid of it.

There are many methods of "do-it-yourself" cleansing to use during a fast. I have provided three recommendations, three separate books and authors with three different but effective methods in the Recommended Reading List at the end of this book for those who would like to learn more and/or pursue this type of cleansing. There are many other methods and systems available on the market today. For both financial and safety concerns, I would not purchase or do any of them until you thoroughly investigate their efficacy and safety.

Let's address some of the "nuts and bolts" of fasting, a subject usually not covered in churches but one whose issues keep many Christians from ever experiencing the blessings of this cleansing method. First of all, many people believe they "can't fast" because they get so sick when they try, the most common complaint being horrible headaches. The main source of these headaches is usually sugar or caffeine withdrawal. If sugar is the culprit, you can greatly diminish the fasting headache by preparing your body. Two to three days before entering your fast, gradually cut back on your "sweet intake" (desserts, candy, cookies, sodas, etc.). During this same two- to three-day period, cut back on the size of your meals and cooked foods, eating primarily raw fruits and vegetables as much as possible.

The probable second cause of a headache, caffeine withdrawal, is much more difficult to deal with. The only way to avoid the caffeine headache is by breaking the caffeine addiction prior to fasting, and this can take *days*—days filled with dreadful headaches depending on how heavy your addiction is. The positive side of this is that experiencing this withdrawal should convince anyone of the harmful effects of caffeine on their body, and perhaps keep them from bringing it on again after the fast. Unfortunately, I can offer no suggestion for a gentler way to enter the fast with regard to caffeine. However, the good news is that as you increase your fasting time (by your fourth or fifth fast), you will usually experience no more hunger pangs or headaches after the third day and can continue safely (if fasting properly with bowel elimination aids) for as much as forty days, just as Jesus did. However, for longer fasts (more than seven days), I believe it is imperative to be Spirit-led, certain of *why* God wants you to be fasting.

When you are ready to begin, start your fast *after* lunch, beginning by skipping the evening meal. By doing this, when you get up the next morning, you are nearly two-thirds of the way through your first day. If you have never fasted before, it is also better to start with just a one-day fast. Break your fast with dinner that night, but a dinner of raw fruits and vegetables, not a heavy meat-and-potatoes meal. The following day you can eat normally again. During your fast, you should also be drinking a daily minimum of 64 ounces of pure water, and even as much as 128 ounces. This will greatly assist in purifying your body and keeping your stomach "full," which helps alleviate hunger pangs.

The next time you fast, enter it the same way and increase your time to three days. Break the fast with raw fruits or vegetables again, and slowly over the next day or two get back to regular eating. Preparing your body to enter a fast in this way, you will experience far less of a headache and perhaps escape it entirely. With the absence of a headache, you will be able to concentrate on prayer and Bible reading much better and glean spiritual insights as well as feel better during your fast.

Remember, if you are taking prescription drugs or have a degenerative disease, *always* seek a health professional to help and monitor you during your fast. For such individuals, True North Health Education center proclaims: "Do it right or *don't do it!* Complete rest, a supportive environment and professional supervision are necessary in order to be a safe and effective experience." I echo these sentiments.

If you are fasting independently and it is for more than three days, *please* do so with supplements to aid in your body's elimination of toxins. And always break the fast *slowly* over a couple days or more (even longer for longer fasts), adding broth, eating small amounts of raw or lightly steamed fruits and vegetables and drinking *lots and lots of pure water* to get your body's digestive system up and working properly again. Your stomach and intestines haven't processed any food for the entire fast and will need to be reawakened *gently*! Overall, the benefits of fasting are *wonderful*, spiritual and physical, when done properly. And most important - Fasting is part of God's plan for your well being!

Dieting

In searching out a healthy diet, we need to look for biblical principles once again rather than the latest fad. Our society's idea of dieting is usually drastically cutting back on our food consumption for a short time until our weight loss is achieved, then resuming our old habits all over again. This would be more correctly labeled a perverted fast. When God told Adam what he should eat, He also told him he should *eat freely* (Genesis 2:16). When we are eating God's ordained foods when we feel hungry, *stopping when we are full*, we can eat freely. We do not have to limit our intake.

Most modern diets not only deprive our bodies of calories but of vital nutrients necessary for health. Temporarily starving ourselves until we reach our desired weight or get tired of the diet, only to return to the same habits that brought about the problem in the first place, does not address the real problem. Limiting our caloric intake for a season is addressing a symptom, not the problem. If we are overweight, it is either due to a lack of discipline in our flesh or an imbalance in one of our body's *natural functions* (such as our digestive or endocrine system), or a combination of the two. The first, a lack of discipline, can be overcome through strengthening our spirit to overcome the flesh through the Word, through prayer, and through fasting, because self-control is one of the fruits of the Spirit. The second, an imbalance in our system, can often be corrected through detoxification, supplemental nutrients, and changing our dietary choices to God-ordained foods. The Greek word for diet means *life-style,* not a temporary starvation.

Furthermore, temporary starvation does not work because God designed our bodies to tolerate occasional famines, which is precisely what your body thinks is happening when you deprive it of food for a season. There are several examples in the Bible of times of famine due to lack of rain, enemy destruction of crops, insect infestations, etc. During a famine (self-induced or otherwise), our bodies experience a quick initial weight loss for a week or so, but then our metabolism slows down radically and our bodies cling to any fat deposits they can find to prevent starvation! This is part of God's design, and our body's fat stores are part of God's plan to keep us alive in hard times. This design allows for your body to live a *long* time on very little food (and lose very little weight over this *long* time), allowing for another season's crops to be harvested and normal eating to resume.

Think through and apply what I just said. Today's diet plans are by and large *self-induced famines*: Such diets bring about quick initial weight loss followed by the "plateau" period in which most dieters become completely disheartened because they are no longer losing weight, or are losing it way too slowly for all the suffering they are enduring. This discouragement inevitably leads to stopping the diet and returning to previous eating habits without ever realizing their bodies are performing just the way God designed them to perform during a time of famine.

According to a recent report in *USA Today*, when men and women diet without strength training (*exercise – it's not a dirty word!*), about 25-30 percent of the weight they lose is from water, muscle, bone, and other important lean tissue, while the body fat often stays. Ironically, this means dieting can actually reduce your body's ability to burn fat, as the loss of lean muscle causes your metabolic rate to drop. (It takes 25-50 calories to maintain a pound of muscle but only 2 calories to maintain a pound of fat!)[1] Furthermore, your energy is greatly depleted when dieting this way.

But the worst news of all happens when you stop the diet. You will not only gain back the weight you lost but usually *even more* because your weight loss changed your body composition to more fat and less muscle, which means your metabolic rate is diminished. In other words, the new and higher level of body fat burns dramatically fewer calories (as cited above) than the decreased muscle mass. The devastating result is that even if you eat *less* than you did before your diet you will probably still *gain* weight. In addition, the muscle you lost will not naturally return, but only with a lot of hard work and specific exercises. It is a vicious cycle of *increasing* weight and fat, in spite of the fact that you are *eating less and less!* Sadly, those desiring to lose weight will repeat this cycle many times with ever-growing levels of defeat. Yo-yo dieting is horribly counterproductive and is *not* part of God's eating plan or body design.

What About Low-fat, Jenny Craig, Atkins...?

Eating less fat does not reduce your fat deposits. In addition, you don't have to eat fat to get fat. Part of the problem with a low-fat diet is that we are substituting sugars and carbohydrates for fats. Our bodies convert the sugars from these carbohydrates into saturated fats, which are then added to our body's fat stores, thus exacerbating the problem. This also leads to hormonal imbalance, which in turn *adds even more to our fat stores!*

One reason our bodies are in such a state of imbalance is because there are also diets on the market today that do "work" (meaning you *do* lose weight) but still don't address the root problem. Jenny Craig has put together a program that yields weight loss, but you have to eat her specially prepared foods to succeed. Weight Watchers is similar; however, they do include some dietary *principles* that can be applied outside their brand-name food products.

There are also diets that "work" but are incredibly dangerous. The current rage is the high protein/low-carb diet such as Atkins and South Beach. The Physicians Committee for Responsible Medicine refers to such diets as health-destroying and has created a website called www.atkinsdietalert.org to address concerns about the diet and accumulate data about its health effects. People who have registered with this site reported that they have experienced the following health issues since beginning the diet:

- Loss of energy – 50%
- Constipated – 50%
- Bad breath – 34%
- Difficulty concentrating – 31%
- Gall bladder problems – 14%
- Heart problems – 10%
- Reduced kidney function – 9%
- Kidney stones – 9%
- Elevated cholesterol – 8%
- Gout – 6%
- Osteoporosis – 6%

This website has also documented the first actual death while on the Atkins diet, plus other horrendous reports of developing colon cancer, Irritable Bowel Syndrome (IBS) flare-ups, etc. If your purpose for weight loss is health-related, this is clearly not the correct path to take! These statistics indicate you lose a lot more than just weight.

In addition, Dr. Atkins' recent death has cast the brightest light of all on the merit of his dietary advice. Dr. Atkins is reported to have died from head injuries from a fall on the ice. However, the release of his autopsy showed evidence of an overweight, very unhealthy man. Dr. Atkins was 6 feet tall and weighed 258 pounds at the time of his death, and he could properly be classified as obese. He suffered from severe heart damage known as cardio-myopathy, and his history included congestive heart failure and hypertension. The most common cause of each of these maladies is a high-fat, high-cholesterol diet, precisely what the Atkins diet recommends. I share these facts with you not to malign a dead man but to help you see that his diet is a program that results in short-term weight loss, at best, but eventually causes extremely poor health.

Another problem with this diet is that it is exactly the opposite of what is recommended by the American Heart Association. You may be losing weight, but you are dramatically increasing your risk of heart disease because of all the saturated fats consumed. A study conducted at the University of California, San Francisco, found that too much protein consumption also increases the risk of osteoporosis, bone loss and fractures in elderly women.[2]

The primary reason and bottom line for rejecting this diet is that it violates multiple biblical *principles* regarding eating:

❑ God specifically commands people *not* to eat the fatty parts of the animal, and this diet is loaded with fat.

❑ Jesus indirectly refers to the importance of bread (carbohydrates) in our diet through His analogy of Himself as the Bread of Life and praying daily for God's provision of our bread.

❑ God's original design in the garden was for man to live on a vegetarian diet. Meat was added later as a supplement to fruits and vegetables, *not* as a replacement!

In addition, the U.S. Department of Agriculture has determined percentages of food groups for an optimum diet that also shoots down the Atkins diet in principle. (Though these percentages vary slightly from expert to expert, they are very close to one another):

❑ 70% complex carbohydrates
❑ 20% fats
❑ 10% protein[3]

There are literally dozens (hundreds?) of diets and diet pills available to the consumer today. Your job is to research and reason through any you may be considering to determine whether they are biblically sound. Balance is almost always the answer. God gave us fruits, vegetables, grains, and meat to eat (carbohydrates, fats, and proteins). To exclude or overindulge in one or more food group is to venture outside of good eating parameters.

*God's dietary principles are balanced, contribute to good
health, and contain a variety of food groups.*

A permanent, healthy lifestyle is the bottom line in eating habits,
not a temporary "diet fix." God's design for us is to have a daily diet
that brings life and maintains health. A balance of protein, carbohydrates, and fats should be eaten daily, with a special emphasis on
fresh fruits, vegetables, and whole grains. A weight-loss diet needs
to be *balanced, sensible lifestyle eating*, not temporary starvation. In
contrast, most weight-loss diets are temporary in nature and based
either on gluttony or extremism: You can eat all the carbs you want
(high-carb/low-fat) but little or no protein; or you can eat all the
protein and fat you want (high-protein/low-carb) but little or no
fruits and vegetables. In addition, these types of diets are usually not
concerned about the quantity of food consumed. When restructuring
your eating habits, begin with the word *balance* and the knowledge
that this is the beginning of a new lifestyle, not self-torture through
temporary deprivation until you reach a desired goal.

Exercise – Your Body Will Thank You!
Part of a healthy lifestyle also includes the "E" word – EXERCISE.
No matter what those magazine advertisements promise, no pill can
magically change fat into muscle while you sleep! Right eating can
reduce body fat, but muscle mass is created through *movement!*
Strength training also builds bone density far better than taking a
calcium supplement, which makes exercise a valuable addition to
everyone's program to fend off osteoporosis. As stated previously,
it takes 25-50 calories to maintain one pound of muscle. It takes
2 calories to maintain one pound of fat. You do the math. Muscle
mass not only feels better and looks better, it burns more fuel. But
what kind of exercise should you do, and how much? Jack Medina,
an Olympic fitness coach, has said, "The best exercise in the world
is the one you will do."

Most experts today agree on a combination of aerobic and resistance exercise for optimum health and strength. Walking at a very
quick pace for 30-60 minutes every other day provides wonderful
cardiovascular movement. Ted Broer, a university-trained

biochemist, exercise physiologist, and licensed nutritionist, has produced an outstanding video series for resistance exercise called "Eat, Drink & Be Healthy." This series is designed specifically for reducing body fat and increasing lean muscle mass, and it can be personalized to your age and gender. It begins with only 10 minutes a day and increases, at your own pace, to a tailor-made, every-other-day resistance workout. You can check it out at www.healthmasters. com or call 800-726-1834.

Another excellent video exercise program you can do from the privacy of your own home is Pilates. There are many versions, but Mari Winsor has produced a tutorial video series that trains beginners in the different moves, and her videos include modifications for those who have various physical limitations. You can check it out at www.winsorpilates.com. Her series takes you from the beginning program through to more advanced and challenging exercises as your body stretches and grows in strength. She also has "target exercise" programs for various body areas, and they really do work. Once you are familiar with these exercises, most libraries have other Pilates videos you can check out. I would *not* recommend doing any of these exercises without first going through a tutorial so as to avoid personal injury!

By the way, it is possible to lose inches without losing weight if you are working out consistently. A pound of muscle takes up about 22 percent less space than a pound of fat![4] A woman participating in an experimental weight loss group (results published in the 1998 *Journal of American Nutraceutical Corporation*) lost only one pound of scale weight in eight weeks—gaining eight pounds of muscle, but losing nine pounds of fat. *But she also lost two dress sizes.* So it is important not to judge your body by the scale when you start to exercise regularly.

By now, I'm sure it is clear that spiritual and physical detoxification, diet, and exercise are all components of a healthy lifestyle. But the food we ingest is not all that goes into our bodies. Most, if not all, of us have taken, are taking, or will take some type of drug in the form of prescriptions or over-the-counter medications. Our body's health is profoundly impacted by the drugs we use. For this reason,

I want to address drug use and alternative medical practices before we begin discussion of principles regarding specific foods.

END NOTES

1. N. Hellmich, "Strength Training Pumps Up Weight Loss Regimens." USA Today, June 1, 1998.
2. Deborah Sellmeyer, "High Animal Protein Intake May Increase Risk of Bone Loss and Fractures in Elderly Women, UCSF Study Finds," UC San Francisco, 22 December 2000
3. Gordon S. Tessler, The Genesis Diet, (Raleigh, NC: Be Well Publications, 1996), p. 156
4. Michael O'Shea, "Parade's Guide to Better Fitness," Parade Magazine, 7 December 2003, p. 21

PART FOUR

MAKING BIBLICALLY BASED MEDICAL DECISIONS

Whose ways are you seeking first –
God's or man's?

Jeremiah 46:11b – In vain shall you use many medicines;
for you shall not be cured.
Matthew 6:33 – But seek you first the kingdom of God
and His righteousness; and all these things shall be added
to you.

Chapter 11

"Good" Drugs

We all know that the food we ingest goes through our digestive tracts and makes up our diet. But few of us think about the fact that the drugs we take also pass through the digestive tract (and our livers), becoming part of our "diet" and contributing to the toxic overload our body organs and systems must deal with.

The toxic nature of drugs is overlooked to our peril. According to the *New England Journal of Medicine*, the percentage of personal health care dollars spent on prescription drugs has grown faster than any other segment, including doctor and hospital bills. The *Journal of the American Medical Association* (the most widely circulated medical periodical in the world) declared in its July 26, 2000, issue that "Doctors Are the Third Leading Cause of Death in the U.S." Within that statistic, the largest number of deaths by far was attributed to *"non-error, negative effects of drugs."* Do you understand this statement? These were not drug or medication errors. These were the *right* drugs for the *right* disease prescribed *correctly* for the patient, who died anyway as a result of the negative effects of this "good" drug!

The vast majority of medical professionals in America today are allopathic doctors, those who are trained to fight disease with drugs and surgery. It is extremely rare to go to an allopathic doctor and leave his office without a prescription for one or more drugs. Indeed, that's what we have come to expect, and we would probably demand our money back if we were sent home without a prescription drug, as we perceive this is the answer to our medical challenge. But there is a basic underlying problem with always using this approach. "Pharmaceutical salesmen point out that about 95 percent of all medicines sold deal only with symptoms and to relieve discomfort and pain. Almost none of them deal with the root cause of the illness."[1]

Drugs that attack or cover symptoms in your body are not addressing the **root cause** *of your disease and do not heal or cure.*

Let's look at an example in the natural world to illustrate: You are driving your car one day when the red indicator light on the dashboard comes on. You know there is a problem somewhere but don't have the knowledge to figure out where it is or what to do about it. You go to your local mechanic so he can examine your car, diagnose the difficulty, and fix it. When you arrive, you explain to him what has happened. Your mechanic goes out to your car, turns it on, and sure enough there's that pesky red light, shining brightly. Your mechanic reaches into his coveralls, pulls out a roll of masking tape, rips off a small piece, and puts it over the red indicator light, concealing it completely.

"There you go!" he says. "You're all set. Have a nice day." And he presents you with a $100 repair bill. Are you happy with this solution? Did he fix the problem? Are you going to take your car back to this mechanic? I'm betting your answer to all three questions is a resounding NO—and you're probably laughing at how ludicrous this would be. But isn't this often what happens when we go to a doctor and walk out with a prescription?

When I suffered from migraine headaches the doctors always sent me home with a powerful painkiller and *never* attempted to find or eliminate the *cause* of the migraines. David's doctors did try to determine the cause of his ongoing infirmities, but in the end they always resorted to drug therapies, which covered the symptoms (temporarily) but never cured the problem (which always returned). The physical root of David's difficulties (and of so many other medical ailments) was wrong eating habits, environmental pollutants, and too many drugs, all of which led to one or more backed-up elimination, cleansing, or filtration systems. He needed to make some lifestyle changes and have his body detoxified. He did not need to be given the latest and greatest legal (prescription) drug.

Unfortunately, Americans have become accustomed to the "unnatural fix" drugs *seem to provide*. In his book *The Pleasure Trap*, Dr. Doug Lisle asserts that one of modern medicine's goals is too often to relieve pain without determining the underlying cause of the disease. Many times the best path to health would not be taking a pill to relieve symptoms, but rather dietary change, exercise, stopping smoking, etc. Patients are given a prescription and then equate feeling better with getting better. *They are not the same!* He cites two examples:

❑ Fever is a natural defense of the body to a predator. When you suppress a fever in most instances, you are interrupting the healing process. But most people associate the fever-breaking with a recovery, so they look at medical intervention as a positive thing, when actually intervention should only be used when there are obvious risks of the fever continuing.

❑ Medications are available to block nausea, diarrhea, or vomiting when these are signs that something is wrong with either the gastrointestinal tract or what you're putting in it. In a study conducted at the University of Texas, researchers infected two groups of people with a bacteria that induces diarrhea. In one group, no drugs were used to stop the diarrhea. In the other, subjects were given medication. In the treated group, the participants were feverish and toxic for twice as long as those in the untreated group. This is a very clear example of relieving uncomfortable symptoms while the cause of the disease lingers and can cause more damage. We are much better off to let the body heal itself.

Drug relief is instantaneous, but it often encourages the continuation of damaging behavior and confuses the patient into thinking that healing is occurring—it may even cause horrendous side effects.

The truth, according to Dr. Lisle, is that the public has been lured into thinking modern medicine has a cure that will save them from any disease they develop. The reality is quite different, he says, as evidenced by the fact that over 75 percent of the population will die prematurely from some degenerative disease that is preventable and treatable with natural means.

In addition, since the medical *industry* (not *profession*) has become contaminated by greed, "legal drugs" have become as profitable as illegal drugs. And the fact remains that drugs, "good" or bad, "legal" or illegal, are terribly toxic to your body. It is only logical, therefore, that we should actively investigate alternative, safer, and more natural forms of treatment in non-emergency situations.

Attacking symptoms in a body that has not been recently detoxified is an exercise in futility. Chances are high that the disease you are experiencing was at least brought on partially by a lack of eliminating toxins in one or more areas of your body. Rather than treating or covering the symptoms, we should be searching for the *source* of the symptoms, *why* the symptoms are happening, and then making whatever purification, diet changes, or physical adjustments are needed to assist our bodies in returning to healthy balance. As stated before, God designed our bodies to heal themselves. Just as an external wound such as a cut finger will heal itself (bleed to cleanse the wound, scab to protect it from germ invasion, then grow new skin, all part of our *natural functions*), so will our internal bodies begin to heal themselves and come into balance as they are supplied with the right nutrients, environment, adjustments, and internal cleansers.

By and large, the prescriptions given us by allopathic doctors are comprised of chemicals and manmade substances that mask symptoms or "trick" our bodies into producing or not producing certain substances. Treating diabetes with insulin is a good example. While a diabetic needs insulin to live, the fact remains that the root problem has not been addressed. Insulin does not *cure* diabetes. A diabetic will *always* need insulin unless their body functions are returned to normal through cleansing, possibly some remedial supplementation, and proper diet. While drug solutions are very often necessary as a temporary fix, they should not be considered a "life sentence."

Attempts should always be made to help the entire body return to balance, to health, ultimately eliminating the need for the drugs.

Examples abound when it comes to misuse, abuse, or over-consumption of pharmaceuticals, but for the sake of brevity I would like to share just three very common prescriptions used in America today – hormone replacement therapy for women with "female problems," Ritalin (and similar drugs) for children with Attention Deficit Disorder (ADD), and antidepressants such as Prozac, Paxil, Luvox, and Zoloft.

Hormone Replacement Therapy

Many natural options are available today for managing difficulties experienced during a woman's monthly cycle and at the time of menopause. But because these symptoms affect so many women today, they have become a highly sought after drug "market." The first thing to acknowledge is that menopause and the monthly menstrual period are *not* diseases. They are natural functions of a healthy female body, not maladies requiring pharmaceutical intervention. However, the plethora of problems associated with these functions have made it an easy case for the allopathic medical world to target for drug rehabilitation. The drug most commonly chosen for menopause problems is Premarin, which is made from **pregnant** horses' (**mares'**) **urine**.

Premarin became exceedingly popular in a very short period of time due to both the pharmaceutical company's marketing plans as well as the initial "good" results women experienced when taking it. However, because of the vast amount of women using this drug, it didn't take too long before problems started surfacing. Kaiser-Permanente reported an increase in endometrial cancer in women taking Premarin. In 1975, the *New England Journal of Medicine* published results of a study that showed that 57 percent of women with cancer had used estrogen replacement drugs, while only 15 percent of the control group had used them. The article's stark and startling conclusion was that **the risk of cancer increased by 760 percent** in women on estrogen replacement therapy, and long-term users were at even greater risk.[2]

When these statistics went public, the drug company's response was to make the drug more desirable. To them, the issue was one of marketing, not women's health or safety. To promote the sales of this drug after the cancer scare, it was decided by the pharmaceutical company to claim that the drug Premarin had additional value in reducing the risk of heart disease and osteoporosis. At the time these claims were made there was little or no evidence as to the drug's effectiveness in these areas, but the claims did their job, made the drug more desirable, and by 1995 Premarin was the most widely prescribed drug in the United States, with $940 million in annual sales.[3]

In reality, studies have not shown Premarin to be useful for the prevention of heart disease or osteoporosis. The Heart & Estrogen/Progestin Replacement Study (HERS) concluded that four years of treatment with both estrogen and progesterone did not reduce the risk of heart attack in women who had already experienced some form of cardiovascular disease. The most optimistic study showed only that hormone replacement therapy may slow the loss of bone but does not reverse existing bone loss, while we know that proper diet and exercise do. Premarin has become popular only through extensive marketing, and not because of its proven efficacy.

[Note: As of this writing, hormone replacement therapy is receiving much more negative publicity due to ongoing negative test results, and doctors are responding by offering it less often. Being an outspoken consumer *does* make a difference! In addition, more doctors are becoming aware of "bio-identical" hormone replacement, a method proven to be safer and work better. For more information go to www.hormonebalance.org

Ritalin and Attention Deficit Disorder

Today, millions of children are under the influence of a drug called Ritalin. According to Dr. Pam Popper, the number of prescriptions written for people with Attention Deficit Disorder (ADD) has tripled since 1990 and **includes children under age three!**

Dr. Ted Broer reports that when he does a health seminar and asks how many people know someone with ADD, virtually 70 percent of the crowd raises their hands. What is ADD? Ask ten different people and get ten different answers. One of the most interesting things

128

about the study of ADD is that America is one of the few countries whose children suffer from the disorder. Diseases like heart disease and cancer affect people from Asia, the Far East, Europe, and Africa. But some countries' native languages do not even have a term for children who are out of control because it is not a problem! Here in America the treatment is almost solely limited to drugs that suppress the behavior, not attempts to find out why these children behave the way they do. Is it possible that some of these children are suffering from a lack of parental discipline, others from allergies to certain foods or chemicals, and still others from missing vital nutrients in their daily diets? This is a real problem in adults and children that needs to be addressed, but do drugs address it properly?

In the 1960s and 1970s, Dr. Benjamin Feingold conducted research on children who, at that time, were called hyperactive. He found as many as 40-50 percent of these children had a hypersensitivity to food additives like artificial colors and flavors, preservatives, and even some naturally occurring preservatives.[4] While the majority of studies in America have not supported Dr. Feingold's claims, this is probably due to the disconcerting fact that they were funded by the Nutrition Foundation, an organization which receives its funding from food manufacturers!

I would issue a strong warning to parents: What you put into your child's mouth may decide what you are able to put into his head! Ritalin is an amphetamine-type drug which has been shown to decrease the amount of blood flow to the brain by as much as 20-30 percent according to a study conducted by Brookhaven National Laboratory. Withdrawal can cause anxiety, depression, irritability, sleep problems, fatigue, and agitation, which can lead to suicidal tendencies or outright violence. **These are very similar to the effects that cocaine produces.** Ritalin usage can lead to upsetting glucose metabolism and the possibility of **permanent brain damage (atrophy).**[5]

Equally disturbing in the ADD/Ritalin story is the seemingly clandestine, cooperative collusion between a large pharmaceutical company, the federal government, and an NGO (non-governmental organization). In 1996, John Merrow, host of the PBS television series *The Merrow Report*, produced a program titled "Attention

Deficit Disorder: A Dubious Diagnosis?" In this program he uncovered a long-term, unpublicized, financial relationship between the company that makes Ritalin (Novartis, and its forerunner Ciba-Geigy) and the nation's largest ADD support group – Children and Adults with ADD (CHADD).

This pharmaceutical company has given almost $1 million to CHADD, which has over 650 local chapters with monthly meetings in which they render free medical advice featuring Ritalin as the drug of choice. CHADD also received a $750,000 grant from the U.S. Department of Education in 1996 to produce a video titled "Facing the Challenge of ADD," which mentions the drug Ritalin by name.[6] Could this possibly account for those teachers and administrators of tax-supported schools who pressure parents to put their children on Ritalin? Some parents have even reported threats from social agencies: "If you don't allow us to prescribe Ritalin for your ADD child, we may decide that you are an unfit parent. We may decide to take your child away."[7]

Ritalin is classified as a "selective serotonin reuptake inhibitor" drug (SSRI). I mention this fact because it forms the terrifying bridge to antidepressants, which are also classified as SSRI drugs.

Antidepressants – the Untold Stories

Depression is a very real, and at times, a very debilitating malady which needs to be investigated jointly by the medical and nutritional communities. To date, the solution of choice is nearly always drugs such as Prozac, Zoloft, Luvox, Paxil, and others. For many, these drugs seem to have provided a livable solution, but the facts concerning these drugs' connection to horrible tragedies have been largely hidden from the public:

- ❏ Eric Harris, one of the shooters in the Columbine High School massacre, was taking Luvox at the time.
- ❏ Andrea Yates, the mother who drowned her five young children, was taking Prozac. Her doctor had just recently increased her dose before this unspeakable tragedy.
- ❏ Kip Kinkel, age fifteen, was taking Prozac when he killed his parents, stayed with them all night, then killed two students

and wounded twenty-two others at Thurston High School the next day.

While the argument could be made that these are just coincidences, I could list more than a dozen other incidents but will instead summarize with a few quotes from highly reputable people and unrelated sources clearly connecting these drugs and the accompanying catastrophes:

"...Virtually all of the gun-related massacres that have made headlines over the past decade have had one thing in common: they were perpetrated by people taking Prozac, Zoloft, Luvox, Paxil or a related antidepressant drug." Dr. Julian Whitaker [8]

"...Nearly a dozen court cases involving Prozac have disappeared from the court record." [9] These are lawsuits against Prozac manufacturer Eli Lilly which "have apparently been settled, without trial, in such a quiet and final way, with such strict confidentiality, that it is almost as if they never happened."[10]

"This smoothness, this invisibility, keeps the Press away and also, most importantly, does not encourage other people to come out of the woodwork with lawyers and Prozac horror-stories of their own, because they are not reading about $2 million or $10 million or $50 million settlements paid out by Lilly."[11]

The undergirding principles are stewardship, government, and education: God has commanded us to take dominion over this earth and our bodies, and to hold our elected officials accountable.
With all the knowledge and resources we have today, it is our responsibility to find a treatment for depression and ADD that **will not harm** *either the individual taking the medication or bring harm to others around them!*

This responsibility extends into our civic and political involvement, as another aspect of drug popularity is the influence pharmaceutical companies exert over our legislators. In 2003, drug makers spent $108.6 million on federal lobbying activities.[12] They hired 824 individual lobbyists who do nothing but twist your legislator's arm to keep their drugs on the market, whether or not they are effective, and regardless of how much harm they cause. *This amounts to more than eight lobbyists for each member of the U. S. Senate!* The end result for all of us ranges from extra expenses or diminished well-being, up to and including massive and tragic deaths, murders, and suicides that do not have to occur! This is an issue I pray you will become involved in – both in educating yourself and others – and forming or joining citizen action groups to bring about reform. (I will provide you with a couple of suggestions in later chapters.)

Dr. Julian Whitaker makes a poignant appeal for citizen involvement in this arena, speaking in reference to the many stories involving murder, suicide, and antidepressant drugs:

"Look folks, these are the acts of monsters. The accessibility of guns and violent movies alone does not create monsters out of children. But prescription drugs that markedly alter brain chemistry can — and do! Particularly drugs like Prozac, which are in my opinion, the chemical equivalent of a ghoulish Stephen King monster hiding in the closet. A few people have tried to warn the neighborhood, but no one is listening."[13]

Please listen.....and get involved.

END NOTES

1. James McKeever, Whatever Happened to Hope? (Medford, Oregon: Omega Publications), 1989, p. 15
2. Pam Popper, "Take Charge of Your Hormones," Recorded lecture, 2002 PB Industries, 800-761-8210
3. Ibid.
4. Ted Broer, "Attention Deficit Disorder: The in-depth health and nutrition analysis," Eat, Drink & Be Healthy Report, Volume 1, Number 1, 1995, p. 2.
5. Tom Rose, "School Violence: Littleton Revisited," The Christian Statesman, March-April 2000, p. 28.
6. Ibid.
7. John Rappoport, "School Violence; The Psychiatric Drug Connection," Nexus, August-September 1999, p. 23.

8. Tom Rose, "School Violence: Littleton Revisited," The Christian Statesman, March-April 2000, p. 25.

9. Michael Grinfield, "Protecting Prozac," *California Lawyer,* (December 1998), as cited by Rappoport, "School Violence," 27.

10. Ibid.

11. John Rappoport, "School Violence; The Psychiatric Drug Connection," Nexus, August-September 1999, p. 27.

12. Public Citizen's Congress Watch, "The Medicare Drug War: An Army of Nearly 1,000 Lobbyists Pushes a Medicare Law that Puts Drug Company and HMO Profits Ahead of Patients and Taxpayers," June 2004, www.citizen.org.

13. Julian Whitaker, "The Scourge of Prozac," *Health and Healing 9* (September 1999), p. 2

Chapter 12

Antibiotics and Vaccinations...Good Idea or Bad?

Now let's investigate an aspect of antibiotics and vaccinations that you may not have considered or known about previously.

Antibiotics – Link to Disease Perpetuation?

One of the outcomes of ongoing "good" drug intervention, most particularly antibiotics, is the perpetuation of disease. If the body is not occasionally internally cleansed, friendly flora reintroduced and established, and dietary or lifestyle changes made, chances are huge that the disease problem will reappear again and again.

> *Overmedication has actually caused many of us to create our own chronic or degenerative diseases.*

That's a *radical* statement! Let me explain. When you go to an allopathic doctor about an ear infection, bronchitis, or sinus infection, he will send you to the pharmacy for an antibiotic. (The word *antibiotic*, by the way, actually means *anti life*. This definition alone should make you seriously think about ongoing drug therapy.) When my children were being treated for ear infections, the doctor had us come back for a recheck in ten to fourteen days. Why? Because the drugs kill friendly bacteria, one of your body's biggest defenses against illness, right along with the harmful bacteria. The antibiotic cannot distinguish between the two, so while it kills the bad bacteria of your ear, sinus, or other infection, it also kills the good bacteria making up your body's natural defenses, leaving you open to any number of other diseases or germ invaders, not only for as long as you are on the antibiotic, but for several days or weeks afterward until your body replenishes the good bacteria that was destroyed by the very medicine you were taking to cure you.

The Centers for Disease Control recently made a startling and revealing admission regarding antibiotics: **In the year 2001, 235 million doses of antibiotics were prescribed. Of those, they declared 20-50 percent were unnecessary!** In addition, even when an antibiotic is needed, it never kills all the germs. Even if it kills all but one, that lone microbe can immediately reproduce itself in industrial quantities. Only the immune system does away with 100 percent of the invaders.[1] This would seem to indicate that the superior way to fight these types of diseases would be to boost our own body's natural defense mechanisms to kill off these germy assailants.

One of the more frustrating and frightening problems the allopathic world faces today is the mutation of bacteria when treated with an antibiotic. Stronger and stronger antibiotics are being rendered impotent as bacteria continue in endless mutations. Furthermore, antibiotics have never been effective against viruses.

But God has provided us with natural healers to kill disease, *including viruses* (which will be discussed later), while they simultaneously help build up the body's immune system to fight off future disease. The difference is profound: We can help our bodies help themselves **naturally**–using *internal* cleansing and nutrients to boost our immune systems, leading to *external* symptoms vanishing—or we can use **drugs** to destroy the *external* symptoms and often the *internal* defenses as well.

I am not against allopathic doctors or medicines but am vehemently opposed to them always being our first and only line of defense, or a way of life! And for good reason: While cancer and heart disease are the top two killers in America today, the third highest killer will probably shock you: *"Doctors are the third leading cause of death in the United States, causing 250,000 deaths every year."*[2] This revelation was not printed by someone attacking the medical profession, but rather appeared in the most widely circulated and highly respected medical periodical in the world, the *Journal of the American Medical Association* (JAMA). While the causes of these doctor-induced deaths are varied, the single largest percentage (nearly half) is due to *non-error, negative effects of drugs!*[3] In other words, the right drug prescribed for the right disease is often *killing the patient!*

> *The underlying truth about all drugs – over-the-counter, prescription, or illegal – is that they are toxic substances that your body would be better off without.*

Drugs can also *cause* disease. How? Unfortunately, I can again use my son David as an example: When David was first diagnosed at age seven with asthma, it began to manifest through allergy symptoms, mostly a stuffy or runny nose. After a week passed and these symptoms did not disappear, we went to the doctor, who gave us medicine to clear up his breathing passages. Several days later these drugs had brought no relief and infection had usually set in. So the doctor prescribed antibiotics. This drug seemed to clear up the infection, but in a couple of weeks the nasty nose would reappear and we would repeat the above scenario. As the years went by, stronger and stronger antibiotics had to be used—as the bacteria mutated—until David became immune to the effects of every antibiotic on the market. Undaunted, the doctor reached deeper into his bag of pharmaceuticals and introduced David's body to steroids. These knocked out all the symptoms for another couple of weeks, only for the symptoms to return *again,* starting the whole cycle over again! Why did this happen? Why was the return of his symptoms as predictable as sweating in a sauna? Because both involve natural laws.

To avoid overheating, one of our body's natural functions is to perspire to maintain a normal body temperature. In like manner, a cough or runny nose is also a natural result of your body attempting to eliminate toxins. [NOTE: Allergies are the exception to this case. Allergies are an acquired, abnormal immune response to a substance – pollen, food, dust, or micro-organisms - in amounts that do not affect most people. An individual with a strong immune system will not have allergies.] Toxins can exit through every body opening we have. You can cough them out, sneeze them out, sweat them out, pee them out...you get the idea. When we take drugs to stop the sneezing and dry up the running sinuses, we are stopping the *natural function* of the body ridding itself of toxic substances. We seem to get better, but the $64,000 question is, *Where did all that toxic stuff go that was trying to escape?*

It did not magically disappear. When we use medications to stop detoxification, some of the poisons stay inside our body in various locations and in various forms. They become trapped in our lungs in the form of mucus and phlegm; they enter our bloodstream as germ-laden cells in need of cleansing; they adhere to our colon walls as extra waste matter that our colons cannot entirely eliminate.

Every time we use drug medications to stop our body's *natural function* of elimination, we have just added to the accumulation of trapped waste products and internal toxins that can bring about further health problems down the road. Other elimination systems in our body will try to clean out some of these toxins, and to a small degree they will succeed. But most toxins will simply become stored within our bodies, making them weaker and more susceptible to future disease or the return of the same problem over and over again. After the medication is no longer giving a false reading to our body, sooner or later our body will try again to purge itself of these leftover toxins through sneezing, coughing, etc. The problem continually recurs because it was never truly resolved in the first place.

In addition, since God designed our bodies to assimilate and eliminate natural plant products, and most pharmaceuticals are not natural but chemical in makeup, our bodies cannot properly assimilate or eliminate these medications. Therefore, even the medicine we take to help us becomes an additional part of the toxic build-up that made us sick in the first place. This is how overuse of medications causes us to create or contribute to our own chronic or degenerative disease. What a vicious cycle!

Do not misunderstand me. I am not against allopathic doctors. We need them desperately. Medication has its place. Surgery is often necessary. Both can be life-saving at times. But drugs should be used to get us through a crisis, not as a way of life. If we had explored natural healing methods from the beginning, most medications and surgeries would be unnecessary. And it is *never* too late to begin exploring alternatives. (Coming up in the next two chapters!)

What About Vaccinations?

Childhood immunization is a very hot topic today. As with everything in this book, I strongly urge you to research this area *very carefully* before you allow any medical professional to inject your child with a vaccine. There are very strong feelings on both sides of this issue.

Like drugs, immunizations enter your body, going into your bloodstream and various tissues and organs. They may or may not help bypass childhood and other diseases, but current research indicates they are likely to bring about other long-term problems of much more serious consequences than the disease you hoped to miss. Often parents do not understand the risks involved in vaccination. As you study I think you will find the possible ill-effects of these vaccinations *far* outweigh any perceived positive impact in preventing childhood diseases (or flu). In fact, as you study you may decide you don't want to prevent childhood diseases! There are more and more medical professionals today who will tell you childhood diseases are important to long-term health as they help to build a child's immune system and should not be totally suppressed.[4]

Over the last few decades, the number and types of vaccinations given to children has increased dramatically. As recently as the 1970s and 1980s, children were required to receive twelve to fifteen shots before they entered kindergarten. *Today the average child is mandated by law to receive thirty-seven doses of eleven different vaccinations by the age of five!* Newborn infants are injected with Hepatitis B before they are sent home from the hospital. Hepatitis B is usually contracted by drug users and people with multiple sex partners. Can anyone explain to me the logic of why we should inject this dangerous substance into every tiny newborn infant?

Just reading a list of the standard ingredients found in all vaccinations, including diphtheria, pertussis (whooping cough), tetanus

(DPT), and Hepatitis B vaccinations, should be sufficient motivation to cause a parent to investigate further before allowing their precious little ones to be inoculated. Have a look:

- mercury
- aluminum
- pus from sores of diseased animals
- fecal matter
- urine
- cancer cells
- formaldehyde [*embalming fluid*]
- phenols
- monkey virus #40.[5]

The semi-good news is that the above list was compiled in 2002. By 2004, so much uproar had been generated by concerned parents that California passed a bill banning mercury in vaccines for young children and pregnant women. Iowa did the same earlier in 2004. Shortly after this, the federal government mandated removal of mercury from childhood vaccinations. (This mandate did not include flu or tetanus shots.) However, any child who received all the government-recommended vaccinations prior to 2004 had four shots by the time they were eighteen months old, each with thirty to seventy-eight times the "safe level" [as established by the Food & Drug Administration (FDA)] of mercury injected into their little bodies![6] Unfortunately, the absence of mercury in most of today's vaccines still does not address the problems with the rest of this ingredient list, which contains nothing I would want in my body or my child's body.

Mercury and aluminum are both highly toxic substances that build up in our bodies over time. They are not eliminated. (Mercury is also in dental fillings.) This build-up has been shown to produce cognitive dysfunction. Harvard Medical School and the FDA conducted a test at Children's Hospital in Boston that showed "severe neurological problems could follow the administration of DPT vaccinations."[7]

The use of vaccines has been implicated in such diseases as autism, hyperactivity, AIDS, multiple sclerosis, cancer, Alzheimer's, and Sudden Infant Death Syndrome (SIDS).[8]

In addition, the efficacy of vaccinations preventing the targeted disease is also in question today. Several studies show disease rates falling and sometimes nearly eradicated *before* the introduction of vaccines, mainly due to better nutrition and sanitation practices. Even the World Health Organization (WHO) says, "The best vaccine against common infectious disease is an adequate diet." Incredibly, there are studies that show epidemics occurring *after* vaccines were begun. In 1998, JAMA reported that whooping cough frequently occurs even in populations with high immunization rates. In 1986, *90 percent of 1300 pertussis cases in Kansas were "adequately vaccinated."*[9] What does this tell you about the capability of vaccinations in preventing disease?

Adults should carefully consider the ramifications before they are inoculated as well. According to Dr. Hugh Fudenberg, a highly respected doctor and author of more than eight hundred papers that have been published in peer-reviewed journals, "Individuals who have had five consecutive flu shots between 1970-80 have a **ten times higher chance of getting Alzheimer's Disease** than if they had one or two or no shots."[1]

The anthrax vaccination was highly sought after we were attacked on September 11, 2001. The fear of germ warfare looms. The anthrax vaccine has been shown to be contaminated and ineffective.[11] (Have you noticed we are no longer hearing about being vaccinated for anthrax?) According to Dr. Gary Young, anthrax is on every farm in the world. If you've ever been around a cow or horse, you've been exposed to anthrax. If you didn't get sick when you were exposed, you already have a natural immunity! Truly, the best protection we have against any disease is a strong immune system, and putting the principles you learn in this book into practice will help you build a great immunity. Putting these chemical and heavy-metal-laden vaccinations into our bodies *weakens* the immune system. Educate yourself about vaccinations before you get them or consent to have your children inoculated!

The biblical principle is stewardship of our body, which is the temple of the Holy Spirit:

> Or do you not know that your body is the temple of the Holy Spirit who is in you, whom you have from God, and you are not your own? For you were bought at a price; therefore, glorify God in your body...
>
> 1 Corinthians 6:19-20 NKJV

How can God possibly be glorified when we are putting toxic substances, up to and including animal feces into our bodies or the bodies of our children? There are other principles involved as well:

The principles are again stewardship, government, and education:
Learn to take care of your body and your child's body in the most natural way possible. Hold the government in check to its prescribed purposes, which do not include your personal or family medical decisions.
Educate yourself and others on these vital issues!

In this country, we have government-mandated vaccinations before our children are allowed to attend government schools (another good reason to homeschool). Parents need to know that they have the *right to refuse* vaccinations for their children based on either philosophical or religious views. Going to the website www.mercola.com will give you a step-by-step *legal* and safe way to do so if this is your desire. Another website – www.nvic.com – the National Vaccine Information Center—contains listings of each state's *recommendations* versus *requirements* regarding these shots.

Upon investigation into vaccinations, you will learn that pharmaceutical companies are behind the mandatory vaccination requirements in this nation. Vaccinations are not about health. They are about making money for the drug companies that produce them. News stories about flu vaccine shortages in the 2004-05 winter season caused alarmed adults to line up for hours waiting for the shots that were available. *News Flash*: Inoculation with *last year's* flu virus will not protect you from *this year's* flu virus, which is an entirely different "animal."

As more and more parents learn the truth – *that these vaccines do not stop disease but can actually perpetrate the ones they claim to eradicate, as well as bring on other horrible, non-related "side-effect" diseases*—the drug companies are becoming alarmed and trying to cover their backs. Education is powerful, and an educated parent is an entity the drug companies fear! A true story to illustrate:

On November 15, 2002, USA Radio News reported that one of the barriers to the passage of President George Bush's Homeland Security Bill was a totally non-related amendment that would *protect pharmaceutical companies from lawsuits regarding childhood immunizations.* Does this tell you they *know* these immunizations are creating problems? Does this also tell you that as more parents become aware of the dangers vaccines pose, they *can* make a difference? The pharmaceutical giants are beginning to run for cover. Let's keep this ball rolling. Get involved!

A non-profit organization, People Against Vaccines, has been created by a man named Gary Young to help educate on the possible hazards of vaccinations so parents can make informed choices in this dangerous arena. *Mandatory vaccinations are a billion-dollar business. It's about making money, not saving children's lives.* Gary Young's credentials and credibility in the area of natural remedies are both intriguing and impressive. If you would like more information about his vaccination research (it is fascinating, infuriating, and documented), his lectures, or this organization, you can call 800-336-6308 and request it, or visit www.essentialscience.net.

Ancient and modern sciences are often combined in today's medical world. Let's look at some alternative medical practices next.

END NOTES

1. Francisco Contreras, Health in the 21st Century: Will Doctors Survive? (Chula Vista, CA: Interpacific Press, 1997), p. 317

2. Barbara Starfield, "Is the U.S. Health Really the Best in the World?" Journal of the American Medical Association (JAMA) (July 26, 2000) : Volume 284

3. Ibid.

4. Philip Incao, "Childhood Diseases Are Important to Long-Term Health," Alternative Medicine, July 2001, p. 84

5. D. Gary Young, "Find Healthy Life in a World of Toxins," Training Tape #40, Audio Book, Essential Science Publishing, 2002

6. Ibid.

7. Ibid.

8. Amy Boothe Green, "Convention Report from Amy Boothe Green," La Canada Flintridge, California, Three Sisters Apothecary – Aromatic Thymes, Summer 2002, p. 1.

9. Ibid.

10. D. Gary Young, "Find Healthy Life in a World of Toxins," Training Tape #40, Audio Book, Essential Science Publishing, 2002.

11. Ibid.

Chapter 13

The Role and Importance of "Alternative" Medical Practices

Why They Must Be Explored!

Today there are more than a dozen alternative medical arts, but most insurance companies will not cover their diagnostic methods or treatments. Have you ever wondered why? At times, this is due to a lack of scientific evidence to validate these treatments, but even more often it is due to the unhealthy relationship between the Food & Drug Administration (FDA), the American Medical Association (AMA), and pharmaceutical giants. Each of these organizations has a powerful bias against and control over insurance payments for "non-traditional" treatments. They consider drugs and surgery as the accepted "normal" remedies for sickness and disease and have even brought about legislation to protect that stance. It was not always that way. Ancient cultures used natural plant substances derived from stems, foliage, bark, or roots to treat various maladies. As I began to search Scripture in this area, I was very surprised to find *dozens* of references to the use of trees, leaves, oils, incense, and plants for medicine.

> ...all kinds of trees....their fruit will be for food and their leaves for medicine.
>
> Ezekiel 47:12 NKJV

"Alternative" medicine pre-dates allopathic medicine by many centuries. The Egyptians and Chinese used herbs and plant oils very successfully in treating disease. Other ancient cultures thought demonic spirits brought on headache pain, so they drilled a hole in the sufferer's head to allow the demons to escape. Alternatively, they used animal droppings to keep the apparitions at bay. Hippocrates believed that migraines started as a gas in the liver which worked its way up to the head. His treatment: bleeding to bring out the gases.[1] Thankfully, much progress has been made through the years in the medical world so we are no longer subjected to such treatments as these! Many natural remedies and cures have been found and documented through the ages, but recently (within the last century) nearly all have been cast aside for manmade drugs.

Unfortunately, progress and a patient's well-being were not the only reasons for our culture's journey from natural healers to drugs. Around 1910, pharmaceutical companies began investing heavily in medical schools. To increase the return on that investment, these companies published a report titled "Medical Education in the United States and Canada" that was highly critical of all forms of healing other than allopathic, with its reliance on surgery and drugs. The tragic result was that practitioners of herbal and naturopathic medicine were basically run out of town. Medical schools began training solely on the basis of fighting disease with drugs, and the subject of maintaining health began a disappearing act.[2]

Today, far too many individuals are trusting the government to assist in medical decisions. Many unsuspecting people regard the FDA favorably, erroneously believing it protects them from quackery or "snake oil" remedies. After all, we are told, "independent experts" are hired to advise the FDA which medicines should be approved for sale. However, *USA Today* found that these "independent experts" weren't as independent as one would hope. Indeed, more than half of them have a direct financial interest in the drug they are asked to evaluate.[3] As a result, FDA drug approval is more likely to be profit-motivated than it is to prove safety.

Even worse, it has come to light that the FDA and Pharmaceutical Advertising Counsel (PAC), which represents some thirty-five major drug companies, have formed and co-funded a corporation under a joint letterhead, calling itself the National Council Against Health Fraud. *Under this aegis, individuals are paid to publicly discredit as unscientific or unknown any or all viable herbs, vitamins, homeo-pathic remedies, or non-allopathic therapies, particularly those that are proven to have the most promise and present the greatest threat to the PAC members.*[4]

In addition, pharmaceutical companies are often guilty of rewarding doctors who are willing to help introduce their latest drug: Pharmaceutical giant Wyeth Ayerst, the maker of synthetic hormones, found a willing gynecologist named Robert A. Wilson and set him up with positive "studies" (contracted and paid for by Wyeth) and the means to write a book called *Feminine Forever*, published in 1966. Dr. Wilson's Fifth Avenue office was a gift from Wyeth.[5] This story is the backdrop for the introduction of Premarin (for hormone replacement therapy) on the market. I previously stated that the *New England Journal of Medicine* has found that this drug increases a woman's risk of cancer by 760 percent! *Patient beware!* Don't be afraid to ask your doctor pointed questions about the drugs or treatment he is prescribing.

A group of medical professionals has started a website – www. medicaltruth.com – that I would highly recommend to anyone who is serious about investigating health problems through a non-allo-pathic perspective. This group lists their mission statement at the top of their website:

> Our Mission: To communicate truth and hope by encour-aging the ill and disabled to pursue their healing through proven effective treatments, and to educate and inform the public about the state of the medical system in the U.S.[6]

This website contains truly astonishing articles and information about allopathic and alternative medicine, medical practices, doctors, and drugs, all backed up with names, dates, and places for verifica-tion. The documentation is a necessity due to the inflammatory nature of much of what is written there, as many would otherwise dismiss it. Their intent (and mine) is not to discredit allopathic medicine or doctors, as evidenced by their opening statement on the website:

"The sincerest motives of the medical __profession__ are derailed by the greed and power of the medical __industry__." [7]

This distinction *must* be made and understood. Their intent and mine is not to abolish allopathic medicine, but rather to demolish the monopoly (stronghold?) allopathic medicine holds as a result of government and pharmaceutical company manipulation. This monopoly manifests in many terrible ways. To list just three:

❑ By withholding insurance payments from viable non-drug or non-surgical procedures

❑ By keeping effective alternative medical practices and practitioners out of the mainstream and sometimes even out of the country

❑ By approving *unsafe* drugs for the profit of special-interest groups or even selected individuals

A Closer Look at the FDA

Few people are aware of both the biased nature and the extreme tactics used by our government (FDA) and the AMA. I don't wish to belabor this point but will cite two "life and death" examples for credibility purposes:

"Will Block, in an article in *Life Enhancement* relates how Richard Wurtman, a prominent medical doctor connected with the Massachusetts Institute of Technology, and who is a large stockholder of Intemeuron Pharmaceuticals, Inc., was influential in getting the FDA to approve a new drug called *dexfetifluramine* (trade-named Redux). The first FDA panel refused to give approval because of concern for its adverse effects—like permanent brain damage and pulmonary hypertension. But another panel was set up shortly after and approval was given by a 6-5 margin. Mr. Block points out that the price of Intemeuron stock rose by more than 24%, thereby increasing the worth of Dr. Wurtman's stock in Intemeuron by $1.68 million. Since reading Will Block's article, I found out that Redux has been responsible for some deaths and that the FDA has pulled it off the market."[8]

Stanislaw Burzynski, M.D., doing his own private research discovered a cure for cancer. The process, which I will not detail here, acts as a tumor suppressor that stops the growth of cancer.[9] Dr. Burzynski's treatment has literally saved hundreds of cancer sufferers from death. The only problem is that his successful treatment threatens established special interests and has not been approved by the FDA. In reality, the FDA has attacked him viciously over the years. At a cost of over $1 million, he has successfully defended himself in two long-lasting trials, during which time the FDA made raids on his office, confiscating his records.[10]

America's War on Cancer

The question that is begging to be asked from these two stories is, Why would the FDA and Texas Medical Board levy such strong attacks against a successful cure for cancer, particularly when the accepted treatments of radiation, chemotherapy, and surgery have killed more cancer patients than can be numbered? Is America's war against cancer or against alternative treatments for cancer?

The fact is, the "FDA approved" approach to treat—notice I did not use the word cure—cancer is a multibillion-dollar industry. Whenever non-orthodox approaches crop up they are consistently attacked by the FDA, pharmaceutical companies, and the orthodox medical establishment. The sad answer to the first question is simply "to follow the dollar."

The April 22, 2004, issue of Fortune magazine carried an article by Clifton Leaf titled "The War on Cancer." He noted that the 12 latest cancer drugs being studied were no better at curing cancer than the ones they replaced; however they did cost as much as 350 times more. The expected outcome was that patients would live 4-6 months longer. Erbitux, for example, does shrink tumors, but shrinking tumors does not translate into being cured or even lengthening patients' lives. In spite of this, insurance companies are paying as much as $2400 per week for such medications.

Ralph Moss has done extensive research on complementary and alternative cancer therapies. He has authored a book detailing more than 100 unconventional therapies for cancer, most of which have not even been considered by the National Institutes of Health or the National Cancer Institute. If you or a loved one is suffering from cancer I highly recommend the website www.cancerdecisions. com. Here you will find many of the Moss Reports - treatment plans, costs, locations, evaluation of the plan by its cost and efficacy, individual cases, nutrition suggestions, etc.

One of Ralph Moss's books, The Cancer Industry, discusses eight promising therapies that were dismissed, some of which had the developer being persecuted by the medical establishment. Don Haley, a former senator from New York, has published a book titled Politics and Medicine which addresses various cancer therapies and what happened to them and the people who developed them.

The World Health Organization recently published some startling statistics showing the size and scope of the "cancer industry" in this nation:

- 1 million people will be diagnosed next year with cancer
- $110 billion is being spent per year (this is 10% of all medical costs or 2% of the gross domestic product)
- The average cancer patient spends over $100,000 on treatments
- More people are making a living in the industry than are dying from it (this statistic may be the biggest indictment against the medical "industry")

Let's Open the "Medical Free Market"

In 2001, approximately one-seventh of the U.S. economy - $1.4 trillion – was devoted to the "health care business."[11] "Health care" is actually a misnomer as this industry is in reality devoted to the "sickness or disease" business. *Forbes Magazine*, March 31, 2003, ran an article titled "The New Drug War." This article discussed the fact that employers are not going to be able to continue to pay the medical expenses they are currently paying. Employees are going to have to pay a much larger share. Average costs of the most commonly prescribed drugs range from $750-$10,000 per year per drug! Radiation treatments for cancer patients can run into *several thousand dollars per month!*

The bulk of our population (the baby boomers) is now stepping onto the degenerative disease treadmill. Do the math: If 80 percent of us are getting cancer and heart disease (not taking into account other common diseases like diabetes), the conclusion is obvious:

> *We cannot afford to only treat disease with allopathic methods!*
> *We must focus on prevention first, in addition to opening up the "medical free market" to explore alternative and complementary procedures.*

As a general rule, the allopathic medical profession pays little attention to diet as part of treatment, recovery, or prevention. A recent article in *The Journal of Preventive Medicine* stated that three-quarters of patients surveyed following a doctor's visit reported receiving no nutrition advice at all. The other quarter reported that their physicians spent less than one minute on nutrition while they were in the office. The survey included 3,475 patients and found that dietary advice was most often given to the elderly and to patients with diabetes and other chronic conditions.

This report emphasizes a couple points. First, it tells how important, or in this case unimportant, doctors think nutrition is. For most, it's not even worth mentioning. The medical system overall is not placing enough emphasis on patient education, diet, and prevention. This brings us to the main point:

> *People need to take matters into their own hands*
> *and get educated on their own in order to make good decisions on their own about their health.*

This principle is backed up by Scripture: In the Old Testament, when an Israelite got sick he went to the priest for cleansing and purification – part of the definition of healing. In the New Testament, all believers make up the kingdom and priesthood!

You also, as living stones, are being built up a spiritual house, a holy priesthood...

> 1 Peter 2:5 NKJV

...from every tribe, language, people and nation. You made them to be a kingdom of priests for our God and they will rule on the earth.

> Revelation 5:9-10 NCV

But if anyone does not provide for his own, and especially for those of his household, he has denied the faith and is worse than an unbeliever.

> 1 Timothy 5:8 NKJV

The principle is one of personal character and govern-mental jurisdiction. The choice of healthcare for you and your family is **your responsibility** *– not the government-funded FDA's – and that includes the type of care, the procedures selected, and the payments made.*

Your health and the health of your family is *your* responsibility – not the doctor's and not the federal government's. It is time for citizens to take control of the healthcare arena and break down the government barriers that keep us and insurance payments from authentic, credible, alternate practitioners. It is also time to educate yourself on how to wisely select these practitioners. Love for your family and a few learning principles will lead you well. Unlike the FDA, your "special-interest group" is (and should be) your own family.

END NOTES

1. "Viewpoints on Health, Taking Control of Migraine," Supplement to Reader's Digest," 3rd in a Series (Bristol-Myers Squibb Company, 2000), p. 4

2. Patrick Quillin, <u>Healing Secrets from the Bible – God Wants us to be Healthy, and the Bible Tells us How,</u> (Tulsa, OK: The Nutrition Times Press, Inc., 1996), p. 16

3. Dennis Cauchon, "FDA Advisers Tied to Industry," <u>USA Today</u>, 25 September 2000, p. 01.A

4. "A Revelation about Modern Medicine in the USA," Medical Truth Online, <u>http://medicaltruth.com/FDA-AMA/story2.htlml</u>, 9/19/02.

5. "Hormone Replacement Therapy: A Theory Run Amok," <u>The Essential Edge</u>, November 2003, p. 2

6. "A Revelation about Modern Medicine in the USA," Medical Truth Online, 9/19/02.

7. Ibid.

8. Tom Rose, "The Many Faces of Tyranny and How To Establish Godly Rule," <u>The Christian Statesman</u>, January-February 1998, p. 30.

9. Julian Whitaker, "Medical Heroes of 1997," <u>Health & Healing</u>, Special Supplement, December 1997, p. 1, ed. Tom Rose, "The Many Faces of Tyranny and How to Establish Godly Rule," <u>The Christian Statesman,</u> January-February 1998, p. 30.

10. Tom Rose, p. 30.

11. Paul Zane Pilzer, <u>The Next Trillion</u>, Video Plus, 2001

Chapter 14

Scrutinizing Medical Practices

First Things First

Most people's first encounter with an alternative medical professional comes only after their frustration with allopathic doctors. If you are suffering from a disabling, degenerative, "incurable" disease that the medical establishment has been unable to cure, I want to point you to a very important resource book *before* you go to another medical professional.

In an earlier chapter I mentioned Pastor Henry W. Wright's book, *A More Excellent Way – Be in Health.* The subtitle is "Spiritual Roots of Disease – Pathways to Wholeness." Pastor Wright began his college years studying to be a physician and therefore has some background in medicine. That knowledge combined with his study of Scripture as a pastor has provided him with a unique perspective on disease. He has read the *Physician's Desk Reference* (PDR), which describes how diseases manifest, and cross-referenced biblical descriptions of various maladies to come up with the spiritual roots of diseases and various "blocks" to healing.

He believes the vast majority of auto-immune and incurable diseases are spiritually rooted, and as you read his book it is difficult to disagree with him. As an example, the spiritual root to many diseases is fear, a twenty-first-century word for *stress* and a subject that comes up a lot in the Bible. Both the medical and psychiatric communities acknowledge that fear, anxiety, and stress cause many diseases. God created our brain and body to *respond* to fear, but He did not create us to *stay* there.

The fight/flight syndrome is a body/brain chemical response resulting in adrenaline release to give us extra strength and stamina to run away from a sudden encounter with a bear in the woods or any other life-threatening situation. However, this same mechanism of adrenaline release happens when we are stressed out for any reason. Our brains send a message to the master gland, the hypothalamus. The hypothalamus does not reason through the brain's stress message to determine whether there is a bear in your path or if you're just upset because your husband is late for dinner again. It is a responder, not a thinker. It receives the brain's messages and acts accordingly, communicating to the pituitary and adrenal glands to secrete whatever hormone is necessary to deal with this thought of stress/fear. Many of us are living in ongoing stress/fear to the point that our glands are exhausted from overuse and begin misfiring or malfunctioning, causing imbalances throughout our bodies' various systems or natural functions. This is the beginning of disease that drugs cannot heal because the *root problem* is the fear itself, not whatever disease is manifesting itself as a result of the fear.

This is a great oversimplification of the contents of Wright's book, but the core message is powerful. I believe Pastor Wright has found the answer to why so many Christians pray and are not healed. It is not a lack of faith. It is simply that they have an *unknown spiritual and/or sin issue* to deal with before God can heal them. Indeed, I have seen many people healed of cancer, fibromyalgia, and other horrible ailments, only to have it come back in a few weeks or months. The explanation is simple: their faith was strong enough to make the disease leave, *but the underlying conditions that brought about the disease remained.* They are still stressed out, and their adrenals are still being exhausted, causing chemical imbalances throughout their bodies and bringing back the same disease they prayed away. The root issue was not faith. This is a matter of sanctification or holiness, or being more conformed to the image of God. The root issue was stress/fear, or our lack of trusting God. Until the fear is dealt with, the disease will return.

God is more concerned with our holiness than He is with our health because He knows that our holiness will lead to our health.

As previously mentioned in chapter 4, Chester and Betsy Kylstra's ministry, Restoring the Foundations, and their book, *An Integrated Approach to Biblical Healing Ministry*, also deal with finding the root spiritual cause for physical and spiritual dis-ease. Their personalized ministry and follow-up are powerful tools for a *lasting healing* at the spiritual level that manifests in physical healing for your body and personal relationships as well. To order the book or speak with the Kylstras, call 888-324-6466 or go online at www.ftftrainingcenter.org.

I *cannot overemphasize* the importance of reading either the Kylstras' or Henry Wright's book or attending one of their week-long seminars. Pastor Wright's church has an unsurpassed track record in the worldwide Christian community of healing physical and mental illness along with incurable diseases (such as environmental sensitivities) which the medical world cannot touch. His organization can be reached at www.pleasantvalleychurch.net or by calling 800-453-5775.

A Closer Look at Alternative Modalities

Whether or not you are dealing with a spiritually rooted disease, it is also very important to educate yourself on how to carefully and wisely select alternative practices and practitioners. (Note: A better term might be "complementary" rather than "alternative." Alternative medicine insinuates *replacing* conventional therapy, whereas complementary medicine would be *prescribed along with it*.)

What criteria do you use to separate the weird and wacky from the tried and true? We are in the midst of a paradigm shift in medicine due to the inescapable fact that allopathic medical practices of drugs and surgery are slowly bankrupting the system. This has resulted in a huge wave of new medical technologies emerging on the scene. The "playing field" is huge and growing, making it imperative to find a godly sorting method of what's good and what's not.

Chiropractors and osteopaths are becoming more well-known and accepted in today's medical arena. Naturopathic physicians have made a comeback, as have herbologists and homeopathic practitioners. We have reflexology, iridology, naturopathy, magnet therapy, applied kinesiology, accupuncture, accupressure, bio-feedback, many kinds of therapeutic massage, and so forth.

As you scrutinize these various practices there must be criteria and some unchangeable principles to help you find solid footing, as not all practices are viable and not all practitioners competent—some may even be dangerous. I began my investigation into alternative (complementary) methods with fear and trembling, having been taught that most "other" medical practices were demonic or New Age and should therefore be avoided entirely. It was clear that drugs were not the answer to my son's health difficulties, but where else was I to look and not be walking outside God's established order? I found freedom to search when I received a prophetic word directly from the Lord and was able to verify it was truly from Him.

While deep in prayer about whether or not to try and rely on muscle testing (used in applied kinesiology), the Lord spoke clearly to me: "Get out of your box! Stop being so afraid! I am *not* the author of fear. Pray and put on My armor every day, then step out of that box and *think*. I have given you the mind of Christ, the most logical mind in the universe. Use it!"

In matters of the spirit world, it is always good to verify whose voice you are hearing. God is not the only one who can "speak" to you. There are times when there is no doubt, but others when you aren't so certain. My pastor unknowingly reworded the admonition I had received from the Lord when he was teaching on how to search out truth:

> *The principle is education – God is not offended by our searching out the truth. When you come across anything of unknown origin or merit, check it out! Test it – "Chew it up" (a definition of "meditate") – You don't have to swallow…you can spit it out!*

The second, and best, verification came in God's Word:
Beloved, do not believe every spirit, but test the spirits,
whether they are of God...

1 John 4:1NKJV

This doesn't say to "avoid" the spirits but to "test" them. So the question now becomes, what are some basic principles to use to test the validity (or even possible validity) of various practitioners and their treatments? Simply because something is unfamiliar or unknown to you is not a fair yardstick to use for rejection. When Louis Pasteur first introduced the idea of germs – invisible creatures that carry disease! - the most knowledgeable doctors of his day laughed at him. How ridiculous! (I wonder if the accepted churches of the day considered him to be demonically inspired?) But time and science proved Pasteur to be right, and uncounted lives are saved today just from the simple practice of hand washing and/or use of rubber gloves.

On the other hand, the warning remains that the spirits must be tested. For the truth of the matter is there *are* medical practices available today that *do* have their roots in the occult. True healing comes from God and His methods, but we are warned in Scripture that Satan has the ability to imitate God's power. For example, when Moses performed wonders with God's help, Pharaoh's sorcerers were able to duplicate many of them. The principle behind this example is ominous, of paramount importance, and must be judiciously and prayerfully considered:

Just because a particular medical practice works does not mean it is of God.

Some of today's alternative medical methods involve ancient practices with modern applications. Others use modern technology that was unknown in Biblical times. Furthermore, determining the scientific or Biblical principles behind these various practices can often be very difficult. For this reason, the *Principle Approach* (a method of applying a Christian philosophy of life consistently in every area through the application of Bible principles, definitions, and leading questions) is the best way to discern the truth.

Let's consider some key questions and definitions and use them to evaluate several modern medical practices.

- What is _____? (Name the practice and define it.)
- What training is involved in learning this practice?
- What is the origin of _____? Is its origin related to an Eastern religion?
- How does it work?
- Does the treatment follow God's design of the body?
- Does legitimate proof (other than testimonials) exist to validate this treatment?
- Is it scientifically proven (or disproven)?
- What are possible concerns with this practice?
- Are there other factors that should be considered?

Now let's answer these questions as they relate to five medical practices.

ALLOPATHY

Allopathy is the term given to traditional medicine and uses drugs and surgery in the treatment of disease.

> **Allopathy** – treatment of disease by remedies that produce effects different from or opposite to those produced by the disease: opposed to homeopathy. *(Webster's New World Dictionary, 1960)*

Allopathic practitioners must complete four years of college, four years of medical school, and two to five years of residency. Cicero is usually credited with the introduction of allopathic medicine in the first century B.C. It is based on the "Doctrine of Contraries," which purports the idea that the body is not able to heal itself or rid itself of sicknesses. Therefore, a situation must be created in the body that will solve the problem. For example, if a patient has an infection, he should be given an antibiotic.

The diagnostic techniques of allopathic medicine are based on solid science and are usually observable, repeatable, and measurable. Much legitimate proof exists that some allopathic treatments work (such as taking antibiotics for infection); *however, the underlying premise of the body being unable to heal itself is contrary to the way God created us.* There are times when boosting the body's ability to heal itself would be a better option than introducing drugs to cover a problem. Enhancing the immune system or changing lifestyle habits (to stop smoking or to eat more fruits and vegetables, e.g.) may often enable a body to fix itself.

I strongly believe that allopathic medicine is the best alternative in an emergency or life-threatening situation. However, when using an allopathic doctor, always consider what he is prescribing and its immediate and long-term effects. In addition, the question must always be asked whether a diet or lifestyle change will bring about the desired change instead of drugs or surgery.

HOMEOPATHY

What's in a name? Homeopathy is a name that is used (and MIS-used) by many people today. It is a very good example of misunderstanding or confusion in a healing modality. There are many medicines and ointments available today that are called "homeopathic." However, they would more aptly be called "home remedies." Simply because something is derived from an herb or created by substances found commonly in your home (like baking soda pastes, mustard plasters, etc.) does *not* make it a homeopathic remedy. We need to answer the questions set forth to determine what true homeopathy really is.

> **Homeopathy** – A system of medical treatment based on the theory that certain diseases can be cured by giving very small doses of drugs, which in a healthy person and in large doses would produce symptoms like those of the disease: opposed to allopathy. *(Webster's New World Dictionary, 1960)*

Some special education is required to learn this modality. A homeopathic practitioner is generally qualified by local training seminars that teach a system of diagnosis and treatment developed by Samuel Hahnemann in the nineteenth century. Homeopathy was originally based on four laws (set out below), but the fourth is often missing in current literature:

- The Law of Similars: "Like cures like," meaning any substance which produces symptoms in a healthy person will in minute doses cure a sick person with the same symptoms.
- The Law of Minimum Dose: Curative substances are made more powerful by dilution and shaking.
- The Law of Single Remedy: Proper treatment entails one remedy at a time.
- The Law of Spiritual Cause: Homeopathy is founded on the belief that disease has no physical cause; rather it is an imbalance of the spirit-like power or "vital principle" within the body. (It is noteworthy that few adherents to homeopathy know of or acknowledge this fourth law, which happens to be a component Christians need to be especially aware of.)

Hahnemann believed that physical sicknesses are results of disturbances within the "vital force" and can be cured only by restoring this vital force to its original state. He was a follower of Emanuel Swedenborg, a spiritist and medium who blended the world of nature with the occult, thus leading Hahnemann to believe that disease and illness were energy issues, not matter issues, and should be fought on a spiritual level.

Diagnosis is made by taking a lengthy history while searching for unique symptoms. Muscle testing or applied kinesiology is often used for diagnostic purposes. One example of muscle testing involves placing a substance to be tested in one hand, then having the person tested hold their other arm out at a right angle to their body. The practitioner or tester will then attempt to push the arm down while the patient resists this pressure. If the arm falls easily, the substance being tested is determined to be detrimental to the body. If the arm holds firmly, however, the substance is determined to be beneficial. (There are variables within this technique, but the basic testing method is the same.) Muscle testing has no basis in science. Though it is observable and repeatable, it is *not* measurable. How hard is the person pushing? How strong is the person resisting? How severe is the reaction? Is the substance simply not good for your body, or will it do great harm? These are all immeasurable variables.

Historically, treatment sometimes involves the use of various substances such as herbs, plants, bacteria, or diseased tissue. One drop of these substances is diluted with 99 drops of water or alcohol. This solution is shaken for a long time. Then one drop of that mixture is mixed with 99 more drops of water or alcohol to be shaken again. This process is repeated several times until there is virtually no original substance left. A medium homeopathic remedy dilution known as C12 (1 part to 100,000,000,000,000,000,000,000,000 – 10 to the 24th power) is roughly equivalent to dissolving one pinch of salt in a volume of water the size of the Atlantic Ocean.[1]

Today, however, homeopathic practitioners employ more modern methods of testing using electricity, which *is measurable*, and making remedies based on those electrical results, not with the extreme dilutions mentioned above. Homeopathy is a stellar example of a medical practice that has its roots in the occult, but today has some practitioners who are using much more scientific, measurable methods to diagnose and prescribe. The principle of education emerges as very important in this instance, along with asking the practitioner many questions.

While the beginnings of any medical practice are important, redemption is more important. Ask questions. Check it out carefully and prayerfully.

Bottom line: Remember that the success of a treatment is *not* the measure of whether it is acceptable to God and/or scientific in nature. It is incumbent upon the individual to be an investigative consumer and determine the safety, efficacy, and acceptability in God's eyes of everything and anything we put into or on our bodies. Ask questions. Do research. Check it out meticulously and prayerfully!

NATUROPATHY

Naturopathy – a system of treating diseases, largely employing natural agencies such as air, sunshine, etc., and rejecting the use of drugs and medicines. (Webster's New World Dictionary, 1960)

Naturopathy was not used until the late nineteenth century, but its philosophical roots date back thousands of years, drawing from the healing wisdom of many cultures, including Indian, Chinese, Native American, and Greek. It follows six basic principles:

- First, do no harm – by employing safe, effective natural therapies.
- The healing power of nature – therefore the role of the naturopathic physician is to facilitate the natural process with natural, nontoxic therapies.
- Treat the cause rather than the effect – symptoms are viewed as expressions of the body's natural attempts to heal while causes can spring from physical, mental, emotional, or spiritual realms.
- Treat the whole person – disease is multi-factorial and involves spiritual, mental, emotional, and physical dimensions, all of which should be considered in treatment.
- The physician is a teacher – educating, empowering, and motivating the patient to assume more personal responsibility for their health by adopting healthy diet and lifestyle choices.
- Prevention is the best cure – accomplished through education and a lifestyle that supports health.

Naturopathy treats health conditions by using the body's inherent ability to heal itself. After identifying conditions causing the illness, the naturopathic physician advises the patient on the methods most appropriate for returning to health. Naturopathy is not a single modality of healing, but rather incorporates a variety of methods including homeopathy, acupuncture, herbs, etc. Each of the modalities used needs to be assessed by the biblical criteria mentioned previously; however, the underlying premise of treating the whole person and the cause of disease rather than the effect is very reasonable.

Training to become a naturopathic doctor begins with a four-year bachelor's degree, followed by continued education specific to this field of endeavor. It is important to note that there are two types of naturopaths today, one of which is "outside the scope" of naturopathy's original principles. In addition to those trained according to the six principles stated above, today some are also trained to learn traditional medical practice that incorporates alternative methods. This type of training does not follow the six basic original principles of naturopathy as it can involve drugs and surgery. However, to deliver babies, perform minor surgery, or have the capacity to prescribe drugs, this type of education is required. If checking out a naturopathic doctor, it would be very important to know which school of thought they subscribe to since "wellness-centered" diagnosis and treatment would be quite ineffective when confronting acute illness where surgery is truly necessary for saving the patient's life (i.e. immediate removal of an inflamed appendix).

The basic idea of naturopathy is correct in that health is more than the absence of disease. Its basic tenets are reasonable and applicable to many medical decisions. The principles of allowing the body to try to heal itself, treating the person as a whole, dealing with the cause rather than the effect, and viewing prevention as the best cure are all good and true. These are all fundamentals of medicine that everyone should apply when making decisions concerning medical care. However, the definition of "natural" is frequently subjective because "natural" treatment may include methods of medicine which have occultic potential, such as homeopathy, meditation, and yoga. This is why, once again, it is absolutely necessary for you to study and examine carefully to determine the safety, efficacy, and acceptability in God's eyes of every healing modality. Check it out before you try it out!

Bottom Line – Learn to Discern

There are two other healing modalities (aromatherapy and functional medicine) that I want to search out with the above listed discernment questions, but they are of such sufficient and significant importance that I want to dedicate an entire chapter to each of them. I sincerely believe the body of Christ is missing many of God's natural methods of healing because the non-Christians rediscovered it before the Christians did. This ties in directly to another important educational principle:

Bad religion does not invalidate sound science, but sound science can be distorted or overused by bad religion.
Consult God first as your healer and learn to discern!

I encourage you to pray, consider, and ponder through every different medical practice or practitioner, using the questions and principles found in this chapter. Scripture says there is safety (wisdom) in a multitude of counselors. Have other Christians research and pray with you. Check it out. Chew it up. Remember, you don't have to swallow! You can spit it out. If after all your investigation into an alternative medical practice you are still uncomfortable with it, don't do it. Let your conscience be your guide. If you're a Christian, the Holy Spirit lives there (in your conscience). You can trust Him.

Let's study and take back dominion over scientifically based, complementary/alternative medical practices rather than automatically running from them. The next chapter goes into much deeper investigative methods to check out aromatherapy and essential plant oils. Let's take a look!

END NOTES

1. Understanding Homeopathic Medicine," <u>Protect: A Medical Journal...for the Family – The Philosophies Behind Modern Medical Practices</u>, Series 2 – Volume 2 (April 1996) p. 25

Chapter 15

Essential Plant Oils and Aromatherapy - Part of God's Medicine Cabinet

There are two distinct medicinal uses for essential oils. The first is in topical application and the second is in smelling them – true aromatherapy. Plant oils can be legitimate medicines *if* therapeutic-grade oils are being used properly. Aromatherapy has been scientifically proven to assist in healing in some areas, but not all. Further inspection into this particular healing art is a valuable exercise and an example of using discernment to separate legitimate aromatherapy from the illegitimate use of "expensive perfumes."

> **Aroma** – The quality of plants which constitutes their fragrance
> *(Webster's 1828)*
> **Therapy** – [therapeutic] That which pertains to the healing art; is concerned in discovering and applying remedies for diseases. *(Webster's 1828)*

Essential Oils in History

Plants not only play a vital role in the ecosystem and balance of our planet, but have been intimately linked to the physical, emotional, and spiritual well-being of man since the beginning of time. Millions of dollars are allocated for research every year to

167

look for novel therapeutic agents yet undiscovered in barks, roots, jungle foliage, river bottoms, and wilderness regions throughout the world.

Essential oils are the most powerful part of the plant, and *when extracted and distilled properly* they are powerful healers. Why is that? Because they bear a direct relation to our body's blood, our life source. When a plant leaf is torn, usually a clear liquid seeps out, similar to when we bleed from a cut. This liquid has a similar purpose in the plant as the blood does in the body. It cleans the cut, protects the wound, fights harmful microorganisms, and provides nutrients and oxygen for plant cell regeneration. Likewise, when you cut yourself, your blood cleans the cut, protects the wound, fights harmful microorganisms, and provides nutrients and oxygen for cell regeneration. These are *natural healing functions.*

Essential oils are also the oldest recorded medical treatments. Records dating back to 4500 B.C. describe the use of oils for religious rituals and medical applications. Hieroglyphics on the walls of the temples depict the blending of oils and describe hundreds of oil recipes.[1]

The priests were the medical practitioners/doctors in Israel. There are over two hundred references to essential oils, incense, and ointments throughout the Old and New Testaments, such as frankincense, myrrh, galbanum, cinnamon, cassia, rosemary, hyssop, and spikenard. These oil compounds were prepared "after the art of the apothecary" (Exodus 30:25), a term which referred to *perfumers!* Only in more modern times has this term been used in reference to drugstores. These oils were used for anointing in cleansing or ceremonial rites, as well as healing the sick. Just a few examples:

❑ In Exodus 30:23-25, God gives the recipe to Moses for a "holy anointing oil" which was to be used for purifying the various vessels in the temple as well as anointing Aaron and his sons as priests.

❑ In Numbers 16:46-50 Moses instructs Aaron to take a censer and add burning coals and incense to stop a plague. The ingredients used (we know today) are highly anti-infectious and anti-viral. Whether the antibacterial nature of the incense played a part in stopping the plague or not, 14,700 Israelites died of the plague before Aaron brought forth the incense!

❑ The wise men presented the Christ child with the essential oils of frankincense and myrrh, both of which were more valuable and costly than gold at that time in history. These oils were part of the purification practice of the day. (Today, we know that frankincense and myrrh are two of the most powerful anti-viral and anti-bacterial oils available.)

❑ The Good Samaritan treated the wounds of the injured man with oils.

❑ Mary anointed the feet of Jesus with spikenard, "and the house was filled with the odor of the ointment" (John 12:3).

❑ Oils can be used to elevate your mood, or ward off depression: "Ointment and perfume delight the heart..." (Proverbs 27:9). Also, "....Your God has anointed You with the *oil of gladness* more than your companions" (Psalm 45:7).

The use of essential oils for healing was lost for centuries but reintroduced in the late nineteenth and early twentieth centuries. During World War II, a French physician, Dr. Jean Valnet, had exhausted his supply of antibiotics. He began using therapeutic-grade essential oils on patients suffering battlefield injuries and found they exerted a powerful effect in combating and counteracting infection. He was able to save the lives of many soldiers who might otherwise have died.[2]

Expensive Perfumes or Medicine?

The lifeblood of the plant is in the volatile liquid, or resin, that functions like blood in our bodies. When distilled, this life force is called the essential oil. It takes hundreds of pounds to produce a small amount of medicinal quality oil. For instance, *it takes 5,000 pounds of rose petals to produce one pound of rose oil!* This is why the effectiveness of the oil is many times greater than the dried or powdered plant (herbs). One drop may represent the life force of many plants, depending on the type of plant and the distillation process used.

This brings up a very important point. To the best of my knowledge, essential oils found in health food stores are not of sufficient purity for medicinal purposes. There are grades of essential oils, and most are simply expensive perfumes. *Read the labels* and you will find one of four types:

- Pure – This simply means the oil was not diluted with a lesser quality oil. It does not mean it has no chemicals added. It could be 80% vegetable oil and 20% essential oil and still be labeled "100% Pure."
- Natural – This means the oil was not adulterated with vegetable oils, propylene glycol, SD Alcohol 40, or other chemicals, but makes no provision as to how the plants were grown or the oils distilled.
- Complete – Oil was distilled at low heat and low pressure so that all the therapeutic properties were retained, but this still does not address how they were grown (sprayed or unsprayed).
- Genuine or Grade A – These are the cream of the crop. Great care is taken at every step of the process. Seeds – not hybrids – are used, organic soil, no chemicals sprayed on plants, distilled at proper temperatures for proper times.

I personally recommend Young Living Essential Oils because they produce Grade A oils and are the only company I know that grows many of their own plants from seed and distills and bottles all their oils. They are the largest grower of essential oil plants in the world.

How important is proper distilling? There are anywhere from two hundred to eight hundred chemical constituents that make up one single essential oil. *When the oil is not properly distilled, you will be left with as few as ten.* In addition, some of the most powerful healing constituents are derived at the end of a long, slow distilling process.

Young Living Essential Oils are available only through distributors in this organization as the company does not want them confused or intermingled with the lesser quality oils found in health food stores. The reasons for this direct-sales procedure are not just vanity or profits, but safety and the well-being of the consumer.

Illustration: The essential oil lavender can nearly work miracles on burns. If applied early and often enough, third-degree burns have completely healed without scarring, and even the hair growth was restored. A woman heard this story and went to the health food store to purchase lavender. Sometime later she burned herself in the kitchen and applied the lavender she had purchased. Within two days it had turned a second-degree burn into a third-degree burn. Upon further investigation, she learned the lavender she purchased had been "extended" with camphor, which made it smell wonderful, but had altered the burn-healing properties of the oil and instead intensified the severity of her burn. This example truly points out the necessity of therapeutic, Grade A oils in the treatment of disease or wounds. The difference is crucial.

Essential Oils and Emotions

Topical application of essential oils for wounds, stings, etc., is one practical use. Inhalation of essential oils has also proven to be a viable treatment for emotional responses, thinking patterns, and the physiological way in which this effect occurs. God truly designed our bodies in a fascinating way.

When you inhale a fragrance the molecules travel up the nose where they attach to receptor cells in the olfactory epithelium (aka inner wall of the blood vessels of your nose lining). They stimulate the lining of nerve cells that trigger electrical impulses to the olfactory bulb in the brain. The brain then transmits impulses to three places, including the amygdala (where emotional memories are stored), and other parts of the limbic system (the emotional control center of the brain). Of our five senses, only the sense of smell is related directly to the limbic system. Fear, joy, depression, anger, and all other kinds of emotions come from this region of the brain. This is why smells can provoke powerful memories, positive or negative. You may have had an experience where you inhaled a particular scent and it made you think of an event from earlier in your life.

Additionally, the limbic lobe can activate the hypothalamus (our master gland) which among other things serves as the hormonal control center. Odor also has a powerful effect on other physiological functions such as breathing, heart rate, and blood pressure. It is these connections that are responsible for the powerful relationship between inhaling an essential oil and the reduction of stress or an emotional trauma, the stimulation or production of hormones, an increase in energy levels, and other positive effects. There are several published studies showing the profound and positive effects that inhaling essential oils can have on both the body and mind.

Past and Present-day Applications

A study of plants and oils of the Bible reveals they were used for medicines as well as food. Plants and oils are God's natural disease killers. As stated previously, these oils can be applied topically to your body, but they can also be diffused into the air to kill bacteria *and viruses*. Researchers working with (Therapeutic/Genuine or Grade A) essential oils such as frankincense and myrrh have yet to find a virus or bacteria that these oils will not utterly destroy. This is not new knowledge.

In the Old Testament - Exodus 30:22-38 - God gives the recipe for holy anointing oil and incense (which includes frankincense), and states that the purpose of this oil was to **purify** both the priests and the utensils of the tabernacle. When someone in Israel got sick, he went to the priest for *cleansing and purification!* (This takes us right back to the definition of healing – "to purify from corruptions.")

Deciding with Discernment

Many European doctors and hospitals routinely use these oils when treating their patients. In America this type of treatment is relatively new; however, the evidence of efficacy of therapeutic-grade essential oils in treating various disease conditions continues to grow. The greatest obstacle we face in using these oils for any serious ailment is finding a knowledgeable practitioner who truly knows the proper use of them.

Training is available to distributors for less serious ailments – at either local seminars or through a book known as the *Essential Oils Desk Reference*. This book is published by Essential Science Publishing and is a virtual layman's encyclopedia of the different oils available, along with their various uses for many maladies.

This book is a great place to begin your re-education process. You can inquire as to its price and availability at 800-336-6308 or go to www.essentialscience.net. More and more physicians are slowly incorporating these oils into their treatment arsenals.

Gary Young, founder of Young Living Essential Oils, started life on a ranch in central Idaho with no indoor plumbing or electricity. At age seventeen he moved to Canada to follow his dream of wilderness living, working as a rancher and logger. It was there that a near-fatal logging accident changed his life forever. Paralyzed and confined to a wheelchair with no hope of recovery (according to his attending physicians), he took control of his own fate. He was determined to either get out of the wheelchair or end his life.

His search led to a total recovery of a busy and at times strenuous lifestyle. He is vibrantly healthy: walks, runs, skis, rides horses, enters jousting competitions, and teaches others what he has learned of the ancient and modern sciences of natural medicine. Due to his extensive research over the last thirty years, he is perhaps the premier authority on essential oils today. Gary Young is a devout Mormon, and though you may not share all his religious beliefs this does *not* diminish his knowledge, expertise, or the quality of the product he produces. (You probably don't agree with all of *my* religious beliefs stated in this book. It is my hope you will continue reading and studying to fine tune and deepen your *own* personal belief system and not turn away from others' teachings simply because they do not *all* line up with yours. We all need to practice grace in this regard as we are all "works in progress.")

I am slowly resupplying my medicine cabinet with essential oils for the more common first aid remedies such as bee stings, cuts, and burns. I also use essential oils for common and simple maladies like headaches, upset stomachs, or cold and flu symptoms. Young Living Essential Oils also carries an extensive line of dietary supplements and personal care products such as soaps, shampoos, toothpaste, etc., that are *all natural* without harmful chemicals or additives. The main website for information about any of these products is www. youngliving.com.

While I firmly believe these essential oils are a valuable addition to the medicine cabinet, I would advise caution in *overuse* of them for every disease, malady, or mood. First things first: In conjunction with *whatever* medical modality you choose, be sure to keep God, your mind, and your heart involved in the process. Pray for wisdom and discernment first!

There is yet one more medical practice I want to evaluate, and I believe it holds much promise for our future health and prevention decisions. Read on...

END NOTES

1. PDR – Essential Oils Desk Reference, Compiled by Essential Science Publishing, (United States of America), First Printing July 1999, p. 4
2. Ibid, p. 6.

Chapter 16

Functional Medicine – A Fresh Approach

Functional medicine is a relatively new arrival on the medical scene, and I believe it is the threshold to a new model of medicine whose goal is to heal the body and prevent disease, not simply treat and manage symptoms. Its approach is refreshing.

> **Functional Medicine** – A science-based healthcare approach that assesses and treats underlying causes of illness through individually tailored therapies to restore health and improve function.

The promotion of functional medicine has been the lifelong work of Dr. Jeffery S. Bland. Dr. Linus Pauling can also be credited as being on the forefront of functional medicine as he was a visionary who saw the value of vitamins as therapy when given in mega-doses for short periods of time. Though his contemporaries laughed at him (much like Louis Pasteur), his therapies worked, and he personally lived healthfully to the age of ninety-two.

Functional medicine has been around for approximately thirty years and has gained sufficient numbers of practitioners and patients to have recently held its 13th International Symposium. A functional medicine teaching university, the Institute for Functional Medicine, located in Washington State, has recently celebrated its ten-year anniversary.

Functional medicine is science-based and employs many of the same diagnostic techniques as allopathic medicine. A functional M.D. completes the same schooling as an allopathic M.D., but rather than simply looking to drugs to treat or cover symptoms, the functional M.D. is also trained to employ clinical nutrition therapy and lifestyle changes that will assist the body in healing itself. Drugs are not necessarily eliminated from the course of treatment, but they are rarely the only prescription.

The Principles of Functional Medicine

1. Biochemical individuality based on genetic and environmental uniqueness
2. Patient centered versus disease centered.
3. Dynamic balance of internal and external factors
4. Web-like interconnections of physiological factors
5. Health as a positive vitality – not merely the absence of disease
6. Promotion of organ reserve – healthspan

Let's look just a little closer at each of these principles to better understand how they relate to the traditional way of viewing medicine and health.

1. *"Biochemical individuality based on genetic and environmental uniqueness"* is a fancy way of saying that your genes are a *factor* in determining your health, but they *are not a life sentence.* Simply because your mother and grandmother died from breast cancer does *not* mean you will. While there may be genetic factors involved, we also "inherit" our eating habits and lifestyles, which also can be main players in the breast cancer scenario. You can't change your genetic predisposition, but you *can* change how those genes express themselves by making dietary and lifestyle habit alterations. Functional M.D.'s will advise and assist you in that pursuit as part of your treatment.
2. *"Patient centered versus disease centered"* – in other words, the individual – not the disease – is the target of treatment. If

you've ever heard yourself or a loved one referred to in your doctor's office as "the chest pain in Room Three," you know that many doctors regard patients as the sum of their symptoms and treat them accordingly: identify the symptoms, name the disease, prescribe a treatment. Yet no two people with the same diagnosis will respond to treatment in the same way. So why focus on the disease instead of the person? Research has linked effective *patient-centered interviewing* with improved health outcomes. This interviewing needs to include the whole person, including emotional needs and life issues. What are the "triggers" – what keeps this thing going? And what are the "mediators" – what could shut it off?

3. *"Dynamic balance of internal and external factors"* – or homeodynamics. Cells are speaking to one another 24/7. When communication is interrupted, here comes the problem! Genetic (internal) and environmental (external) factors both contribute to heart disease, cancers, and other major causes of mortality, but evidence indicates that environmental factors are most important. This is great news because you can often *change* your environment, whereas you are stuck with your genes.

4. *"Web-like interconnections of physiological factors"* – what organs and systems work together? There is a gut-liver connection; also a gut-liver-neuro (mind) connection. There is a neuro-endocrine (hormone) connection, an immuno-cardiology connection, and even a psycho-somatic one. What we eat, how we exercise, and what we think are all integrated factors leading to ease or dis-ease. This is a search for "total health" – body, mind, and spirit all working in harmony.

5. *"Health as a positive vitality – not merely the absence of disease."* This is such a powerful principle I hope everyone reading this book can begin to truly grasp it. Health is so much more than the absence of disease. To maintain and enhance health requires a proactive approach marked by behaviors, choices, and interventions that maximize our body's natural functions and wellness. The twin forces of biology and behavior will be stronger if we comprehend the fact that they work together.

6. *"Promotion of organ reserve – healthspan."* Functional medicine believes chronic illness may be postponed and/or shortened by changes in lifestyle, including markers of aging. In other words, not only do persons with better health habits survive longer, but in such persons disability is postponed and compressed into fewer years at the end of life. *I love this aspect!*

Functional medicine is not just about adding years to your life but adding life to your years!

Concerns with this Practice

There are two major concerns with functional medicine. The first is similar to that of naturopathy in that some practitioners in this field use techniques other than the tried and true, scientific, measurable lab work with bodily fluids. Thus, careful questioning or interviewing of the physician to determine their methods of diagnosis and treatment is very important. The term "natural treatments" could possibly employ New Age remedies that are not scientifically based, so as always keep your discretion in the forefront.

The next concern contains both good news and bad news. The good news is that a functional doctor's office visits and tests/lab work will almost always be covered by your standard insurance since their diagnostic techniques are generally the same as allopathic doctors'. The bad news is the availability of functional doctors. The field is growing but is still in its infancy as of this writing. To find this type of physician in your area or study more about the field, go to www.functionalmedicine.org.

"Total Health" Seminar

Dr. Bill Gothard is a highly respected Bible teacher in the Christian community who has conducted seminars for forty years exploring the relationship between health problems and spiritual causes. He has recently developed a seminar which he refers to as a "new" approach to "Total Health." The teachers at this conference include functional doctors and other health professionals who are looking for cures to disease, not just management. For those who desire to take part in a research study and health evaluation, Dr.

Gothard includes blood and urine testing at the seminars which is then sent to Dr. Broekhuyse, a physician in the Netherlands.

In the past thirty years Dr. Broekhuyse has discovered and is refining the technology of formulating many different dietary supplements to naturally boost the immune system to assist the body in overcoming some adverse health conditions. He has conducted thousands of these studies for people from all over the world and achieved success in defeating many diseases the Western world has been stymied by for years (such as Lyme disease). This is an excellent example of functional medicine at work.

I highly recommend that everyone investigate and attend Dr. Gothard's "Total Health" seminar. His organization is called the International Institute for Health and Research and can be contacted by calling 615-865-7400 or e-mailing medicalregistrar@iblp.org. In addition, his general website is www.iblp.org where you can find more details about these health conferences.

In Summary

In conclusion, Dr. Mark Houston is a clinical professor of medicine at Vanderbilt School of Medicine. His comments in a recent *Journal of American Nutraceuticals Association* publication summarize my thoughts about functional medicine:

> The wise healer uses that which works. Health-oriented medicine utilizing a bio-chemical nutrient-genetic approach to prevention and treatment of disease and dysfunction will be the medicine of the future. The physician who can transcend the quantum leap from basic science to clinical nutritional and functional medicine, within the framework of the mind, body and spirit of the human, will synergize the healing powers inherent in all of us.

I believe functional medicine is the medicine of the future. It follows God's design of the body, is scientifically based, and works toward helping the body help itself. In conjunction with whatever medical modality you choose, be sure to keep your mind and heart involved in the healing process.

I feel there is a need to discuss drugs one more time in the context of functional medicine. Since drugs, supplements, and other medication can be a part of functional medicine as well as any other healing art, I would like to take one final but *very important* look at them in the next chapter.

Chapter 17

A Time and Purpose for Medication

As stated previously, diet and lifestyle are very important components to health and the main thrust of this book. However, dietary changes are sometimes not enough to allow our bodies to heal themselves, and there are times when needed lifestyle changes will not only be physical in nature, but spiritual as well. The fact is that the root to *chronic* disease is very often *spiritual*. This is one reason why taking drugs for a prolonged malady such as an allergy or high blood pressure does not "cure" it. If it did, you would be able to stop taking the drugs and the allergy or high blood pressure would be gone and your body's health restored.

Discerning the spiritual root of persistent disease could be the subject of an entire book in itself, but I will address it briefly here due to its importance. Finding the spiritual root of disease is the beginning of the *cure* for an "incurable" malady. Scripture is clear. Disease is a curse, not a blessing (see Deuteronomy 28). This curse cannot come without a reason:

n curse without cause shall not alight.

Proverbs 26:2 NKJV

The causes for a curse to come into our lives are sin—disobedience to God's Word—(read Deuteronomy 28) or evil spirits. (Jesus cast out many evil spirits in order to heal people. The four Gospels—Matthew, Mark, Luke, and John—are full of examples.) Therefore, the cause of the curse – sin and/or evil spirits – which brings about habitual disease in this case, must be dealt with before the blessings – healing and health – can come from God.

I can almost hear you arguing, "That's Old Testament! Christ paid the penalty for the sins of the world and saved us from the curse by His sacrificial death and resurrection, as recorded in the New Testament." True!

> Christ has redeemed us from the curse of the law, being made a curse for us....
>
> Galatians 3:13 NKJV

> Who His own self bore our sins in His own body on the tree, that we, being dead to sins should live to righteousness; by whose stripes you were healed.
>
> 1 Peter 2:24 NKJV

BUT....AND THIS IS HUGE...

> *The blessing of health is a gift, but we must actively, not passively, receive it. We must* **appropriate** *God's gifts and blessings – including health—by knowing His Word and applying it to our daily lives.*

So how does this relate to our taking prescription drugs or other medications? Let's look at what the Bible says.

The Bible and Medications

Surprising to many Christians, the Bible addresses the subject of taking medicine, and it is *very important* to learn and apply what we see on this point. The use of Scripture will allow the Word of God to define this so it is clear that it is *not* just "my opinion." Please read this section carefully and prayerfully as it will be a challenge to your mind and heart due to our dependence on and easy access to drugs (prescription and over-the-counter).

Now the works of the flesh are manifest, which are these: adultery, fornication, uncleanness, lasciviousness, idolatry, **witchcraft**, hatred, variance, emulations, wrath, strife, seditions, heresies, envyings, murders, drunkenness, revellings and such like; of the which I tell you before, as I have also told you in time past, that they which **do** such things shall not inherit the kingdom of God.

Galatians 5:19-21 KJV

What a list! But be of good cheer. We're only going to look at two words in these verses: "do" and "witchcraft." (You can deal with the others on your own time.) Reading this list could make anyone believe that *no one* will inherit the kingdom of God. Who hasn't done at least one of these things? This is a great example of the importance of looking up the meanings of words. Fortunately for all of us, this is the *Strong's Concordance* definition of *do*:

do – to perform repeatedly or habitually, thus differing from a single act. (*Strong's Concordance*)

That's a relief to many, I'm sure, as this is stating the difference between Christians who habitually practice one of these issues *as a way of life* versus those who *occasionally fall* into it. But don't get too comfortable yet. Now we're going to tackle "witchcraft."

Witchcraft – (Greek word – *pharmakeia*) – medication, pharmacy – from the root word *pharmakeus* or *pharmakon* meaning a drug, spell-giving potion, druggist, pharmacist or poisoner (*Strong's*)

Ouch! This word "witchcraft" in Galatians is medications prescribed by a physician or over-the-counter drugs found in any pharmacy or department store. Remember, it is not just the taking of these drugs that is the issue, but rather *how* we "do" the drugs that is of paramount importance. Does this mean we should never take drugs? *A resounding* – NO! There are times when drugs will save your life. Does this mean it is *wrong* (dare I use the word....sin?)

to take drugs on a "repeated, habitual" basis? Pastor Henry Wright has written a booklet on this subject, and I'd like to quote him at this point as his explanation is clear and concise:

> There is a place for doctors. There is a place for medication. But when you use medication to give you ease or give you an altered state of soul or biological consciousness, the old enemy goes undealt with while you are chemically managed and altered, **and that is why it is sin.** Now most people take medications because they need relief. Most medications for pain, for example, are beta-blockers. This drug shuts down the pathway of pain. You still have the pain, you just do not know it. So it is an occultic delusional safety. As long as you take the medication then you do not feel the pain.[1]

This quotation is strong, so to further back it up I want to define the word *occult* for your deeper understanding:

> **Occult** (*Webster's 1828*) – hidden from the eye or understanding; invisible; secret; unknown; undiscovered. In astronomy – the time a star or planet is hidden from our sight when eclipsed by the interposition of the body of a planet.

Proper Use of Medication

Please think through these definitions and applications slowly and carefully. This means *anything* I am using (drugs, herbs, supplements, medicinal oils, etc.) that is *blocking* my relationship with God, or is used in place of, or is obscuring my relationship with God is "occultic." This is so important! *Medications* (drugs, herbs, supplements, medicinal oils, etc.) *are not inherently evil* (though they all need to be searched out to be certain), *but any of them can* become *evil if I am using them to* replace *what God wants me to do or deal with.*

My understanding is that *anything* (drugs, herbs, supplements, medicinal oils, etc.) that I am using on a *regular* basis to combat an *ongoing*/chronic condition (i.e. allergies, headaches, high blood pressure, etc.) is occultic because God's Word promises me good health *if* I meet specific physical and spiritual conditions. To suffer from any chronic disorder means my life is out of alignment with God in one or more areas.

My search for healing from this *chronic* disorder must begin with God, His Word, and prayer. Any spiritual root that is discovered must be dealt with whether it is a sin issue to be repented of or a change in heart and thought patterns such as bitterness or unforgiveness, etc. Discerning and dealing with the problem on the spiritual plane may eliminate the problem, but if not, then I must also search for a physician to help me find the physical *cause* of my disease. I want a physician who will prescribe remedies to help my body come back into balance, not simply prescriptions for daily "disease management" for the remainder of my life.

This does not mean that I *never* take drugs or other medications. It does mean that our ultimate goal should be taking *no* medications *permanently*, either pharmaceutical or nutraceutical in nature. Please note - I did *not* say to never take medications. I am *not* telling you to stop medications you are currently taking. *I am saying* our goal should be to *keep searching until we find the cause*, the spiritual and physical root of our disease, so we will be taking *no medications permanently!* God wants to heal us and make us whole. His best for us is *not* to be taking medication forever. According to the Galatians passage above, medication is something we can use, something we can "do" as long as it is not "repeated and habitual." We can use it with a clear conscience to get us through the time of crisis while at the same time diligently searching for the root cause and healing.

> *Taking drugs isn't about how evil you or I are,*
> *but about how good God is. God's Word wasn't written*
> *to condemn us but rather to set us free.*

If we are habitually taking medication without simultaneously seeking the solution to our disease, we are not experiencing God's best. We are living under the curse instead of under His blessings. He wants to cure you of whatever ails you, not have you "manage your disease" with drugs for the rest of your life. The truth is that traditional medicine attempts to manage symptoms with drugs. The problem with this approach is that most drugs have side effects, which eventually produce new symptoms that require more drugs. And on goes the decline and deeper goes our dependence on drugs rather than our loving Father. This is why my first recommendation for medical intervention is functional medicine because it addresses the *whole person*, including *mind and spirit*, and is truly searching for a cure for disease, not simply symptom management.

Please don't "beat yourself up" on this point. (Don't beat me up either.) God's Word was not written to condemn us but rather to set us free from the sins we discover as we walk through this life. I've been on a fifteen-year search and have just recently become free of "doing" medication on a daily basis.

As you search, use whatever newfound information you discover as the hacksaw to begin to cut off the ball and chain of any diseases or medications that are a part of your daily life. Freedom is available, but there is a cost. It will require personal effort and perhaps years of investigation to learn how to *obey* and apply what you have learned. Scripture refers to this as "working out your salvation." But you can do it! God doesn't put time limits on us. He will help you as you read, study, and apply. The reward of *freedom* and *health* is worth it!

> Wherefore, my beloved, as you have always obeyed, not as in my presence only, but now much more in my absence, work out your own salvation with fear [respect] and trembling.
> Philippians 2:12 NKJV

This said, we've finally reached a turning point! At last our foundation of history, definitions, detoxification, and medical care choices are in place. Let's begin to apply these principles and newfound knowledge and find out how best to maintain health at the dinner table. Now it's time to eat!

END NOTES

1. Henry W. Wright, <u>Insights into Pharmakeia and Sorcery</u> (Thomaston, Georgia: Pleasant Valley Publications, 2002), p. 10.

PART FIVE

SO…..WHAT CAN I EAT?

God's Dietary and Environmental Principles Explored for Meat, Seafood, Dairy, Sweeteners, Fruits and Vegetables, Grains and Processed/Refined Foods

Galatians 6:7 – Do not be deceived; God is not mocked; for whatever a man sows, that he will also reap.

Chapter 18

Meat and Leviticus 11 – Jewish Dietary Laws or God's Dietary Principles?

As we begin to explore what it is we are to eat, we will keep God's Word at the forefront. After all, God created your body and knows what's best to use for fueling it. Unfortunately, what we find in Scripture often differs from our opinions and what we find at our church potluck dinners. As we go through this section, please remember we are dividing the Word of God, not setting forth my ideology. In other words, "Don't shoot the messenger." If you react strongly to any of these tenets, take it up with the Lord for it is His Word you are objecting to, not mine.

In Chapter 2, we already discussed God's first instructions about food – that we are to eat a lot of fruits, vegetables, grains, and nuts. There is no mention of meat until Noah returns to land after the flood. I'm not sure why that is, except perhaps Noah would have found no vegetation to eat for several months after the flood, so meat became a staple out of necessity and remained so after vegetation returned, possibly because of what had now become habit. Apparently man's new meat-eating habit needed some guidelines, which God gave to the Israelites in Leviticus 11:1-23, a literal treasure trove on dietary regulations regarding meat and fish.

God's Law and God's Grace – the Dynamic Duo

Many Christians argue that these Leviticus regulations are part of the Old Testament law and that we are no longer under the law, but under New Testament grace. They say these are just Jewish dietary laws that do not pertain to us today. There is an important point here that needs to be discerned. According to my understanding:

There are three types of God's law: moral, civil, and health/dietary.
Disobedience in any of the "types" will bring negative consequences, some of which are temporal, some eternal.

The *moral law* is composed, generally, of the Ten Commandments, and specifically of many others found throughout the Pentateuch (first five books of the Bible). Disobedience to these commandments is sin and carries physical, spiritual, and even permanent consequences, up to and including eternal separation from God (hell).

The *civil law* is made up of statutes and ordinances for the smooth functioning of society – such things as just punishment befitting the crime committed, or, more often, equitable restitution for property loss. Non-adherence to these laws will lead to varying degrees of civic injustice or civil unrest but does not directly involve the spiritual realm of everlasting punishments.

Then we have God's cleanliness, *health*, and *dietary laws*. Violating these laws reaps negative consequences for the environment in general, which sooner or later also impacts the individual through sickness, the spread of disease, and even death. Disobedience to God's dietary and cleanliness laws will not send you to hell, nor will obedience get you into heaven, but each option carries its own set of consequences. Obedience will result in your living a longer, healthier life where you can fulfill your God-ordained destiny with vigor! Disobedience may get you to heaven faster, but at what cost? Your strength and ability to perform God's divinely decreed purpose for you will be diminished because of sickness and short-circuited by premature death.

Another aspect of God's law is that it was not intended to be burdensome, but rather keeping (obeying) it is to be a delight and a blessing that brings personal prosperity:

> Blessed is the man...[whose] **delight is in the law** of the
> Lord. And in His law he meditates day and night. He shall
> be like a tree planted by the rivers of water, that brings forth
> its fruit in its season, whose leaf also shall not wither and
> **whatever he does shall prosper.**
>
> Psalm 1:1-3 NKJV

A final argument: Jesus Christ's death and resurrection on the
cross—taking us from the old covenant/Old Testament to the new
covenant/New Testament, from being under law to being under
grace—did not change our human anatomy and physiology, the real
reason God gave us these dietary laws. They were *safeguards, not
just regulations.* He knew what our digestive systems could handle
and what they couldn't.

The Israelites accepted God's Word without understanding
"why" some meats were classified as "unclean" and others as
"clean." Since we have so grossly violated some of these laws, I
believe it is imperative to explain some of the "whys" of this culi-
nary code. Hopefully, these explanations will give you both understanding and sufficient incentive to make some healthful changes,
and even to view these "laws" as God's "grace" in His care and
concern for your health.

Old Testament Guidelines

> And the Lord said to Moses and Aaron, "Say to the Israelites,
> 'These are the animals which you may eat among all the
> beasts that are on the earth. Whatever parts the hoof and is
> cloven-footed and chews the cud, among the animals, that
> you may eat.'"
>
> Leviticus 11:1-3 NKJV

The only animals that have both divided hooves and chew
their cud are the *vegetarian* animals or herbivores (plant eaters).
Herbivores are the healthiest of all the beasts of the field because
they don't eat the flesh of animals and, thereby, avoid the many
diseases, parasites, and worms that are in the flesh and blood of

those animals. Not only are vegetarian animals free of most diseases and parasites associated with the eating of flesh foods, but their long digestive tracts, which are six to twelve times the length of their bodies, ensure that they will completely process and eliminate any unfavorable toxins and poisons. Cow, buffalo, deer, and sheep all fit into the category of the edible animals mentioned in Leviticus because they have divided hooves and chew their cud.

> *An edible or "clean" animal is defined by what it eats*
> *and the length and cleanliness of its digestive tract.*

There is another important Scripture principle that relates to eating meat:

> And the priest shall burn them on the altar as food, an offering made by fire for a sweet aroma; all the fat is the Lord's. This shall be a perpetual statute throughout your generations in all your dwellings. You shall eat neither **fat nor blood.**
> Leviticus 3:16-17 NKJV

The body fat of mammals is where many toxins deposit themselves. Blood carries nutrients to the cells but also removes toxins and wastes. Hence, the admonition against eating neither fat nor blood. God's instruction to the priests for preparing animals for sacrifice was not strangulation, but rather to slit the animal's throat and then immediately drain the blood out before it was cooked. Before I began research on this book I often wondered why God bothered to include details about how to kill the animals for the sacrifices. What difference could it make? It is because failure to drain the blood immediately gives it ample opportunity to settle in various organs and tissues of the dead animal, thus decreasing the purity.

This chapter in Leviticus also gives additional instructions regarding certain parts of the animal we shouldn't eat.

> Then he shall offer from the sacrifice of the peace offering ... made by the fire to the Lord. The fat that covers the entrails and all the fat that is on the entrails, the two kidneys and the

fat that is on them by the flanks, and the fatty lobe attached
to the liver above the kidneys he shall remove.

Leviticus 3:3-4 NKJV

The parts mentioned are not to be eaten, but burned up as an offering to the Lord. The entrails are intestines. The fatty lobe attached to the liver is the gall bladder. The liver, kidneys, and gall bladder are all part of the elimination system, which means they process toxins. To eat any of these organs is to ingest a mega-dose of bodily poisons. These are "filter" organs and should not be consumed.

[A side note on this subject: Today, many doctors quickly remove our tonsils, our appendix, and our gall bladders, not giving sufficient credit to their value as protective filters. Our tonsils keep many diseases out of our lungs and throat. Our appendix is not a vestigial or useless organ as many of our biology books say it is. (Is it in keeping with God's character to put an organ in our body that is useless? I don't think so.) Both the appendix and the gall bladder perform very important functions for purifying our systems of toxins. The reason an appendix becomes inflamed and must be removed is due to toxic overload!]

Nevertheless these you shall not eat among those that chew the cud or those that have cloven hooves: the camel, because it chews the cud but does not have cloven hooves, is unclean to you; the rock hyrax, because it chews the cud, but does not have cloven hooves, is unclean to you; the hare because it chews the cud but does not have cloven hooves, is unclean to you; and the swine, though it divides the hoof, having cloven hooves, yet does not chew the cud, is unclean to you. Their flesh you shall not eat, and their carcasses you shall not touch; they are unclean to you.

Leviticus 11:4-8 NKJV

Fasten your seat belt—here comes the one nobody likes to hear: The inedible or unclean animals include the camel, horse, hare or rabbit, rock badger (this class includes all rodents, rats, squirrels, and mice), and swine. This "swine" class includes bears, monkeys, and **pigs (bacon, ham, and sausage)**. This entire group of unclean animals is called omnivores. Omnivores eat both vegetation and animal foods.

Omnivores will, by their very biological nature, eat anything!
Their digestive tracts are much shorter than the herbivores because the decaying flesh and by-products are potentially toxic and must be removed quickly from their bodies.

Let's look specifically at pigs since pork is a staple on most American tables. First of all, the indiscriminate eating patterns of omnivores such as pigs make them disease carriers. Pigs are known to carry up to **200** diseases and **18** different parasites and worms, including the one that brings trichinosis.[1] Contrary to what most of us have been taught, *these parasites are **not** removed by thorough cooking*. Heat and cooking will kill bacteria but not these little worms. These worms are so small and transparent that only trained inspectors using high-powered microscopes can detect their existence; yet trichinosis is so potent it can cripple or even kill anyone who eats *as little as a forkful* of contaminated food. Trichinosis can also mimic other diseases such as arthritis, rheumatism, or typhoid fever.

Pigs have more incidences of arthritis than any other known animal in the world. Dr. Gordon Tessler and other nutritionists believe arthritis may be a virus or a parasite that is transmitted from pigs to humans as a direct result of eating their flesh and blood. Dr. Tessler believes many diseases are misdiagnosed and their real cause is roundworm, gullet worms, hookworms, thorn-headed worms, trichina worms, stomach worms, nodular worms, tapeworms, as well as many other parasites found in the flesh of the unclean swine.[2] A person may be committing slow suicide by eating a steady diet of bacon, ham, sausage, or pork chops.

Okay, you say, but today's hogs are corn fed; there is no more "slopping the hogs." True, but even hog farmers who insist that corn-fed hogs are safe cannot give you a guarantee that their indoor hogs haven't eaten any rats, mice, *their own fecal waste*, or maggots within the past few days.

The metal doorknobs in a pig nursery become corroded after a year or so due to the gases produced by the pigs' urine and feces. The same gases and pig dander that eat away metal doorknobs have been found to be harming the respiratory tracts of hog farmers. These farmers have an unusually high incidence of respiratory ailments, ranging from coughing and sniffles to lung scarring and pneumonia. These ailments can no longer simply be attributed to weather and allergies alone. Hog waste spills from hog farms are contaminating our land, our rivers, and our water supply. Pork should be considered a human poison and the probable cause of many common sicknesses and degenerative diseases. Pork is not "the other white meat." A more accurate advertisement would declare, "Pork—the parasitic meat."

Whatever argument you may have for eating pork, the bottom line and principle involved is God's sovereignty: He said – "DON'T EAT IT!"

New Testament Food and Freedom - Let's Look Closer

I'd like to take this opportunity to close the door on the New Testament arguments that are often brought into this debate, passages that are cited as making the distinction of "unclean and clean" meats of the Old Testament null and void.

- First of all, Jesus said the New Testament was not written to overrule the Old, but rather to fulfill it.
- Second, we need to look at the *context* of the passages cited.
- Third, both the *Webster's 1828* dictionary *definition of food*, as well as the definition of the Greek word for food/meat – *broma* - used in the New Testament, need to be understood:

food - flesh or vegetables eaten for sustaining human life; whatever is or may be eaten for **nourishment**. (*Webster's 1828*)

broma – food sanctified by the Levitical law of God. (*Strong's Concordance*)

With these three criteria in mind, now let's look at a few of the most contested passages.

> The next day as they went on their journey and drew near the city, Peter went up on the housetop to pray about the sixth hour [noon]. Then he became very hungry and wanted to eat; but while they made ready, he fell into a trance and saw heaven opened and an object like a great sheet bound at the four corners, descending to him and let down to the earth. In it were all kinds of four-footed animals of the earth, wild beasts, creeping things, and birds of the air. And a voice came to him, "Rise, Peter; kill and eat." But Peter said, "Not so, Lord! For I have never eaten anything common or unclean." And a voice spoke to him again the second time, "What God has cleansed you must not call common." This was done three times. And the object was taken up into heaven again.
>
> Acts 10:9-16 NKJV

Many Christians use this passage as their proof text that God has removed the clean and unclean standard for meat, and everything is okay to eat today. This is a misrepresentation of Scripture. The intent, or context, is clearly seen if we continue reading:

> While Peter thought about the vision, the Spirit said to him, "Behold, three men are seeking you.... Then [Peter] said to them [the visiting Gentiles], "You know how unlawful it is for a Jewish man to keep company with or go to one of another nation. But God has shown me that I should not call **any man common or unclean**.
>
> Acts 10:19, 28 NKJV

God was using the food illustration as an *analogy* that Peter would clearly understand as it related to man and God providing salvation for *all* men of *all* nations. *No man of any ethnic back-*

ground would be considered "unclean" or excluded from the salvation message that had previously been the exclusive property of the
Jewish Christians.

Here is another passage that is also used to "prove" that God has
removed Old Testament eating restrictions:

> Therefore let no one act as your judge in regard to food or
> drink or in respect to a festival or a new moon or a Sabbath
> day – things which are a mere shadow of what is to come;
> but the substance belongs to Christ.
>
> Colossians 2:16-17 NAS

The context of this passage is in reference to food that was
offered to pagan idols. This practice presented a huge stumbling
block in the early church. Some Christians refused to eat it, calling
it unclean, while others declared that idols were meaningless, and
therefore the food offered to them was not made unclean. Hence,
the basis of the argument was what the food was used for (an idol
offering), not what the food was!

Yet another verse, with the same explanation:

> I know and am convinced in the Lord Jesus that nothing
> is unclean in itself; but to him who thinks anything to be
> unclean, to him it is unclean.
>
> Romans 14:14 NAS

If we are to take Paul's words at face value, he sounds like a
twenty-first-century man—situational ethics rule. Whatever you
think is right and okay. Who needs an absolute God to make absolute rules? But the reality here is again a matter of conscience over
eating meat offered to idols, not a meat declared unclean due to its
nature as described in the Levitical law.

Neither do either of these next two passages negate God's prohi-
bitions on unclean meats, but rather refer to the definition of food:

> ...some are going to give up on the faith and chase after
> demonic illusions...Men who forbid marriage and advocate

abstaining from foods, which God has created to be grate-
fully shared in by those who believe and know the truth.
For everything created by God is good, and nothing is to be
rejected, if it is received with gratitude; for it is sanctified by
means of the word of God and prayer.

1 Timothy 4:1, 3-5 NAS

...because it does not go into his heart, but into his stomach,
and is eliminated? (Thus He declared all foods clean.)

Mark 7:19 NAS

In the first passage from Timothy, it looks as though the author
(Paul) believes you can eat anything (cockroaches, snakes, dirt?)
as long as you pray over it first. In the Mark passage, the quotation
from Jesus also seems to rescind any and all limitations on eating
– "*He declared all foods clean.*" But as we refer to the *Strong's
Concordance* definition of food/*broma*—"*food sanctified by the
Levitical law of God*"—the meaning becomes clear: The writers
are once again referring to food offered to idols, leaving God's Old
Testament dietary guidelines intact in the New Testament as well!

Still unwilling to give up your pork? Consider the following:
Did God re-invent pigs after Jesus rose from the dead? Did pigs
suddenly look at the calendar, gasp, and stop eating maggots and
their own waste when they realized that 40 A.D. had come and
gone? Did Christ's resurrection spontaneously stop causing worms
and parasites to enter our bodies when we eat pork? I don't think so!
Clean and unclean food is not a question of legalism, dates, or grace
versus law. It is an issue of the nature of the animal, what they eat,
and whether or not they will poison our system or provide nutrition
to us.

As a final New Testament argument, what was Jesus' response
to pigs? In Matthew 8:32, He filled them with demons and *drowned*
them in the lake! How could Jesus, who miraculously fed five thousand people and then warned His disciples not to waste any of the
scraps, be so unfeeling about "wasting" two thousand pigs? The
answer is simple: He did not consider the pigs to be a food source.
Neither should you.

The Great Physician, the Creator of all life, admonishes us to separate the clean animals from the unclean for physical health and well-being. Many faithful church people who would never defile God's temple with cigarettes (even though smoking is not mentioned in the Bible) continue to regularly ingest bacon, ham, and pork chops, which are disease-carrying, parasite-infested, unclean foods that God *commands* His children not to eat! It would be futile and absurd to ask God to bless a cigarette before we smoke it, yet we pray that He will bless a pork chop on our dinner plate! The choice is yours, but you will reap what you sow.

The principle for eating pork (or any other unclean meat) is God's sovereignty.
Can we expect our Creator to disregard His Word to us so we can indulge our appetites?

Next category in Leviticus—fowl:

These, moreover, you shall detest among the birds; they are abhorrent, not to be eaten: the eagle and the vulture and the buzzard, and the kite and the falcon in its kind, every raven in its kind, and the ostrich and the owl and the sea gull and the hawk in its kind, and the little owl and the cormorant and the great owl, and the white owl and the pelican and the carrion-vulture, and the stork, the heron in its kinds, and the hoopoe, and the bat.

Leviticus 11:13-19 NAS

The unclean birds are birds of prey that eat the flesh of man and beast, taking into their feathery bodies every disease and parasite of the animals they devour.

It is just plain common sense not to eat such birds. Obviously, the "health fad" touting ostrich as a nutritious meat is also in error, according to God's standards. The birds that are clean and *edible* are chicken, turkey, duck, quail, and geese.

The last section on "meat" in Leviticus actually refers to clean and unclean insects.

> All the winged insects that walk on all fours are detestable to you. Yet these you may eat among all the winged insects which walk on all fours: those which have above their feet jointed legs with which to jump on the earth. These of them you may eat: the locust in its kinds, and the devastating locust in its kinds, and the cricket in its kinds, and the grass-hopper in its kinds. But all other winged insects which are four-footed are detestable to you."
>
> Leviticus 11:21-23 NAS

I find it interesting that God considers some insects to be more edible than pork products! John the Baptist lived on locusts and wild honey, if you recall. I don't know of very many people today (any?) who ingest insects. I have done no studying in this area and so will not attempt to expound on the value of eating bugs at this time. If you have questions in this regard, as always, let Scripture be your guide.

Shopping for "Clean" Meat and Eggs

Sadly, we face additional problems and criteria today regarding "clean" beef and fowl. Factory farming is fouling our food, both beef and poultry. Practices such as injecting hormones for quick growth, and widespread use of antibiotics to preclude disease in feedlot pens and henhouses that are overcrowded puts harmful substances in the flesh of these otherwise good meats. The U.S. Department of Agriculture (USDA) has a legal code of health, safety, and cleanliness standards for our slaughterhouses, but these laws are often grossly under-enforced or entirely ignored.

Chemically enhanced feeds, genetic engineering, drugs, and hormones are some of the tools used by the modern livestock industry to create the super chickens that lay eggs around the clock and monster cows that grow twice as fast with one-fourth the feed.[3] Bovine growth hormone and estrogen are the most abused. Together, their synergistic effect provokes human problems like arthritis, obesity, glucose intolerance, diabetes, heart disease, and other less serious but annoying conditions like headaches, fatigue, vision impairment, dizziness, menstrual problems (like PMS, unheard of fifty years ago!), and loss of sexual drive.[4]

Fortunately, there is a solution. A growing number of poultry farmers and cattle ranchers are raising their animals either organically or giving them "free range" (not crowded in pens, but free to roam pastures or barnyards). Both of these practices remove the "need" for large and continual doses of antibiotics, and those who raise animals in this way usually *choose* not to use hormones for quick or unnatural growth and production. Because it is harder work to find these meats, and usually more expensive as well, I want to give you sufficient details on the distinctions between these two types of meat to motivate you to search out the good and spend more money if necessary.

Factory-farmed cows live in crowded, filthy feedlots and are fed the pulverized remains of other animals, stale pastries, cardboard, and even chicken manure! No wonder they are constantly sick and need regular doses of antibiotics. (More than 20 million pounds of antibiotics per year are fed to livestock.) While the hormones they receive accelerate their growth, the extra weight is *saturated fat* (the bad fat). When they make it to the slaughterhouse, some of their manure often gets mixed in with the meat.[5]

Free-range cattle, on the other hand, eat real grass, hay, and cattle feed. They are much less likely than their factory-farmed friends to get sick or have the deadly sort of E. coli because their intestines have a healthy mix of all the bacteria needed to break down their food. (This bacteria is destroyed in the factory-farmed animals from all the antibiotic use.) These cows are smaller and leaner than the others, and what fat they have is filled with healing omega-3 essential fatty acids, which actually *fight heart disease.*[6]

Free-range chickens have 20 percent less fat than conventional, confined chickens. A USDA-funded study found that eggs from three pastured poultry farms (free range) contained a third less cholesterol than the average for commercial eggs from confined birds. Free-range chickens lay eggs with up to *20 times more omega-3 essential fatty acids than are found in supermarket eggs!* [7] This answers the much-debated question as to whether eggs are healthy food: Free range – YES. Confined – NO. Eggs are a natural, God-created food and a wonderful protein source, but they need to be raised naturally!

For those of you who want more information, I recommend a book by Jo Robinson titled *Why Grassfed Is Best!* It is completely documented with tests and accompanying statistics. This book also contains listings of farmers across the country who sell grass-fed meat and dairy products. However, since this list would be updated constantly, I recommend you go to her website for current data: www.eatwild.com

Consumer demand for grass-fed is growing, and many small-scale farmers are responding by adding natural pasture-based animal production to their farms. When these show up in the supermarkets, they are usually very expensive, but if you can buy directly from the local producers, the cost may be comparable to what you're paying now for "conventional" meats. Please try to search out and support these farmers. They are truly America's finest and need our business to stay afloat.

Also, check your local markets for "free range" poultry or organic beef. (In the Midwest many Amish farmers supply local supermarkets, and their meat is excellent – hormone and antibiotic free.) *Laura's Beef* is an organic brand name carried by Kroger. If you don't see it, ask for it. Major grocery store chains are becoming much more amenable to carrying "health food store" items. If enough of us insist on buying only "clean poultry and beef" (no hormones or antibiotics), maybe Tysons, Holly Farms, and cattle ranchers will be pressured to institute cleaner and more humane methods of raising their animals.

The principle is stewardship: Taking dominion over animals as God intended is beneficial for both the creatures and man.
Free-range farming methods are obviously better for the animals, but also immeasurably safer for human consumption as well.

There are three key principles about eating that will serve you well as we continue in our search for good, healthy eating:

- Eat only substances God created for food.
- As much as possible, eat foods as they were created, *before* they were changed into something man thought might be better. (Examples in coming chapters)
- Avoid food addictions. Do not let any food or drink become your god.

Next, let's go fishing and see what we catch!

END NOTES

1. Gordon S. Tessler, <u>The Genesis Diet: The Biblical Foundation for Optimum Nutrition</u> (Raleigh, NC: Be Well Publications, 1996), p. 51
2. Ibid, p. 52
3. Francisco Contreras, <u>Health in the 21st Century: Will Doctors Survive?</u> (Chula Vista, CA: Interpacific Press, February 1997), p. 106
4. Ibid., p. 107
5. Maria Rodale, " Front Gate - The Story of Jim and Sam," <u>Organic Gardening</u>, November/December 2000, p. 2.
6. Ibid.
7. Bryan Peterson, "New Ground – Factory Farming is Fouling Our Food," <u>Organic Gardening</u>, November/December 2000.

Chapter 19

Seafood and Leviticus 11 – Delectably Delicious or Absolute Abomination?

Fins and Scales – Yes!

Seafood, as you will soon see, is a consumable about which God is very passionate. There are few places in Scripture that use extreme language when speaking about what we are to eat or avoid, but seafood is the notable exception.

> These you may eat, of all that are in the water: whatever in the water has fins and scales, whether in the seas or in the rivers—that you may eat.
>
> Leviticus 11:9 NKJV

Clean, or edible fish, can be found in rivers, lakes, seas, and oceans, and have both fins and scales.

Examples of clean or edible fish having both *fins* and *scales* are: bass, cod, flounder, grouper, haddock, halibut, herring, mackerel, orange roughy, perch, sole, salmon, red snapper, trout, tuna, and any other fresh or saltwater fin and scale fish.

But all in the seas or in the rivers that do not have fins and scales, all that move in the water or any living thing which is in the water, they are an **abomination** to you. They shall be an **abomination** to you; you shall not eat their flesh, but you shall regard their carcasses as an **abomination**. Whatever in the water does not have fins or scales – that shall be an **abomination** to you.

Leviticus 11:10-12 NKJV

And just in case you didn't get the idea, he repeats the admonition in another book:

You shall not eat any abominable thing.

Deuteronomy 14:3 KJV

Most of us don't eat crocodiles, snakes, or dolphins. But the list of unclean fish also includes some of our favorite main courses—shark, swordfish, and catfish, which have no scales. However, the list without fins and scales that always raises the loudest howls of protest includes *shrimp, lobster, crab, oysters, clams, scallops, and snails.* God repeats Himself in these short four verses: *Three times* He uses the identifier of "fins and scales" as absolute criteria for edibility. *Four times* in the same amount of space He uses the word "abomination." This is the passion I referred to at the opening of the chapter! Nowhere else in Scripture is there such a compact and stern warning regarding what we are *not* to eat! Does God think we are deaf or blind, or did He foresee our lustfulness for these *scavenger* fish?

> *Creatures without fins and scales - shrimp, lobster, crab, oysters, clams, scallops, snails, etc. - God declares* **four times** *to be not just "unclean" but an abomination!*

The use of the word *abomination* also makes an obvious distinction from simply referring to these creatures as unclean. God also calls idolatry an abomination. During the reign of King Josiah, all those things which were an abomination were broken down and cast out at the king's command. Just how strong is the word *abomination?* Let's compare it to *unclean.*

unclean – (*Strong's Concordance*) to be foul
foul (*Webster's 1828*) – impure or polluted.
abomination (*Webster's 1828*) - anything that arouses strong disgust; a revolting thing; a loathing, hatred of, strong dislike for or detestable.
detestable – extremely hateful or abominable; deserving abhorrence.
abhorrent – expressive of extreme opposition.
abhor – to set up bristles, shiver or shake. To hate with contempt.

What a distinction! Would you choose to eat impure meat or drink polluted water? I don't think so! And yet these descriptions are a "cake walk" compared to the severity of the description of abomination. This is *stern* language—something that is so upsetting we should "hate it with contempt." And yet many of us do choose to eat those things God says are so horrible they should make us "shiver or shake" from our revulsion to them. Let's investigate what we know today of both these types of water dwellers – those with fins and scales and those without – and learn *why* God is so adamant.

Fins allow fish to steer a definite course without being at the mercy of the tides and currents. With its fins in full use, the fish will swim even more against the tides, avoiding all the infected parts of the water, instead of drifting with any scum that might be washed down by the unclean water.

Scales act as a protection from the corrupt conditions of the waters. Any fish losing a scale is immediately in danger of infection. A fish breeder knows that the fish that has lost a scale must be separated from the others and placed in a specially prepared solution in order to prevent disease. He will then have to be carefully tended and observed until a new scale is formed.[1] It is interesting to note that the Hebrew word *qasqeseth*, translated *scale*, is the same word used in describing the impregnable coat of armor/mail worn by Goliath!

In addition, we also know today that fish contain half the fat of animal meats, and 5-40 percent of the fats they do contain are called omega-3. These are also known as essential fatty acids – *good fats!* Scientific evidence suggests that omega-3 fatty acids can actually *decrease the risk of coronary disease and cancer!* [2] The conclusion is simple and straightforward:

Fish with fins and scales are well protected from disease and will even help protect us from disease!

No Fins and Scales – No!

What do we know about shellfish, those without fins and scales? These are all scavenger fish containing high levels of cholesterol, mercury, disease, worms, chemicals, and parasites. High levels of mercury have been associated with various neurological diseases, such as Lou Gehrig's disease (see vaccination information in Chapter 10.) If you have a filthy pond the fastest way to clean it up is to buy a load of shrimp. They'll eat all the scum and other debris. These creatures are literal cesspools of filth, and consuming them is like eating secondhand pond scum.

From the following passage, it is clear that God knew how perverted our taste buds would become:

I have stretched out my hands all day long to a rebellious people, who walk in a way that is not good, according to their own thoughts...who eat swine's flesh and the broth of abominable things in their vessel.

Isaiah 65:2-4 NKJV

There's that word *abominable* again. Could our Lord be referring to clam chowder in those vessels? Oysters, clams, and mussels are immobile and also known as "filter feeders."

These and other shellfish sit in one spot in shallow areas near population centers and pump water through their bodies to soak up nutrients. An oyster can filter up to 50 gallons of sea water every day, including all the pollutants in it. Along with their lunch, they often accumulate a dangerous dose of bacteria and viruses from human sewage.

Can you imagine a person slurping down whole, raw oysters, clams, or mussels, including the entire digestive tract which includes this human sewage? Raw oysters, clams, and other such shellfish may also harbor hepatitis. If that isn't enough to keep you away from these shellfish, deadly nerve toxins called "red tides" can strike eaters of even well-cooked shellfish. Symptoms range from paralysis to memory loss.

Paralytic shellfish poisoning comes from algae that are a food source for filter-feeding shellfish. The toxin from this algae has been found in crabs.[3] When something dies in the ocean, it is the scavenger creature that eats it.

How about a biology lesson? Who remembers what family the lobster comes from? For those who can't recall, it's the "arthropod" class. Know what else is in the arthropod class? Steel your stomach—cockroaches! A lobster is nothing more than a giant aquatic cockroach!

Dr. Ted Broer had the following story in one of his books:

I'll never forget a time in the Florida Keys when I was preparing to go diving. When the previous client's boat came in with a fresh catch of lobsters I watched the divemaster pull lobster after lobster out of large buckets, break off the tails (which contain most of the "edible" meat) and throw the heads back into the water. Behind this man were dozens of cats begging for the lobsters. It looked as if the dive ship supported the entire cat population of the Keys. This was so intriguing that I had to ask the man, "Why don't you feed these lobster heads to the cats instead of throwing them back in the water?"

"Oh, no," he said, 'We can't give them to the cats. The poison in the lobsters will kill the cats."[4]

Why Did God Create Shellfish?

Need I say more? The problem with all shellfish stems from their very nature.

> *God's purpose for creating shellfish – these "cockroaches of the ocean" – was to clean up the waters,* **not for human consumption!**

In summary, we can see in God's regulations about sea creatures, not only divine wisdom, but great mercy as these ordinances aim at *prevention rather than cure.* The diseases brought on by these shellfish are particularly devastating. By choosing not to eat anything God calls "unclean" or an "abomination" we are helping our bodies to maintain a correct standard of fitness so that we can better serve Him in the best physical sense.

That's it for the Leviticus passage. I know this passage is hard to receive, but remember:

> **The principles are God's sovereignty and our stewardship of our bodies: Just because something tastes good does not mean we are to eat it. God's Word is the final authority, not our taste buds.**

We are supposed to be holy, sanctified, set apart, chosen by God as His peculiar people. God sternly warns us not to defile the temple:

> If anyone defiles the temple of God, God will destroy him. For the temple of God is holy, which temple you are.
> 1 Corinthians 3:17 NKJV

defile – to make unclean; to render foul or dirty; to pollute

He further admonishes us on the care of our temple:

> Or do you not know that your body is a temple of the Holy Spirit who is in you, whom you have from God, and that you

are not your own? For you have been bought with a price: therefore glorify God in your body.

1 Corinthians 6:19-20 NAS

We are getting into the heart of explicit diet changes now. In the subsequent chapters, we will talk about dairy products, sweeteners, grains, drinks, more shopping strategies, recipes, and alternatives to those things we eat that are killing us. Let's move on!

END NOTES

1. Raphael Gasson, <u>Food for God's Children</u> (Plainfield, NJ: Logos International, 1977) p. 63
2. Gordon S. Tessler, <u>The Genesis Diet – The Biblical Foundation for Optimal Nutrition</u> (Raleigh, NC: Be Well Publications, 1996), p. 54
3. Ted Broer, <u>Maximum Energy; Top Ten Foods Never to Eat; Top Ten Health Strategies to Feel Great</u> (Lake Mary, FL: Creation House, 1999), p.119
4. Ibid, pp. 119-120.

Chapter 20

A Land Flowing with Milk and Honey...
Dairy Products

When God led the Israelites to the Promised Land, a wonderful place to raise their families and livestock, He told them it was "flowing with milk and honey." This was obviously a very positive aspect of what this land had to offer. So if God gives milk such a rave review, why is it receiving so much negative press in the health food community today? Let's look closer.

"Milk Does a Body Good!"—Not!

Sixty percent of the allergies afflicting people in this country are directly attributable to the consumption of dairy products.[1] After the age of four years, most people naturally lose the ability to digest lactose found in milk, simply because they no longer synthesize the digestive enzyme lactase. *This condition, known as lactose intolerance, is not a disease but a normal state of every person over age five.* Some of us just manifest more allergy symptoms than others as a result of it! It is especially common among adult blacks and Asians, occurring in as many as 90 percent of them.[2] So, I ask again, why did God consider it a blessing to bring the Israelites to a land flowing with milk and honey? What was He thinking?

Relax. God didn't lose His mind. We have simply had ours misdirected through the years from God's original intent regarding the *source* and *purpose* of our milk. A careful search of the Bible reveals that God was referring to goat's milk, not cow's! This conclusion is verified several places in Scripture:

> You shall have enough goats' milk for your food.
> Proverbs 27:27 NKJV

Also, please note the additional implication of the *purpose* for milk - "milk for your food" – as though milk is intended to be used as part of recipes or making cheese, but *not for drinking!* In the New Testament, Paul uses milk as an analogy when speaking of elementary teaching for babes in Christ, while mature believers move on to the meat of the Word (1 Corinthians 3:2). Paul's food comparison supports the knowledge we have today that adults do not even have the digestive enzyme required to digest milk properly (see also Hebrews 5:12-13).

> … Or who tends a flock and does not use [eat of] the milk
> *of the flock?*
> 1 Corinthians 9:7c NAS (emphasis added)

> Butter from the kine [cattle] and milk *of the flock.*
> Deuteronomy 32:14 KJV (emphasis added)

This latter verse approves of making butter from cow's milk but is in agreement with the first verse in that milk itself is to come from the "flock." There is no such thing as a "flock of cows." Sheep and goats come in flocks. Cows come in herds. Further, this passage did not say butter *and* milk from the cattle, but made a deliberate distinction between one source for butter and *another* for milk.

Some dairy products, such as yogurt, are high in friendly bacteria as well as other nutrients and can be beneficial to our health. (You do need to read the label, however, and avoid the yogurts that are either high in sugar content – some as high as 36 grams or 9 teaspoons! - or use Nutrasweet.) Another acceptable dairy product is cottage cheese, the "curds and whey" that shepherds used to eat. However, even with the few "good" dairy products, we are still faced with the dilemma of hormone and antibiotic use in factory farms.

Milk and Calcium Needs

It may surprise you to know that dairy products are not the best source of calcium. Mothers who are breastfeeding are often told to drink lots of milk. Why? Does a cow drink milk so they can give milk? No, the cow's calcium source to produce good milk comes from the greens they eat in the pasture. Nursing mothers who consume a lot of milk products may provoke colic or cow's milk allergy in their babies; more alarming: *some studies also find a correlation between juvenile diabetes and milk intake*[3] (beginning with an allergy to whey protein in cow's milk[4]).

So where are we supposed to get the proper amount of calcium in our diet? Once again, the news is good:

> *Raw almonds and dark green, leafy vegetables are a* **better** *source of calcium than cow's milk.*

Raw almonds should be receiving the greatest reviews and dietary recommendations when it comes to one food providing so many good things. A U.S. Department of Agriculture study determined that almonds have twice the amount of calcium, 2.6 times the fiber, 5 times the amount of protein, phosphorus, iron, riboflavin, and potassium, and 8 times the thiamine of an equal amount of milk![5] There is even almond milk, a very suitable alternative to cow's milk.

In addition, I think I can rest assured that you don't want all the "extra ingredients" in cow's milk today. Fifty years ago, a cow produced 2,000 pounds of milk a year. Today the average milk producers get *50,000 pounds of milk per year per cow!* How is this possible?   Chemically enhanced feeds, genetic engineering, drugs, and hormones are some of the "tools" used by the modern dairy farmer.[6] Also, livestock producers receive preferential treatment when it comes to labeling their products. You may think that "milk is milk," but the terrible truth is that the FDA allows the administration of *up to eighty-two drugs to cows in the production of dairy products!*[7] If you think these drugs magically disappear from the cow's milk before you or your children drink it, think about why a doctor does not want a pregnant or nursing mother to take *even one* medication. What's in the mother's system is in the mother's milk, and the same is true for livestock.

Milk and Allergies

More food allergies in humans have been traced to dairy products than to any other source. More than twenty-five different proteins have been identified in dairy products that can make your body revolt in an allergic reaction.[8] Most of these allergic reactions are respiratory in nature, producing elevated levels of mucous, nasal stuffiness, runny nose, sinusitus, asthma-like symptoms, and inner-ear inflammation. If any of these are plaguing your household, I strongly suggest you consider removing dairy products and see if these symptoms diminish or disappear entirely.

The *East Miami Herald* newspaper ran an article November 12, 1988, on Dr. Fred Pullen of Miami. It reported that Dr. Pullen sees the "tough cases," the children with so many recurrent ear infections they are candidates for surgery to put in tubes. Dr. Pullen's first step with these children is to pull them off all milk products. In 75 percent of the cases, the ear infections go away with no need for surgery.

Good Food or Good Propaganda?

As you have probably guessed by now, contrary to the FDA/RDA requirements and Food Pyramid, cow's milk is not a necessary part of our diet. The reason why we eat and drink so many dairy products today can be traced back to the 1950s and 1960s when the Dairy Council (along with such food-industry giants as Kellogg's, Del Monte, and Pillsbury) first launched their joint public-relations campaign. Their goal was to convince the American people that there are "four main food groups," one of which is milk.[9] This simply is not true, but the campaign worked and revenues of the dairy industry went sky high as conscientious parents, dieticians, school cafeteria workers, and healthcare providers made sure children all had their daily allowance of milk. This illustration points out something else we need to be aware of:

> **When evaluating information that promotes dairy products (or any questionable consumable) be discerning and consider the source:**
> **America's vast consumption of milk was the result of an ad campaign, not scientific data.**

Here's another tidbit to consider before swallowing your next glass of milk: Whole milk is second only to beef as the largest source of saturated fat in the American diet.[10] Indeed, an interesting story from World War II illustrates not only our "lack of need" for milk but the fact that we are probably much better off without it: During World War II many people in Western Europe with established heart disease (coronary artery disease) had to switch from a rich diet high in dairy and meats to a diet of grains and vegetables. The death rate in those countries from heart disease dropped dramatically during this forced dietary change. [11]

Okay, you may argue, but there is low-fat or skim milk. Wouldn't this take care of the saturated fat problem? According to Dr. Pam Popper, nutritionist, author, and lecturer, removing fat from whole milk products exchanges one problem for several others. Fat removal from dairy products causes the amounts of protein and sugars to be concentrated. These are very negative aspects as over-consumption of animal protein is the cause of both colon cancer and calcium loss. According to Dr. Popper, this calcium loss is why consuming dairy products can actually *contribute* to osteoporosis, not alleviate it!

Before I began my independent medical research and subsequent dietary changes, milk was a major purchase for me every week at the grocery store. My family of four consumed nearly a gallon a day! Though I did not realize the connection at the time, my weekly shopping cart was not only filled with gallons of milk but also with about a half-dozen tissue boxes because all of us were constantly battling drippy or stuffed noses. Sneezing and blowing were part of our daily routine. (My son referred to us jokingly as "The Family Phlegm." Yuck...what a legacy!) I had tissue boxes in every room of my house. Today there is rarely cow's milk in my home. Our allergy symptoms and tissue boxes diminished proportionally and simultaneously as dairy products became scarce in our refrigerator. I have an occasional bowl of ice cream (as a treat) and cook with rice milk, soy milk, or almond milk.

What about milk products, such as butter and cheese? The rule of thumb for cheese is simple and straightforward: The harder the cheese, the better. Softer cheese generally means more mucus and more processing, neither of which you want. Cheese products can be eaten in moderation. I wouldn't advocate eliminating them entirely. Let your nose (sinuses) be your own measurement!

Butter, Margarine, and Cooking Oils

The arguments for butter over margarine, or vice versa, rage on through the years, with opinions differing from author to author. Let God's Word and dietary principles point you to the truth. We already saw in Deuteronomy 32:14 that God refers to getting butter from the cow. He doesn't follow that with an admonition about not eating it! In addition, butter is a naturally occurring food. Margarine is not. Remember one of the key principles:

As much as possible, eat foods as they were created,
before *they were changed into something man thought might be better.*

Margarine is a manmade, synthetic product that has no food or nutritional value, and even promotes sickness and disease. Margarine is a "trans-fat"—an example of man trying to "improve" on God's natural product, butter, with disastrous consequences. Margarine is hydrogenated. Hydrogenation is a chemical process that turns liquids into solids and destroys all the natural value of the oil, then creates fatty acids that do not even exist in nature. Our naturally created bodies neither process nor digest chemicals that do not exist in nature, and consequently these products begin to accumulate in our body tissues. *Also, margarine chemically is only one step away from being plastic!* So when you finish your margarine, you can eat the container it came in and receive the same nutrients.

The worst news is yet to come: All hydrogenated oils have been linked in studies showing highly increased risk for both heart disease and cancer.[12] This same study showed women who eat margarine (or any partially hydrogenated oils) instead of butter have an incredibly higher risk of breast cancer.[13] The hydrogenation process involves forcing hydrogen atoms into the holes of healthy unsaturated fatty acids to make them solid at room temperature. This is exactly what happens in your blood vessels as well, plugging them until heart disease manifests.

Olestra is a relative newcomer to the scene of manmade fats, touting the fact that it is "nonabsorbable cooking oil," thereby adding no fat or calories to your diet. The FDA allowed Procter & Gamble to market this new product as a food additive after it performed poorly as a drug meant to control cholesterol.[14] A nonprofit health group called Center for Science in the Public Interest did not believe Olestra was such a great idea as a food source either. According to a news release they issued in December 1998, fifteen thousand customers had already filed complaints about Olestra, saying they experienced problems ranging from gas to bloody stools to cramps so severe they had to go to the emergency room! [15] When will man learn to stop messing with what God created?

The good choices for both buttering your toast or cooking are once again God's natural products. Butter can be used in moderation, or even "lightened up" slightly from the saturated fat content by making what is called "Better Butter." Better Butter is simply equal parts of butter and olive oil or butter and canola oil. (I use slightly more butter just to keep it a little more solid as it warms up to room temperature.)

To make "Better Butter," simply warm butter to room temperature, then beat it in a mixer until creamy, then slowly add an equal amount of olive or canola oil, beating it until smooth. Pour the mixture into a bowl and refrigerate. You now have a *soft spread* that won't tear bread and has half the saturated fat; the other half is actually a *healthy, essential oil* that your body needs (olive oil is an omega-9 essential fatty acid). Better Butter can also be substituted in recipes that call for shortening or butter, again reducing the saturated fat by half and actually adding the "good fat" of olive oil.

Olive oil is well-spoken of in the Bible, relating it to health:

...a land of grain and new wine, a land of bread and vine-yards, a land of olive groves and honey, that you may live and not die...

2 Kings 18:32 NKJV

For the Lord your God is bringing you into a good land, a land of brooks of water, of fountains and springs...a land of wheat and barley, of vines and fig trees and pomegranates, a land of olive oil and honey...a land in which you will lack nothing...

Deuteronomy 8:7-9 NKJV

Today we know that olive oil is a monounsaturated fat that is effective in lowering blood cholesterol levels without any of the dangers in relationship to cancers of polyunsaturated fats. Olive oil assists in bowel regularity and is easily digested, imparting a soothing healing influence to the digestive tract. It does not break down into harmful compounds when subjected to high heat. The only other oil also known for this last quality is canola oil.

Fat in itself is not bad. Our bodies need fat to transport certain nutrients and protect vital organs, to regulate our body temperature, to provide a concentrated source of energy, and to add wonderful flavor to many dishes. Yes, there are such things as good fats. Most of them come from the vegetable kingdom. All fats from vegetable sources contain no cholesterol.

Essential fatty acids (EFAs) like omega 3 found in fish oil actually *decrease* chances of heart disease and cancer. As a matter of fact, major health problems occur from a lack of EFAs. If your diet includes 12-15 percent EFA, you will notice an increase in your metabolism.[16] Salmon, free-range chicken, and free-range eggs are wonderful sources of omega 3 fats.

As always, returning to Scripture and its principles identifies those things we should eat, which in turn identifies those things we should not eat. It is noteworthy that the "good" things are almost always those which are in their most natural form, as God created them, not "messed with" by man.

Now let's check out the truth about sweeteners.

END NOTES

1. Ted Broer, <u>Maximum Energy; Top Ten Foods Never to Eat; Top Ten Health Strategies to Feel Great</u> (Lake Mary, FL: Creation House, 1999), p.137

2. J. Bayless, "Lactose and Milk Intolerance: Clinical Implications," *New England Journal of Medicine,* 292 (1975): 1156. Edited by Ted Broer, Lake Mary, FL: Creation House, 1999.

3. Annemarie Colbin, <u>Food and Our Bones</u> (New York: A Plume Book - The Penguin Group, 1998), p. 54.

4. Udo Erasmus, <u>Fats that Heal, Fats that Kill</u> (Burnaby BC, Canada: Alive Books, 1993), p. 373

5. Gordon Tessler, <u>The Genesis Diet, The Biblical Foundation for Optimum Nutrition</u> (Raleigh, NC: Be Well Publications, 1996), p. 76.

6. Ernesto Contreras, <u>Health in the 21st Century – Will Doctors Survive?</u> (Chula Vista, CA: Interpacific Press, 1997) p. 106

7. Ibid, p. 107

8. Ted Broer, <u>Maximum Energy</u> (Lake Mary, FL: Creation House, 1999), p. 144

9. Ibid. p. 138

10. Dean Ornish, <u>Eat More, Weigh Less</u> (New York: Harper Collins Publishers, Inc., 1993), p. 34. Edited by Ted Broer, Lake Mary, FL: Creation House, 1999.

11. John A. McDougall, <u>The McDougall Plan</u> (Piscataway, NJ: New Century Publishers, 1983), p. 145, citing A. Strom, "Mortality From Circulatory Diseases in Norman 1940-1945," <u>Lancet</u>, 1 (1951): 126; Edited by Ted Broer, Lake Mary, FL: Creation House, 1999

12. Ted Broer, <u>Maximum Energy</u> (Lake Mary, FL: Creation House, 1999), p. 148

13. Ibid.

14. Ibid, p. 175
15. Ibid., p. 177
16. Gordon Tessler, <u>The Genesis Diet</u> (Raleigh, NC: Be Well Publications, 1996), p. 72

Chapter 21

A Land Flowing with Milk and Honey – Sweeteners

Once again, looking to the same Scripture passage as the previous chapter, we see that God led the Israelites to a land flowing with milk and honey. Obviously, then, sweetening our food or drinks is not an offense to God. He considered honey to be a blessing as part of His provision for His children. So what happened? The same thing that happens so often throughout history: Man took something good that God made and perverted it into something terrible! Natural (unheated, unprocessed, healthy) honey was refined into (harmful) sugar. Additionally, what was originally intended for an occasional treat has become a mainstay in the American diet.

We have a terrible "sweet tooth" problem today. According to a 2001 U.S. Department of Agriculture publication known as the *Weekly Statistical Sugar Trade Journal*, our sugar intake has increased more than 20 times over what it was 200 years ago – *from 7 pounds per year to over 147 pounds per year!* Check out the typical American's annual consumption of "sweets":

- 756 doughnuts
- 60 pounds of cakes and cookies
- 23 gallons of ice cream
- 22 pounds of candy
- 200 sticks of gum
- 365 servings of soda

• 134 pounds of refined sugar[1] (This figure is from 1996. By 2001, this figure rose to 147 pounds, an increase in 13 pounds in just five years!)

Sugar's Not So Sweet History

A brief review of the history of sugar is both revealing and alarming. From the Garden of Eden through thousands of years, what we call sugar was virtually unknown to man, and he survived quite well without it. Around 325 B.C., Alexander the Great found East Indian natives partaking of sweet cane juice as a fermented drink. In Nero's time (circa 66 A.D.), a Roman historian gave sugar the Latin name *saccharum* and described it as "a sort of concreted honey." A piece of saccharum was considered a rare and precious miracle drug of the time by both the Romans and the Greeks, and this commodity was heavily in demand during times of plague and pestilence.

By 1573, a German botanist, Leonhard Rauwolf, observed another phenomenon of sugar and published his findings as military intelligence:

> The Turks and Moors cut off one piece [of sugar] after another and so chew and eat them openly everywhere in the street without shame...in this way [they] accustom themselves to gluttony and are no longer the intrepid fighters they had formerly been.[2]

Interestingly, Rauwolf viewed sugar addiction among the sultan's armies in much the same way modern observers viewed American forces in Asia who were hooked on heroin and marijuana. (There is a connection between these two that I'll share shortly.)

From the fifteenth to nineteenth centuries, sugar cane plantations and slave labor to tend them became a major industry for the Portuguese, Dutch, Spanish, and British. Noel Deerr, a British historian, assessed sugar's impact on history during this time:

It will be no exaggeration to put the tale and toll of the Slave Trade at 20 million Africans, of which two-thirds are to be charged against sugar.[3]

Even the clergy were involved. In 1515, Spanish monks offered $500 in gold (a small fortune at the time) as a loan to anyone who would start a sugar mill.[4] Corruption and organized crime accompanied fabulous fortunes, which in turn precipitated the formation of the first Anti-Saccharite Society in 1792 by the British.

It is very noteworthy that the trail of the opium poppy (which was refined to produce morphine, and then again refined to produce heroin) has kept a parallel historical pace with the sugar cane trail. *Both began as medicines.* (Large numbers of morphine addicts from the Civil War brought about further refinement to heroin, which was originally hailed as a non-addictive painkiller to replace morphine.) Both ended up being used to placate purely pleasurable pursuits, as evidenced by the list at the opening of this chapter.

Sugar and Its Consequences

Refined, processed sugar robs your cells of needed oxygen, overworks your pancreas, uses too much insulin, and can even damage the insulin mechanism and lead to diabetes.[5] Your body must actually remove calcium/magnesium from your bones to digest refined sugars. This is why *one of the leading causes of osteoporosis is not a lack of calcium in the diet, but an over-consumption of refined sugar.*[6]

In addition, as calcium and magnesium are removed from the bones, they end up in the soft tissues of the body, including the hair and joints. This accumulation of calcium in the joints is commonly referred to as arthritis. Approximately 75 percent of men and women over sixty have some form of osteoporosis or arthritis, and the culprit is at least in part refined sugar.[7]

Is it old age that causes our degenerative conditions, or can some be attributed to the consumption of the thief called refined sugar?

225

In a report titled "Collateral Effects of Excessive Consumption of Refined Sugar," Dr. Solarsano reported that sugar is dangerous for babies and small children. When sugar was withdrawn from a child's diet, he observed the disappearance of many eruptions, infections, allergic reactions, and problems of the nervous system. Furthermore, he observed a diet with much sugar can bring on many illnesses, including neurosis, hypoglycemia, diabetes mellitus, cancer of the biliary tract, colorectal cancer, arthritis, arteriosclerosis, coronary insufficiency, and others.[8]

Just as with dairy products, there are those who are trying to convince the public that sugar isn't all that bad. They are coming up with ever-novel ways to combat and contradict the evidence that sugar is harmful. One way is to form institutes with names that lead you to believe they are credible, and then issue "official health" statements. For example, the International Life Sciences Institute, which is accredited by the World Health Organization and the Food & Agriculture Association, recently published favorable information about sugar. This could be very confusing until you learn that the International Life Sciences Institute is operated by Pepsi, Coca-Cola (one 20-ounce soda contains 17 teaspoons of sugar!), General Foods, Kraft, and Procter & Gamble. While the dairy industry was able to boost sales with an ad campaign, sugar's reputation was so bad that those who peddle it had to resort to forming pseudo-science institutes and publishing bogus research. Consumer beware:

When research findings are dubious or differ from what is generally known, accepted, or plain common sense, **check out who's doing or funding the research** *before forming new conclusions.*

In July 2004, the Center for Science in the Public Interest and dozens of leading health experts and organizations petitioned the FDA to set a maximum recommended daily intake for added sugar. The U.S. Department of Agriculture advises people to limit their added sugar to 10 teaspoons per day. This may sound reasonable until you realize that one 20-ounce soda contains 17 teaspoons of sugar! The favorite snack of teens today is a Coke and Snickers.

There's enough sugar in this one snack to shut down their immune system for five hours! We truly have our work cut out for us as Americans and parents.

Sugar Substitutes – the Bad News

Okay, okay, you're convinced that refined sugar is a substance to be greatly reduced and avoided wherever possible. You may be thinking, *That's not hard, I'll just switch to aspartame (Nutrasweet or Equal)...there are lots of alternatives* — NO! To borrow an old maxim, that would be akin to jumping from the frying pan into the fire itself. While refined sugar should be consumed in very small quantities, *aspartame (Nutrasweet or Equal) should be avoided entirely!*

The story behind Nutrasweet is shorter on history's timeline, and more modern, but equally abominable to that of refined sugar. What is largely unknown to the general public is the fact that the company that manufactures aspartame (G.D. Searle Company) has been accused of providing falsified test results to the FDA and even unethical deal making with prosecutors from the U.S. Attorney General's office. All the while, reports of adverse patient reactions — including headaches, memory loss, seizures, and *even confirmed death* — continue to mount while these reports are being kept from the general public.[9]

Each of the component parts of aspartame is in itself a known toxin. Methanol, for one, is also known as wood alcohol and is used as a paint thinner and an industrial cleaner. The Environmental Protection Agency (EPA) includes methanol in their "Community Right to Know List," which is a list of toxic chemicals that must be clearly identified on manufacturer's labels when certain hazardous chemicals are used in a product. Amazingly, methanol is not mentioned on any of the labels of products containing aspartame.[10]

Effects in the body from human consumption of methanol include lethargy, fainting, headaches, nausea, vomiting, blindness, cough, breathing difficulties, and other vision problems, along with birth defects in developing fetuses.[11] Once absorbed, methanol is very slowly eliminated and should be regarded as a cumulative poison, according to *Sax's Dangerous Properties of Industrial Materials*.

Results can be worse if the product has been exposed to heat (such as hot chocolate, coffee, or tea), or left for a long time on the shelf, as these factors promote the breakdown of aspartame into its toxic components. (There are those who believe Gulf War Syndrome is the result of diet sodas stored in the hot desert temperatures, thus promoting the above difficulties.)

When aspartame was first approved, consumer watchdog groups, consumer safety attorneys, and researchers filed legal objections presenting documented evidence that animals fed the chemical developed brain tumors.[12] Ingestion in humans could easily result in brain damage and mental retardation since further evidence showed that humans are *one hundred times more sensitive to methanol than are animals![13]*

In the *Journal of Advancement in Medicine,* scientists and researchers have cited that according to National Cancer Institute records, there has been a dramatic rise in the incidence of brain tumors in the United States beginning in 1985, just two years after Nutrasweet became available in diet sodas. During that time the incidence of these brain tumors increased *600 percent, and the rise continues every year since that time![14]*

Authors George Verrilli, M.D., and Anne Marie Mueser published a book for expectant mothers titled *While Waiting: A Prenatal Guidebook.* These writers raised concern over the effects aspartame could have on babies growing in the womb. They wrote, "Aspartame is suspected of causing brain damage in sensitive individuals. A fetus may be at risk for these effects...some researchers have suggested that high doses of aspartame may be associated with problems ranging from dizziness and subtle brain changes to mental retardation."[15]

In February 1994, the Department of Health and Human Services Report on "Adverse Reactions Attributed to Aspartame for 1993" reported 6,888 consumer complaints, including 649 reported by the Centers for Disease Control, and another 1,305 reported by the FDA. Currently, *aspartame accounts for over 75 percent of all the complaints in the Adverse Reaction Monitoring System. Yet the use of this product grows every day, and our FDA does nothing![16]* It is truly startling and disheartening to know that government agencies can have this much documented, scientific research and still turn a blind eye. Once again, I admonish you:

> *The principles of Christian character and education are applicable:*
> **Educate yourself** *in order to protect yourself and your loved ones.*
> *Then apply what you learn:* **Stop using Nutrasweet and other artificial sweeteners! The evidence is overwhelming. Nutrasweet is extremely hazardous to your health!**

There is a relative newcomer on the non-caloric sweetener parade known as Splenda. Splenda seems to be replacing Nutrasweet in many products and is being recommended by many physicians for diabetics. But is it a proven, healthy substitute? At first glance, it would seem that *anything would be better than Nutrasweet!* Let's look closer:

Splenda (also known as Sucralose) is created by replacing three hydrogen/oxygen complexes in table sugar (sucrose) with chlorine. Some refer to it as chlorinated sugar. Its purported advantages over sugar are:

- fewer calories
- less tooth decay
- only 20-30% absorbable with the rest passing out of the body in the stool
- does not cause a rise in blood sugar

Its primary adverse effects appear to be diarrhea in some individuals and reactions in those who are sensitive to chlorine. Some have reported symptoms similar to food poisoning with vomiting and diarrhea. A few have reported increases in muscle or joint pain. Japanese researchers reported recently that Sucralose induced DNA damage in the gastrointestinal organs of animals tested. This is contrary to the safety reports leading to the release of Sucralose, but *post*-marketing studies were the first to show problems with cyclamates, saccharin, and Nutrasweet.[17] This pattern is being repeated with Sucralose. All were introduced as safe, non-toxic alternatives to sugar. Problems were identified only after they had been in use for a period of time.

According to the Sucralose Toxicity Information Center, the manufacturer's studies are clearly inadequate and do not demonstrate safety in long-term use. What basically happens when the FDA approves a product like this is that the clinical trial gets run in the general public as more and more people use the product, and they see how many adverse reactions claims come in. Again, a general principle applies:

> *The more a food substance is altered from its natural state, the more likely it should be avoided.*

Sugar Substitutes – the Good News!

My advice is not to become part of the grand human clinical trial (aka a lab rat!) that is going on right now by consuming this chemical, or any other that comes down the pike, when there is no evidence of safety. Common sense says we were designed and engineered to consume food rather than chemicals manufactured in a laboratory.

Once again, God's natural foods come to the rescue! Raw, unprocessed honey is God's natural sweetener, and there are many, many references to it in Scripture. While sugar-laden foods overload the bloodstream in just 15 minutes, honey is absorbed over a period of four hours.[18] When combined with whole-grain flour or cereal high in dietary fiber and B-vitamins, the body can digest honey very well without depleting stored nutrients. As with other foods, however, honey can be refined. Heating it to over 160 degrees and straining removes valuable bee pollen and some of the nutrients. Supermarket honey and much of what is found in health-food stores is refined. Purchasing honey from a local beekeeper will be the least expensive and best honey you can buy. One caution regarding honey: Wait until a baby has passed their first birthday before feeding them honey. Botulism spores may be in honey and are potentially dangerous for infants, but there is no known danger to anyone older.[19]

While honey is my first choice for sweeteners (it even has antibiotic properties), there are several other natural alternatives as well. Some of these are pure maple syrup, blackstrap molasses, sorghum, date sugar, turbinado, sucanat, brown rice syrup, and stevia. Special modifications would have to be made when using liquid sweeteners in most recipes, but the dry sweeteners are often a simple one-to-one exchange with sugar. All of those named above are either unrefined or far less refined types of sweeteners and can be found in health food stores, and even in some regular grocery stores in their "health food" section.

Stevia is derived from the herb *Stevia rebaudiana*. It is two hundred times sweeter than sugar and makes a wonderful weight loss and weight management food as it contains no calories! Grown and processed naturally, research indicates it significantly increases glucose tolerance and inhibits glucose absorption. People who ingest stevia daily often report a decrease in their desire for sweets and fatty foods. It may also improve digestion and gastrointestinal function, soothe upset stomachs, and help speed recovery from minor illnesses. Stevia also inhibits the growth of some bacteria and infectious organisms, including those that cause tooth decay and gum disease. Many individuals using stevia have reported a lower incidence of colds and flu. The difficulty with stevia is the fact that it is very concentrated, so conversion of recipes calling for sugar would be difficult to impossible. The good news is that there are stevia cookbooks and recipes available.

Young Living Essential Oils markets Agave, a sweetener similar to stevia in that it is also grown and processed naturally. It also has a low glycemic index which makes it preferable for diabetics, is 50 percent sweeter than table sugar, and is high in minerals. Also, like stevia, it has tremendous health benefits, but it is liquid and highly concentrated and therefore needs recipes written specifically for its use.

As you begin making healthy changes in your diet, you will find that you don't want as much sweetener in your foods, especially desserts. When baking, I use only half the sweetener the recipe suggests. In addition, honey is twice as sweet as refined sugar. So if a recipe calls for one cup of sugar, this means I would use only one-fourth cup of honey to substitute. One cup of unsweetened applesauce and one teaspoon of cinnamon can also be a suitable replacement for a cup of sugar. Different recipes will turn out better with different sweeteners. There are several good cookbooks that have been written using God-ordained ingredients, and more and more of them are as concerned about *taste* as they are about *health!*

Don't beat up on yourself for "compromising" on some recipes. For example, I make chocolate chip cookies with half the amount of sugar, using freshly milled whole wheat flour, steel-cut oats and wheat germ, free-range eggs, Better Butter, sea salt, and half the amount of chocolate chips. If I made them with honey and carob chips my family wouldn't eat them—and might even buy store-bought cookies instead. Meeting them halfway means they are eating *better*, even if they are not eating "pure."

Most of all, don't be afraid to experiment! As you grow in your knowledge of *good food*, you will find you can "convert" many of your favorite recipes into healthy dishes that are even tastier than when you were using refined, dead, or chemical-laden, manmade ingredients. Any changes you make will improve your family's health.

Now we are ready to move into the food group with the most choices and variety – fruits and vegetables.

END NOTES

1. Patrick Quillin, Healing Secrets from the Bible (Tulsa, OK: The Nutrition Times Press, Inc., 1996), p. 11.
2. William Dufty, The Sugar Blues (New York: Warner Books, Inc., 1975), p. 30.
3. Noel Deerr, The History of Sugar. Edited by William Dufty, New York, Warner Books, Inc., 1975, p. 31
4. William Dufty, The Sugar Blues (New York: Warner Books, Inc., 1975), p. 34
5. Gordon Tessler, The Genesis Diet (Raleigh, NC: Be Well Publications, 1996), p. 24
6. Ibid.

7. Gordon S. Tessler, Lazy Person's Guide to Better Nutrition (Raleigh, NC: Be Well Publications, 1993), p. 89

8. Francisco Contreras, Health in the 21ˢᵗ Century (Chula Vista, CA: Interpacific Press, 1997), pp. 118-119.

9. Ted Broer, Maximum Energy (Lake Mary, FL: Creation House, 1999), p. 158

10. R. J. Louis, Sax's Dangerous Properties of Industrial Materials – 8ᵗʰ Edition (New York: Van Nostrand Reimhold, 1992), pp.2251-2252. Edited by Ted Broer, Lake Mary, FL: Creation House, 1999

11. Ted Broer, Maximum Energy (Lake Mary, FL: Creation House, 1999), p. 159

12. Ibid., p. 161

13. W. Monte, "Aspartame: Methanol and Public Health," J Appl Nutr 36:42-54, 1984. Edited by Ted Broer, Lake Mary, FL: Creation House, 1999

14. Ted Broer, Maximum Energy (Lake Mary, FL: Creation House, 1999), p. 162

15. G. R. Verrilli, A. M. Muser, While Waiting: A Prenatal Guidebook, (St. Martin's Press, 1986). Edited by Ted Broer, Lake Mary, FL:: Creation House, 1999.

16. Ted Broer, Maximum Energy (Lake Mary, FL: Creation House, 1999), p. 173

17. Dale Peterson, "Sucralose (Splenda)," Health by Design E-Newsletter, 5:4

18. Emilie Barnes, The 15 Minutes Meal Planner (Eugene, OR: Harvest House Publishers, 1994), p. 146

19. Ibid., p. 151

Chapter 22

Fruits and Vegetables
"Let food be your medicine..."
Hippocrates

Most people are familiar with the above quote from Hippocrates, but it is only a partial quote. His statement preceding this famous quote illustrates that he understood the principles of how God designed our bodies, and the relationship between food and health, even if he didn't know about free radicals and antioxidants.

"Natural forces within us are the true healers. Let your food be your medicine. Let your medicine be your food."

—Hippocrates

We looked at the definition of *heal* in an earlier chapter ("Are You Healthy?"). Notice how Hippocrates' understanding of our bodies, and the "natural forces" [functions] within it, corroborates that definition:

heal - to cure of a disease or wound and restore to that state of body in which the natural functions are regularly performed.

Gazing backward again (to Chapter 4 – "What is Food?"), remember that God's original provision of food included fruits, vegetables, seeds, and grains (Genesis 1:28). They were His "prescription" in the beginning for food and health. Even though He later approved meat, it was an addition to the original list, most likely due to the unique circumstances regarding Noah's food supply immediately after the flood.

Americans' Fruit and Vegetable Consumption

This ancient wisdom regarding the power of fruits and vegetables as healers has been "re-discovered" by the modern medical community. I doubt there is an adult alive today in this country who doesn't know that both the American Cancer Society and the American Heart Association suggest 5-9 servings of fruits and vegetables every day as a protective hedge against these killers. (This recommendation was recently raised to 9-13 servings.) Yet very few people even come close to this amount. Marilyn Joyce, a well-known author, lecturer, and dietician, says that in spite of the educational effort of the American Cancer Society and the American Heart Association, the average American has increased their consumption of fruits and vegetables from 1 up to 2 servings since this "5-9 campaign" was begun.

Susan Silberstein, executive director of the Center for Advancement of Cancer Education, says the news is even worse because of what the top three vegetables consumed in America today are:

1. French fries (Give me a break...can we *really* count this as a vegetable?)
2. Iceberg lettuce (classified as the "junk food" of lettuce by nutritionists)
3. Catsup (Yes, I know catsup is *not* a vegetable, but our own FDA has designated it as a vegetable to help our school lunch programs claim they serve nutritious lunches with ample amounts of vegetables. Who am I to argue with the FDA?)[1]

Our bodies need color *(bright, fresh fruits and vegetables) and* living *enzymes. Potatoes are* white *and meat is* dead.

Does this give you an idea of our basic problem with the Standard American Diet? Generally speaking, the more color a food has, the more antioxidants inside. Antioxidants are the inner bodyguards that protect our cells from free radicals. It is a paradox that while oxygen is essential for metabolizing food in our trillions of cells to generate energy and body warmth, and provide nutrition for health, this process also creates free radicals. Free radicals damage protective cell membranes, lessen their effectiveness, and sometimes penetrate cell interiors to sabotage the DNA and corrupt it. Simply put, excessive free radicals are the number one cause for all degenerative diseases and aging itself.[2] Antioxidants die when they attach to a free radical, so it is imperative to constantly replenish our supply.

Falling and Failing Nutritional Values

More and more people are becoming conscientious about eating better, trying to eat a lot more fruits and vegetables. So why do cancer and heart disease continue to kill 80 percent of us, even some of those who are "eating better"? For many reasons, one of which is soil depleted of nutrients due to continuous planting. A piece of broccoli today is significantly nutritionally inferior to what a piece of broccoli was forty years ago. A recent government study revealed that 99 percent of the American population is mineral deficient. Soil in at least thirty states has been shown to be seriously depleted of zinc. Surveys conducted over a five-year period by West Virginia University show the contents of iron, copper, and manganese have dropped in grain in eleven Midwestern states.[3]

This shouldn't surprise those of us who know Scripture. God spoke to Moses about farming:

Six years you shall sow your land and gather in its produce, but in the seventh year you shall let it rest and lie fallow....
Exodus 23:10-11 NKJV

Letting the land rest and lie fallow allows uncultivated growth to flourish, which is then plowed back into the soil the following year, creating fresh organic material for the next six years of crops. Not only have we not allowed the land to rest and replenish its nutrients, but we further contaminate it with pesticides, herbicides, and even fertilizers that destroy iron, vitamin C, folic acid, minerals, amino acids, and many other nutrients.

Another reason we are not getting sufficient nutrients from otherwise *good* foods is the simple fact that produce that is picked when ripe will bruise easily and spoil rapidly. To increase the shelf life, farmers must harvest fruits and vegetables long before they mature, even though it is well established that they absorb most of their vitamins and minerals when they are almost ripe. *NBC Nightly News* ran a program on November 5, 2003, showing Florida oranges being harvested, going down the conveyer belt on their way to trucks for transport to your local grocery store. They were *bright green!* This produce never had a chance to get rich in enzymes. Furthermore, once any produce is picked, it quickly loses its nutrient value. Potatoes lose up to 78 percent of their vitamin C in a week. Spinach, asparagus, broccoli, and peas lose 50 percent of their vitamins before they ever get to the market.[4]

Those green bananas we buy may turn yellow over time, but they will never fill up with vitamins and minerals sitting on the supermarket shelf or your countertop. Hard peaches may soften and get darker orange, but they are still nutritionally challenged. Truly "fresh" produce means picked out of your garden, or somebody else's garden, and sold that day at a farmer's market, roadside stand, etc. There is rarely "fresh" produce at the supermarket.

Organically grown produce is becoming more in demand, and it is even being found more often on regular supermarket shelves these days in addition to health food stores. Though it costs more it is well worth the investment. Rutgers University conducted a study comparing nutrient values of fruits and vegetables that were sprayed with various chemicals to those grown organically. The results were astounding. There were remarkable differences in every area measured, but the most dramatic was the magnesium levels in tomatoes. *A tomato grown by the industry had 2 mg of magnesium, while the organically grown tomato had 2000 mg!*[5]

Yet another problem in getting sufficient nutrition (to ward off disease) from our food is found in cooking techniques. The November 2003 issue of *Journal of Science of Food and Agriculture* published the following test results:

- Microwave your broccoli and you will lose between 74-97% of its antioxidants
- Reheating broccoli in the microwave when it was cooked with another method produces the same results.
- Boiled broccoli – loses 66%
- Pressure-cooked broccoli – loses 47%
- Steaming – loses 11%
- Blanching and freezing – loses 20-30%

Even the most health-conscious individual who consumes 5-9 servings of fruits and vegetables every day must also be eating a wide *variety* to get the full spectrum of nutrients. (Most of us have a few favorites and stick mainly with them.) The bottom line:

What matters is not just what foods we eat, but how they were grown, when they were harvested, how they were processed, packaged, and shipped, and finally how we prepare them.

The Pottenger Cat Study

One of the most thought-provoking [frightening?] studies I found while researching this book was performed by Dr. Francis Pottenger. In 1932, he conducted a ten-year experiment in which he fed a diet of two-thirds *raw* meat, one-third raw milk, and cod liver oil to a group of cats. Generation after generation of cats on this program maintained well-shaped bodies with strong, uniform skeletal structures. They were disease and infection resistant and had no allergies. They produced healthy litters with few miscarriages. They were friendly and predictable in behavior.

Dr. Pottenger fed another group of cats a diet consisting of two-thirds *cooked* meat, one-third raw milk, and cod liver oil. These cats produced kittens with different size skeletons, and by the third generation their bones had become soft as rubber. Infections were common, as were heart problems, poor eyesight, marked irritability, parasites, skin lesions, allergies, underactive or inflamed thyroids, infections of the respiratory system, kidneys, liver, genital organs, and bladder, arthritis and inflammation of the joints, inflammation of the nervous system, paralysis, and meningitis. This diet also seemed to cause role reversal, with females becoming the aggressors and males becoming passive. By the third or fourth generation, these cats were so physiologically bankrupt that *none survived beyond their sixth month, thereby terminating their "family line."*[6]

Dr. Pottenger summed up his own study by saying that the elements in raw food, which activate and support growth and development in the young, appear easily altered and destroyed by heat processing and oxidation. Just one year of this cooked diet could so reduce the vitality of cats that it could take them as long as three years to recover, if they could recover at all. It took three to four generations on the raw diet to reverse these problems genetically.[7]

While human physiology is not the same as a cat's, the parallels to disease resulting from the wrong diet are very worthy of comparison, particularly in regard to generations:

- The first generation of "processed food" cats developed arthritis, cancer, diabetes, allergies, and so forth *toward the end of their lifespan.*
- The second generation developed those same diseases *in the middle of their lifespan.*
- The third generation developed those diseases *at the beginning of their lifespan.*
- There was no fourth generation. Either the third generation parents could not conceive, or if they did, they miscarried.

Now let's look at people's age and health issues relating to the onset of processed and "fast food" as a major part of the American diet.

- The first McDonald's appeared in America in the early 1950s. At that time degenerative diseases were primarily seen in 70- to 80-year-olds.
- Degenerative disease has moved to primarily 50- to 60-year-olds and younger. But, worst of all, we now see what used to be exclusively "old-age diseases" moving in on children: juvenile diabetes, juvenile arthritis; 7000 new cases of pediatric cancer every year.[8]
- Infertility rates in America are the highest in recorded history – *almost 10% or over 7 million people* - with the number *growing at a rate of nearly 3% per year![9]* (Admittedly, this last statistic is growing also due to sexually transmitted diseases, but we cannot discount the role that diet plays as well.)

Does this alarm anyone else, or is it just me? The correlation of these statistics and the similar trend is unmistakable. Particularly noteworthy were the weaknesses passed to the next generation, ultimately bringing about the "death of that family tree." These results bring forward a dramatic question:

Is it possible that our "genetic predisposition to disease"
is at least partially a result of our parents' gene pool being
weakened by a wrong diet, and then further perpetu-
ated *by them feeding their children the same diet?*

What About Our Children?

Younger and younger children are developing diseases we formerly associated with older people. Just a look around the shopping mall or grocery store shows children to be developing serious weight problems at very early ages, even obese infants. According to a study titled "Feeding Infants and Toddlers," commissioned by Gerber Products, children's bad habits are beginning very early in life. The eating habits of more than three thousand children were examined by asking their parents or primary caregivers what their children between the ages of four months and two years ate that day. Here are the results:

Children 1-2 years old require about 950 calories per day. The study showed the average intake of children in that age range is 1220 calories per day, an excess of 30 percent. For kids in the 7-11 month range, the excess was 20 percent. So, while they are still infants and toddlers, they are learning to overeat. One-third of the children under the age of 2 years old had had no fruits or vegetables on the day of the survey. For those who did eat a vegetable, French fries were the most common for those 15 months and older. Nine percent of children 9-11 months of age ate French fries at least once per day. For children 19 months to 2 years, more than 20 percent had French fries daily.

Seven percent of the children 9-11 months old ate hot dogs, sausage, and bacon daily, while 20 percent in the older age group ate those daily. Over 60 percent of the 1-year-olds had dessert or candy at least once a day and 16 percent ate a salty snack. By the time the kids were 19 months old, the statistics were 70 percent for dessert and candy and 27 percent for salty snacks. Some 20-40% of these children 15 months and older had a sugary fruit drink every day, and 10 percent were already consuming soft drinks every day. It is no wonder we are having health problems earlier and earlier in life.

In addition, the average American child takes in three-fourths of a pound of sugar every day! That's sixty-eight teaspoons! Before you protest the impossibility of this statement, consider that the majority of the sugar does not come from the canister on your countertop, but from the prepared foods they are consuming, such as yogurt, cereal, fruit, and soft drinks. Consuming twenty-two teaspoons of sugar is enough to suppress your immune system for *five hours!* Our children are consuming three times this amount every day. Is it any wonder we are seeing such a dramatic incline in adult diseases in children?

Parents, I appeal to you to love your children enough to take the time to instill proper eating habits in them. The ONLY way this will happen is for YOU to develop proper eating habits. *"One in every three children now being born in the United States ultimately will become diabetic.* That's because so many become overweight as a result of all the junk food they eat and the lack of exercise necessary to burn it off."[10] A study from Kaiser Permanente released on

October 28, 2002, showed that 25 percent of children under two years old *have televisions in their room; 10 percent have TV remotes (specially designed for small children to use).* I didn't even know there was such a thing as a remote control for children. Parents, *get your children outside and moving and away from the TV!* Again, the best way to do this is for *you* to get outside, moving, and away from the TV.

Speaking of the TV – turn it off at mealtime. I would also strongly advise you to do whatever you can to reintroduce "family dinnertime" at your house. Many studies show a strong correlation between health and *how* and *where* we eat. Family dinners can provide a relaxed, conversational, low-stress environment to not only strengthen your relationships but to better digest your food.

In addition, please remember the second part of the Pottenger cat study. The bad eating results were able to be *reversed* over time. I am certain the same would hold true for correcting our children's diets and lifestyles (even perhaps correcting our diets so we do not pass on this genetic weakness in the first place, if we have not yet had children). Talk about a legacy to leave your children! If you are of childbearing age, you can begin to rebuild your health and pass on a healthy "predisposition" to your children. If you are already a parent, you can start today to make healthy changes. If you are a grandparent, you can help educate your children along these lines. *Everyone can do something positive.*

We must begin to practice "prevention" rather than just "reactive medicine." Prevention is *not* early detection. A mammogram does not prevent breast cancer. Do we put an ambulance at the bottom of the cliff for quick transportation to the hospital, or do we put a fence at the top to keep people from falling off? It's time to start building those fences. Let's check out some health-boosting and maintenance strategies.

What About Supplementation?

Studies like Pottenger's cats can motivate us to jump on the "dietary change bandwagon," but knowing all that is working against us getting the nutrients we need from our food supply can just as quickly cause us to fall off that wagon in discouragement. So what's a person to do? Many have resorted to supplementation, some taking a simple multivitamin, others trying to formulate their own personal vitamin and mineral regimen that could include dozens of pills, liquids, and other concoctions. Incredibly, there are more than 29,000 supplements available on the market today. If you have not been tested by a medical professional to diagnose specific dietary deficiencies, where in the world does the average consumer begin in looking at these 29,000 supplements? Which ones to take? How much? How often? For how long?

Fortunately, preventative science has made yet another option available: concentrated, whole-food supplements. These are my personal choice and recommendation. While few if any of us are able to consistently consume the recommended 9-13 servings of fresh, raw fruits and vegetables every day, a good fruit and vegetable concentrate can bridge that gap. Augmenting your diet with fragmented vitamin and mineral products falls far short of supplementation with a whole food concentrate. The best multiple vitamin on the market may contain 50 nutrients (usually less), while *one whole fruit or vegetable contains more than 12,000 different nutrients,* the majority of which are not even named at this point in time.

Once again, this bears out the truth of Hippocrates' statement about food as medicine, as well as the definition of *heal.* God put fruits and vegetables on trees and in the garden, not fragmented vitamins. Everyone needs large amounts of fruits and vegetables in their diet as the foundation of all good, healthy eating. Science shows our bodies need small amounts of the thousands of nutrients found in whole food as opposed to large amounts of specific nutrients extracted and packaged in vitamins.

However, all whole-food concentrates are not equally beneficial in the same way that all fragmented vitamin, mineral, or herbal formulations are not of equal quality. In June 2004, a Consumer Lab study released exclusively to *O* readers (*The Oprah Magazine*) found that nearly half the brands of vitamins and whole food supplements they investigated did not live up to their labels, and some could be downright dangerous. So the question becomes: How do you find and evaluate whole-food concentrates and other nutritional supplements for their positive impact on your body?

Evaluating Supplements

In the search for good supplementation, both whole-food concentrates and fragmented vitamins and nutrients, do your "homework" to find a good product that is readily assimilated by your body. How do you do this? First of all, *ignore testimonials*. They may or may not be valid, and even if a certain individual did experience a specific health improvement, there is absolutely *no guarantee you will experience the same improvement!* Your body, your chemistry, everything about you is unique. This is one reason why Tylenol works for some as a headache remedy, but others need Excedrin, or others Advil. Testimonials are largely useless in proving the efficacy of supplements.

Another general rule: Don't buy your supplements from the grocery or drugstore unless you have read *published and measurable* evidence proving what it will do for your body. If a vitamin supplement is turning your urine a different color, this indicates it is not bio-available (getting into your bloodstream where it is needed). There are basically three types of vitamins:

- Test tube or synthetic – usually found in drugstores, has no living enzymes, is manmade with inorganic substances such as tar, plastics, and coal.
- Crystalline or extracted – usual health food store variety, with weak enzymes, uses chemicals and heat extraction, organic substances (but of low-quality raw materials), imbalanced, with harsh binders and fillers.
- Natural/unaltered – usually available through distributors and occasionally in some health food stores, with strong enzymatic action, low heat and pressure process, organic substances with high-quality raw materials, balanced, bio-available.

The best test for any supplement is quality, reliable research done at a well-known medical facility or university. However, caution is still necessary. Simply because a product is backed by research is not as important as the caliber and validity of that research. There are certain criteria to look for when evaluating research:

1. First and foremost, it must be *product-specific research*, as compared to "structure and function" claims. In other words, simply because Vitamin C is in a particular product and Vitamin C has been shown to help the immune system is *not relevant research* to prove the product works. You want research on the specific product (not just an ingredient in it) being taken by individuals, with measured results *before and after* consuming the supplement tested.

2. The results must be *measurable* by a concrete, recognized measurement; i.e. milligrams, international units, percentages – not simply "feeling better," "quicker reflexes," or "stronger muscles."

3. Where are the studies being done? Is it a credible facility or university that is well-known for its quality research, or a little known (or unknown) laboratory or college? Worst-case scenario: Was it conducted by scientists/employees of the company marketing the product? If so, this is blatant conflict of interest – *buyer beware!*

4. Was this study published, and if so where? There are a myriad of "clinical studies" published yearly, but the most reliable, the gold standard in the medical community, are those that appear in "peer-reviewed" journals. These journals are extremely difficult to be published in and exponentially increase the credibility of any study.

5. Consider the source of the information, both the research facility and the funding. Are the results sound science that make logical sense, or are you reading a thinly veiled public relations or ad campaign (such as seen in Chapter 20 regarding the recommendations for consuming far too many dairy products)?

I will share a small part of my research on this subject as it is a good example that met all the above criteria. Juice Plus+® is a whole food-based concentrate containing seventeen fruits and vegetables. The many healthful benefits of Juice Plus+® have been demonstrated through numerous independent clinical research studies conducted in leading hospitals and well-known universities by investigators in the United States, England, Australia, Austria, Italy, and Japan.

None of these institutions has any affiliation with Juice Plus+®. To date, this clinical research has been published in the following peer-reviewed medical and scientific journals:

- *Medicine & Science in Sports & Exercise*
- *The Journal of Nutrition*
- *Journal of the American College of Nutrition*
- *The Journal of the American College of Cardiology*
- *Nutrition Research*
- *Journal of Human Nutrition and Dietetics*
- *Integrative Medicine*
- *Current Therapeutic Research*

Each of these studies' results were measurable, repeatable, and noteworthy. Please visit www.juiceplus.com for complete details, which are too numerous to print here. Juice Plus+® is my whole-food-based concentrate of choice, but you need to do your own homework and learn what is best to feed yourself and your family and where to spend your prevention dollars. Don't be afraid to ask the important questions listed above.

In Summary

- Reliable, product-specific, third-party, peer-reviewed, published research is best
- What about written testimonials? *Ignore them!*
- Bottom line: Talk is cheap – valid research isn't.

The principles are education and stewardship: Get to know what your body needs and buy the foods and other supplements to best care for it.
Spending money on what is good for your body is wise stewardship.

An educated person gets the best medical care. An educated person needs the least medical care. It costs a lot less time and money to stay well than to stay sick. You *will* spend the time and money eventually. Will it be invested in your health today, or to subsidize your sickness later?

*Eating a large variety of fresh fruits and vegetables +
pure water + wise supplementation + exercise and rest +
good relationships = a healthy body that can carry out its
God-ordained destiny. Go for it!*

Next, let's check out those great grains!

END NOTES

1. Susan Silberstein, Prevention Plus+ Lecture, Dayton, Ohio, 11 December 02
2. Stephen Langer, "Cancer and Nutritional Approaches to Health," Better Nutrition, January 1998, p. 33.
3. Ernesto Contreras, Health in the 21st Century, Will Doctors Survive? (Chula Vista, CA: Interpacific Press), February 1997, p. 99
4. Ibid., p. 102
5. Ibid., p, 103
6. Celeste Yarnall, Natural Cat Care (Boston: Journey Editions, 1998), p. 52
7. Francis Pottenger, Jr., Pottenger's Cats, pp. 39-42, ed. Celeste Yarnall, Natural Cat Care (Boston: Journey Editions, 1998), p. 53
8. Marti Jackson, Wellness Workshop Lecture - "Food – A Weapon Against Cancer," Dayton, Ohio, February 10, 2003
9. "Infertility – As Many as 7.7 Million Could Be Infertile by the Year 2025 – National Center for Health Statistics," Women's Health Weekly, July 27, 1998-August 3, 1998, p. 9.
10. Isadore Rosenfeld, "Can We STOP the Diabetes Epidemic?" Parade Magazine, 2 November 2003, p. 16.

Chapter 23

Grains – Whole or Enriched?

Breads and cereals: the FDA Food Pyramid recommends 6-11 servings a day. Then you read about the nutritionists who recommend *no* bread if you want to lose weight, and only 2 servings if you want to maintain. Who is right? Here we go again—back to the Bible.

Back to the Bible

God gave us grains as part of a life-giving diet. In the Old Testament, the "herbs bearing seed" that God commended to Adam to eat in Genesis 1:29 are defined in *Strong's Concordance* as "grass or any tender shoot," a description which includes "grains." When the Israelites were in the wilderness for forty years, God supplied them with daily food. Did He give them meat? Did He give them vegetables? No, He gave them manna. The Israelites did not recognize it as food, proven by the fact that the word *manna* literally means "What is it?" But God told Moses what manna was:

> Then said the Lord to Moses, "Behold, I will rain bread from heaven for you...."
>
> Exodus 16:4 NKJV

In the New Testament, when Jesus was giving an example of a model prayer for His followers it included:

Give us this day our daily bread.

Matthew 6:11 NKJV

He didn't simply pray for our daily "food" but specifically named bread. Jesus also spoke of bread again in a very positive sense when He referred to Himself (in John 6:35) as the "Bread of Life." While this particular passage was an allegory, Jesus could have referred to Himself as the meat and potatoes, or the fruits and vegetables of life. Yet He chose bread. I believe these passages clearly reveal that God considers bread to be a wholesome and valuable part of our daily diet.

Nevertheless, while whole grains are an important part of our diet, you must still learn which ones, in what form, and how much is enough. God designed bread to be the staff of life, but...

Bread [grains] only fulfill their maximum potential when properly ground, prepared, and eaten while they are "alive."

Bread in History

While whole grains are very healthy for you in moderation, unfortunately, they have not escaped man's corruption. A look back into history will tell us how we came to the place where we unintentionally devitalized (killed) this wonderful food. Historically speaking, man has always sought after soft, white bread. The Pharaohs of Egypt had their slaves sift wheat for them, separating the coarse, dark fiber from the soft, white so they could eat a soft, easy-to-chew, comfortable bread. Down through the ages, only the wealthy had servants or slaves who could spend the time necessary to sift flour in this way. Several scriptures make reference to the "king's delicacies," one of which was probably white bread.

White bread actually became a status symbol for the wealthy and nobility of the Western world. In first-century Rome, "to know the color of one's bread was the equivalent of knowing one's place in society; the lower one's place on the social ladder, the darker one's bread."[1] White flour maintained this "social status" until the late 1800s.

Then, in 1876, the governor of Minnesota visited the World's Fair in Paris, where he saw a new invention that would drastically change the world. It was called a "steel roller mill." This mill was different from a conventional stone mill in that it separated the bran, middlings, and wheat germ from the endosperm or the soft, fine inside of the wheat. With this new mill, the governor saw a way to get white flour to the masses of people and, supposedly, raise their standard of living. His intentions were admirable. The outcome was disastrous. All the common people in America could now eat soft, white bread just like the wealthy classes of the world had done for centuries. He brought the steel roller mill back to America and began mass-producing white flour in Minnesota. Little did this governor realize what he was inflicting upon the American people's health. The governor's name, you ask? Governor Pillsbury!

It wasn't until the Great Depression of the 1930s that the first evidence appeared of what this white flour was doing. White flour/bread had indeed become available to the masses, and at low cost. In fact, white bread and jelly sandwiches had become a staple for many of our nation's poor at this time in history. However, they soon began to show signs of severe malnutrition. Investigation eventually discovered the nutritional deficit was due in part to all the empty calories being consumed from white bread. Nearly all the nutrition was lost during this steel-roller milling process. Years later, the FDA forced the flour manufacturers to artificially replace some of these lost nutrients, and "enriched flour" was born.

Is Your Flour Dead or Alive?

Today, most breads, cereals, and pastas boast of having "enriched flour" with iron, niacin, thiamin, riboflavin, and folic acid, leading the average consumer to believe they are eating "healthy." What the label doesn't tell you is that the original twenty-five or more naturally occurring nutrients are either gone entirely, greatly diminished, or dead, and the few they artificially added cannot be used by your body.

It has always been God's design for us to eat *fresh* food, and this includes our grains. In the same way that fruits and vegetables lose most of their nutrition within two to three days after they are picked, and even sooner after they are peeled or sliced, the food value of grains begins to deteriorate as soon as the hull is cracked. However, there is a very interesting quality that grains possess to show themselves more valuable than fruits and vegetables in times of famine. While fruits and vegetables will spoil within a relatively short time after they are harvested, grains maintain their nutritional integrity as long as the hull is intact. How long is their shelf life? At this point in time, we know that whole grains can be stored and will retain their freshness and nutrition levels *for more than a millennium* (as long as they are kept cool, dry, and uncracked). *Archeologists found wheat in King Tut's tomb and it was still good!*

The sad truth behind why Pillsbury and Gold Medal (and others) continue to make "dead" flour and the bakeries continue to churn out devitalized bread is profit. White flour is cheap to produce, it has a very long shelf life (since it is essentially "dead" already, how can it go bad?), and the consumer is generally unaware that bread and flour can be "alive." Since these baked goods (and flour) are already dead, they can't spoil, the supermarket can keep them on their shelves for weeks, and the supplier for months, if necessary. I've heard stories of a package of seven-year-old Twinkees, still in its original wrapping and showing no signs of decay. That's because there is nothing to decay – nothing that is alive. This leads us to a key principle:

If your food won't spoil, it's not good for you, or put another way – if bacteria won't eat your food, why would you?

This is yet another major problem with the FDA/RDA Food Pyramid. While *some* of the food requirements listed are acceptable (many are outrageous), there is no distinction made between whole, intact grains and dead, devitalized grains in the bread and cereal category. Fresh, living grains are *complex carbohydrates*, and fuel your body uses slowly. Dead, devitalized grains are simple carbohydrates that become instant sugar inside your body, which very readily changes into stored fat. The Food Pyramid's suggested 6-11 servings of this dead grain and cereal category will add more fat to your middle than nutrition to your body. Why do you suppose the beef industry boasts of "grain-fed" cattle? Because it fattens them up so quickly and thoroughly.

I am not against bread. I love bread. I have a bread-making business! But it has to be made the right way and eaten in sensible quantities. And the only way it will be made correctly is to buy whole grains, mill them yourself just prior to baking, or find a friend or bakery that does. There are a few such bakeries cropping up.

The question to determine bread's freshness is not "When was the bread baked?" but "When was the grain milled?"

A grain mill is a small appliance (not much bigger than a toaster), and a very good one can be purchased for about $250, a very small investment when you consider grains are a major part of our daily diet. With the variety of grains available, you will be treating your family to a wide range of new tastes that are delicious and healthy. There are many cookbooks available for making wonderful, tasty whole-grain products. (I'll list a few I recommend in Chapter 27 – Where Do I Begin?)

My personal recommendation for a grain mill is either the Ultra Mill or Grain Master Whisper Mill, both of which can be purchased from Our Daily Bread, 10250 Jody Avenue North, Stillwater, MN 55082, or you can call 651-762-4600 or email ourdailybread@mcg. net. If you order directly from them, your price will probably be considerably lower than the $250 mentioned above. I have a small bread-making business, and this mill has a lifetime warranty and has ground hundreds (thousands?) of pounds of grain through the years and still runs like new. I also purchased a heavy-duty Bosch Mixer through Our Daily Bread that kneads bread dough perfectly—a great investment. My family loves me and so do my customers. My bread will spoil in less than a week if it isn't refrigerated, but you want to consume it all within three days anyway to glean the nutrition. The taste is wonderful, the nutrient value even better.

So Many Varieties!

Each variety of grain has its own unique qualities. Here are a few:

- Amaranth - a staple of the ancient Aztecs, known for its nutty flavor and aroma
- Barley – delicate flour, very low in gluten
- Buckwheat – dark, intensely flavored flour used in sourdough breads and pancakes
- Cornmeal – comes in several varieties and colors – white, yellow, and even blue
- Kamut – mild flavored and an excellent alternative for those with wheat allergies
- Oat – soft, delicate flour as an addition to wheat flour in recipes, or can stand alone
- Quinoa – a rediscovered ancient grain, tender, moist, and nutty flavor, highly nutritious
- Rice – available in both brown and white; brown is more healthful
- Rye – more nutritious than whole wheat and great in sourdough
- Spelt – another ancient grain, excellent wheat substitute in case of allergies
- Teff – a staple grain in Ethiopia, has a very assertive flavor
- Whole wheat – cornerstone in baking due to high gluten content, ability to rise, cost, availability, and familiarity

Is wheat or dark-grained bread better than white? Yes, because making wheat flour into white flour removes the ingredients that are most nutritious and "clean" your intestines. White bread becomes a sticky paste in your intestines and will actually constipate rather than clean. Here's a phrase to help you remember:

The whiter your bread, the sooner you're dead!

The sad truth is that any bread made from flour that was milled (even properly milled) more than seventy-two hours ago is nutritionally bankrupt. This means even your "fresh" homemade bread, made from store-bought flour, is dead!

A note on preservatives: Their purpose is to keep your food from spoiling, but they do not stop the nutrition from leaving. Nutrition to maintain a healthy body is the main purpose of food. Without preservatives, most food will spoil within a few days. But by the time it does spoil, the nutrition is already gone. Personally, I believe spoilage was God's way of letting us know that the nutrition is gone, so we need some fresh food. Freezing does stop good food from spoiling without losing much nutritional value – bread or fruits and vegetables - provided the food was harvested, blanched, and quickly frozen. Canned goods have little nutritional value and usually contain way too much salt. Bottom line:

There is NO health benefit to preservatives. Chemically-preserved food is dead food. Eat fresh foods as much as possible.

The fiber found in whole grains is also an extremely important part of a healthy diet, but fiber can be obtained in fruits, vegetables, seeds, and nuts as well. Bread is not the only source or even the best source of fiber. More on that in the next chapter!

END NOTES

1. Medical Training Institute of America, <u>How to Greatly Reduce the Riskof Common Diseases</u>, (Oak Brook, Illinois, 1990), p. 8

Chapter 24

What's Wrong with Refined and Processed Foods?

B y this point in the book, you surely have the basic understanding that the closer food is to its natural state, the better it is for you. But our supermarkets are *full* of foods that have been refined, processed, or adulterated with artificial colors, chemicals, and preservatives. Trying to eradicate or even begin to reduce these corrupted foods from our diets would require a tremendous amount of effort. Is it really that big of a problem to eat refined foods? Let's see what God says:

God's Opinion on Processed Foods

> When you sit down to eat with a ruler, consider carefully what is before you, and put a knife to your throat if you are a man given to appetite. Do not desire his **delicacies** for they are deceptive food.
>
> Proverbs 23:1-3 NKJV

Wow! I guess it *is* that big of a problem! "Delicacies" is another name for refined or processed foods. *God thinks it is better for us to slit our own throat than to eat refined foods!* He calls them deceptive. Why do you think that is? It is because food's purpose is to feed and fuel healthy bodies through proper nourishment. Processed foods not only produce little or no nourishment, they plug up our elimination systems at best and can actually poison our bodies at worst. (Remember the research on Nutrasweet?) The end result is disease and even death.

> *Refined and processed foods [delicacies] perform the*
> *opposite function that God designed food to perform.*

As stated in earlier chapters, God doesn't usually tell us *why* we are to do or not do certain things He commands, but when it comes to refined foods He does illustrate the distinction between good food and delicacies (king's meat) quite clearly in the book of Daniel. You may be familiar with this story. Daniel had been abducted as a teenager and taken along with many other prized young people into the conquering king's palace to be trained as his eunuchs. The training was long (three years), intense, and included a special king's diet.

And the king appointed for them a daily provision of the **king's delicacies** and of the wine which he drank, and three years of training ... But Daniel purposed in his heart that he would not **defile** himself with the portion of the king's delicacies, nor with the wine which he drank; therefore, he requested of the chief of the eunuchs that he might not defile himself ... And the chief of the eunuchs said to Daniel, "I fear my lord the king, who has appointed your food and drink. For why should he see your faces looking worse than the young men who are your age? Then you would endanger my head before the king." So Daniel said to the steward ... "Please test your servants for ten days and let them give us vegetables to eat and water to drink. Then let our appearances be examined before you, and the appearance of the young men who eat the portion of the king's delicacies, and as you see fit, so deal with your servants." So he consented with them in this matter, and tested them ten days. And at the end of ten days their features appeared better and fatter [healthier] in the flesh than all the young men who ate the portion of the king's delicacies. Thus, the steward took away their portion of delicacies and the wine that they were to drink, and gave them vegetables.

Daniel 5:8-16 NKJV

There are several things I want you to see in this passage. First of all, refined foods are nothing new. Not only are they not new, they were considered to be food fit for royalty. But our internal plumbing needs bulk, roughage and fiber - not delicacies. Notice that Daniel says he did not want to "defile" himself with the kings' food. He knew God's commandments not to eat the king's delicacies, but had no way of knowing why, or what went on inside his body when he ate those delicacies. We do.

The Facts About Fiber

The word for vegetables in the King James Version of Scripture is *pulse*. Pulse is not just vegetables but includes legumes—beans, lentils, and seeds—foods rich in nutrients and high in fiber. Fiber is simply the part of food that your digestive system cannot break down and digest. It is most abundant in plant products such as fruits, nuts, seeds, grains, vegetables, and legumes.

Fiber comes in two forms, soluble and insoluble. Soluble fiber (such as pectin and found in most fruits) dissolves easily in water so it can be absorbed in the intestine and then circulated in the bloodstream. Soluble fiber in the blood actually has the ability to attach itself to blood fats and create a complex that will remove these fats from the blood and lower cholesterol. Insoluble fiber absorbs water also, but it is not absorbed in the intestine. It remains there and forms the majority of the bulk necessary to "sweep out" bodily wastes through the intestine.

Without fiber, food waste and bodily processes move far too slowly and can putrefy and rot, bringing on all kinds of disease.

How likely is disease to occur as a result of a lack of fiber? Is it really that important? The British medical journal *Lancet*, September 4, 1982, reported the findings of a 10-year Netherlands study performed on 871 men. The *death rate* among the men on low-fiber diets was 4 times higher from heart disease, 3 times higher from cancer, and 3 times higher from all causes than that of the men who ate about 37 grams of dietary fiber per day. Disease declined proportionately with the increase of dietary fiber.[1]

Most nutritionists today recommend 25-40 grams of fiber daily. The average American gets about 5-20.[2] Is it any wonder our colons are clogged and we are plagued by so many degenerative diseases?

Let's go back to Daniel: He and his friends ate no meat during this time. There was a discernible difference in these young men's physical appearance after only ten days of the differing diets; their health and vitality were *visibly* superior to the other young men's. It is also noteworthy that both the king and the eunuch in charge of Daniel's training demonstrated the same ignorance we have today regarding diet. The king was feeding these young men what he perceived to be the best he could give them, food from his own table! The steward in charge of Daniel was also convinced that Daniel and his friends would be weakened by not eating the king's selections. These were educated men who thought they were eating right (sound familiar?), but in reality they were killing themselves with their diet. Just because food tastes good does not make it good for you. Conversely, some things that taste pretty "rough" will bring life to your body.

Do You Live to Eat or Eat to Live?

We love meat so tender that it "melts in our mouths." But nutritionists know that meat takes nearly seven hours for our bodies to digest as compared to three or four hours for fruits and vegetables. The more we chew, the more digestive juices we produce to better break down whatever we eat. More chewing equals better digestion. Less chewing means more undigested meat in our gut that is not easily removed by our colon. YUCK! Undigested meats (along with refined "delicacies") are the beginnings of degenerative diseases. *The shocking and disgusting truth is that the average adult has between 5-30 pounds of fecal matter in their intestines that is not moving!*[3]

Bill Gothard's Medical Training Institute did an in-depth study of infective versus non-infective disease in our Western culture, between the years 1850-1950. In 1850, non-infective disease-related deaths (like cancer and heart disease) were a rarity. Infective diseases like diphtheria, measles, whooping cough, and small pox were the biggest killers in America. Today, these statistics are completely reversed. These contagious diseases have been nearly eliminated; they are of little or no threat. But *non-infective* diseases have risen to the same levels of death (actually even higher) than we had from the infective diseases a century earlier.[4] [Note: The fact that all forms of cancer and heart disease were not yet recognizable in the 1850s does little to diminish the impact of these statistics.]

The Fiber and Disease Connection

The Medical Training Institute found that constipation is a major cause of Western diseases, and that fiber greatly reduces it. The average person in Africa, India, or the Pacific Islands passes *four times* the amount of bowel movements that we do in America. (Yes, they studied and measured it!) The Africans, Indians, and Pacific Islanders have diets that primarily include foods in their raw, natural state, unrefined, unprocessed, and very high in fiber. They are not plagued with, nor often have they even heard of, the diseases that kill us. Some examples:

- Appendicitis - Though this is the most common abdominal emergency in America, an American medical doctor in Africa saw about two patients per year with appendicitis.
- Diverticulitis - The same medical doctor above *never* saw a patient in 20 years in Africa with this disease.
- Hiatal hernia - In America, one in four adults are affected by this disorder. In West Africa, the number is four out of 1,000.
- Hemorrhoids – Affects nearly half the population of America. Fiber is the best treatment.
- Varicose veins – 40% of American women over the age of 40 have varicose veins. In New Guinea, one woman out of 800 has a slight case.

- Heart disease - In North America, one man in three dies from heart disease. American medical students in Africa did not see one case of heart disease in five years.
- Diabetes - About 5% of Americans are affected by diabetes, and 15% of those over 60. There are no reported cases in African bushmen or Eskimos.
- Obesity - Fiber fills you up so you eat less and is eliminated by your body more quickly than fats, sugars, and salt.
- Colon cancer - Studies show a close relationship between economic development and increase in this disease. It is 12 times as common in black Americans as in Africans, due to *diet*.
- Gallstones - 10-100 times as common in North America as in Africa.[5]

Fiber and the phytonutrients – *living nutrients and enzymes*— which accompany a diet of raw, unrefined, unprocessed foods (aka fruits, vegetables, and whole grains), contribute to the lack of these medical maladies in less-developed countries. Just imagine the diseases and surgeries that could be avoided simply by increasing our fiber intake, eating more food in its natural state, and decreasing our meat and dairy portions. Nutritional experts now generally acknowledge that we need to reverse our portion sizes: eat smaller quantities of meat and dairy products – acid producing foods (make them the side dish)—and larger quantities of fruits and vegetables (make them the *main* course), not only for their fiber and water content, but because they are alkaline forming. The conclusion is obvious:

The more refined our diet, the more disease appears.
The more raw foods we consume, the more health remains.

God echoes these sentiments in Deuteronomy 28 when He speaks of blessings and curses that will literally "overtake you" in accordance with your obedience or disobedience to His revealed law. Many of these are diet- and disease-related. Though this is an

Old Testament promise, the principle of sowing and reaping was not erased by the new covenant.

Over time, the principle of sowing and reaping is mani-fested whether we are eating well and experiencing health or eating poorly and encountering various sicknesses and diseases.

What About GMOs (or GEOs)

There is yet another aspect of fruits, vegetables, and grains that needs to be addressed. A modern and highly controversial practice, Genetically Modified Organisms (or Genetically Engineered Organisms), has entered the new millennium of farming. GMOs shuffle the genetic deck in ways nature never intended.

Genes are being developed to aid growth or protect against insects and disease, then they are inserted in plants such as corn, potatoes, and soybeans to help them thrive. But researchers at Ohio State found genetically modified sunflowers have the potential to spread their genes to related plant species growing nearby. This raises fears that genetically altered plants could crossbreed with related plants and wipe out bugs we *do* want, such as butterflies, along with the pests. Or they could create super-weeds we can't destroy. In Canadian fields, according to the National Coalition Against the Misuse of Pesticides, genetically engineered super-weeds resistant to three herbicides have already emerged.

The health risks of GEO foods are just beginning to be documented. Research points to increased risks of allergic reactions, increased risk of cancer, and possible suppression of immune system functions.[6] No pre-testing is being done on these products because it is not currently required. Incredibly, with this lack of knowledge of safety, an estimated 70 percent of processed foods lining our super market shelves may contain genetically engineered ingredients.[7]

Pollen is drifting for miles from these GEO crops, contaminating organic crops, according to an article in the March 29, 1999, *Wisconsin State Journal*. This causes a huge problem for organic farmers, making their produce unmarketable and even forcing some of them into bankruptcy. Organic groups are calling for legislation to make biotech companies like Monsanto and Dupont liable for drift damages, but nothing has come of it to date. This brings to bear the biggest problem of all with GMOs: Once manmade genes start spreading through the natural plant population, they cannot be contained or reversed. This is not only irresponsible, it borders on criminal negligence.

> *The principle is stewardship of both our bodies and the earth.*
> *Creating such "Frankenfoods" and marketing them without proper research is unwise at best, deadly at worst.*

This is another area that begs our involvement as citizens. There are groups already formed that are fighting this irresponsibility. You can add your voice, and I strongly encourage you to do so.

When shopping for produce, if the code number is four digits and begins with the number 4, this food was grown from seed in a field where pesticides and herbicides were used. If it is a five-digit number beginning with the number 9, it is organic. If it is a four-digit number beginning with the number 3, it is genetically modified. Shop accordingly.

What About Processed Meats?

Dr. Ted Broer has written a book in which he recommends the top ten foods *never* to eat. High-fat lunch meats are *number one* on the list, including all pork products – bacon, sausage, ham, pepperoni, and hot dogs. Dr. Broer is of German descent and was raised on wiener schnitzel, pork chops, mountains of hot dogs and sausage. By age twenty-seven, even though he was a highly trained athlete, in tip-top shape, he nearly died of a heart condition. Doctors were at a loss to the cause or treatment for him. They couldn't touch his condition with any conventional or drug therapies. He says, "When I stopped eating pork and processed meats (and shellfish), my life-threatening heart problems quickly improved and ultimately disappeared."[8]

Why are these processed meats so terrible? They slow down the body's ability to fight off disease and cancer through the immune system.[9] Bacon and hot dogs, probably the most popular processed meat products, are loaded with sodium nitrite. Sodium nitrite reacts with the acids in your stomach to form nitrosamines, one of the most potent cancer-causing agents known to man. Add a low-fiber diet to the equation, which can cause meats to sit in your colon for weeks or *years* at a time, and you have a formula for early death. It is no accident that the most prevalent cancers on the mortality charts are colon, pancreatic, and stomach.[10] Smoked, pickled, or salt-cured meats further compound the problem.

This is not new news. The National Academy of Sciences actually issued a warning as far back as 1982, warning the medical community and American public of the dangers of these processed meats. The Children's Environmental Health Network lists cancer as the leading cause of death among children. How many moms do you know who give their little ones hot dogs as one of their first finger foods? The United States has the highest infant death rate of any industrialized nation on the face of the earth![11] In addition, the active carcinogen in these meats is so lethal that a pregnant woman can increase the risk of brain cancer in her infant by eating hot dogs.[12]

*The principle is Christian character. As parents and grandparents, we **must** begin to assume responsibility for what we are feeding ourselves and our children, and make **right** choices that bring life.*

What we drink is also of great importance. Let's go there next!

END NOTES

1. Emilie Barnes & Sue Gregg, <u>The 15 Minute Meal Planner, A Realistic Approach to a Healthy Lifestyle</u> (Eugene, Oregon: Harvest House Publishers, 1994), p. 93
2. Ibid
3. Dr. Glenn Kirkwood, Prevention Plus+ Lecture, Dayton, Ohio, 11 January 2003.

4. Medical Training Institute of America, <u>How to Greatly Reduce the Risk of Common Diseases</u>, (Oak Brook, Illinois, 1990), p. 10

5. Ibid, pp. 11-16

6. Jim Wyerman, "The Genetically-Engineered Food Debate, " <u>The Cutting Edge</u>, July/August 2002, p. 22.

7. Ibid.

8. Ted Broer, <u>Maximum Energy</u>, (Lake Mary, Florida: Creation House, 1999), p. 106

9. Ibid.

10. Ibid, p. 107

11. Ibid. p. 111.

12. Ibid. p. 112.

PART SIX

WHAT SHOULD WE DRINK?

1 Corinthians 6:19 – Do you not know that your body is the temple of the Holy Spirit, who is in you, whom you have from God, and you are not your own?

Chapter 25

"Coffee, Tea or Milk"...or Something Else?

Choices, Choices, Choices!

Things have gotten a lot more complicated since the 1960s and '70s, when the beverage selections offered by the stewardess were "coffee, tea, or milk?" We are confronted with a plethora of choices, and choices *within* choices: Starbucks has turned coffee drinking into a gourmet experience with dozens of avenues to take—caffeinated, decaffeinated, and latte combinations that probably had employees staying up late nights trying to think of creative names for all of them. Tea also comes caffeinated, decaffeinated, and in as many herbal and flavor varieties as the lattes mentioned above. Fruit drink permutations are endless, as are sodas—diet and regular—and let's not forget Kool-Aid with wondrous flavors like "Roarin' Raspberry Cranberry." Then there's beer, wine, and alcoholic beverages. Decisions, decisions, decisions!

Once again, man has greatly complicated an area that was originally very simple.

> *When God gave Adam instructions on what to eat, He didn't even include beverage choices because there was only one – water.*

Alcoholic Beverages

Wine was added at a later date and was generally greatly diluted with water, and not necessarily fermented (grape juice, in other words). Herbal teas were originally decoctions used for medicinal purposes. Coffee and sodas came much later, and fruit drinks and Kool-Aid are newcomers in the history of beverages.

There are those who argue that wine consumption is good for you because studies have shown Europeans (particularly the French) have a *lower* incidence in heart disease than we do here in America, and they attribute this to the antioxidants in red wine.[1] However, the truth of the matter is that while France's heart disease incidence is lower than America's, it is *still the leading cause of death in France.* In addition, the French people have some of the highest incidences of pancreatic cancer, liver cancer, cirrhosis of the liver, and alcoholism in the world.[2] (Still, science does show that - *in moderation* - red wine is good for you.)

Their lower numbers of heart disease rates are more likely related to their generally superior diet. Despite their taste for rich foods occasionally, the French tend to eat more fruits and vegetables and fresh, whole-grain breads than Americans, who love their fast food. The French also use olive oil, not hydrogenated oils, and sugar is used sparingly.

Historically, the deleterious effects of undiluted wine led man to find other ways to achieve the same "high," and the various types of alcohol entered the scene. Alcohol has a devastating effect on nearly every major system in the human body – not to mention what it does to society. It kills brain cells, eats at stomach linings, inundates kidneys, attacks the pancreas, causes cirrhosis of the liver, slows motor reaction times, grossly deforms unborn babies, contributes to osteoporosis, releases clouds of cancer-causing free radicals, weakens the immune system, robs the body of vital nutrients, radically raises blood sugar levels, causes alcoholism, and helps trigger or worsen cancerous growths in the pancreas, liver, breast, bladder, and esophagus.[3] Even "social drinking" ought to lose most if not all of its appeal when you realize alcohol consumption has this many maladies and diseases associated with it. Enough said.

We Love Our Coffee!

Coffee is one of our favorite drinks – *Americans drink over 200 million cups daily!*[4] — but the question is, why? Did you really like the taste the first time you tasted it, or was it all that was available? Or did you like it because it helped you to wake up in the morning? We've all heard the jokes—"Don't talk to me in the morning until I've had my cup of coffee"—but the final punch line isn't very funny. The pharmacological effects of caffeine include increased stimulation of the brain, hormonal system, brain neurotransmitters, and adrenal glands. When the adrenal glands (the "fight or flight" mechanism in your body) are stimulated, glucose or blood sugar that is stored in the liver is released in mass quantities into the system. This is the "rush of energy" we feel when we are suddenly frightened, confronted with danger, or receive a strong dose of caffeine.

> *Excessive, or everyday moderate consumption of caffeine, can produce some very serious medical problems.*

According to the British medical journal *Lancet,* just five cups of coffee a day will increase a man's risk of heart disease by up to 50 percent.[5] This is alarming! Caffeine can aggravate premenstrual syndrome in women.[6]

A typical 8-ounce cup of coffee contains between 50-150 milligrams of caffeine. (Decaffeinated coffee contains approximately 3 milligrams, but the process to decaffeinate is known to be carcinogenic. Talk about a double-edged sword!) A cup of non-herbal tea contains 50 milligrams of caffeine, and a 12-ounce cola contains 35 milligrams. Excessive consumption of caffeine can produce severe symptoms similar to those found in generalized anxiety and panic disorders. Extreme symptoms such as depression, nervousness, heart palpitations, general irritability, recurrent headaches, and muscle twitching have led health professionals to coin the term "caffeinism" to describe this clinical syndrome. Studies have even shown that caffeine intake has been positively correlated with the degree of mental illness in psychiatric patients.[7] Additionally, a woman's risk of fibroid-tumor formation on breast tissue – fibrocystic disease – is increased.[8]

Although all of these problems happen with *excessive* caffeine consumption, it is best not to have caffeine products at all. However, since they are so difficult to avoid, at least consume them in moderation and avoid partaking on an everyday basis, which can cause your body to become addicted to the artificial levels of stimulation. Caffeine withdrawal is brutal, takes a long time, and is similar to ongoing migraine headaches until your body is totally purged of it. (The fact that there are "withdrawal symptoms" should verify its nature and accompanying danger.)

Although black and green tea have caffeine, they do have some redeeming benefits – working with vitamin C to strengthen blood vessel walls, inhibiting growth of dental plaque, helping to fight colds, and minimizing effects of radiation. Herbal teas are generally safe and enjoyable, but many contain medicinal properties, so knowledge and discernment are essential as to which ones you should drink on a regular basis. For example, peppermint tea can soothe mild stomach discomfort; chamomile can be very soothing for a mild headache or relaxing at the end of a long day.

Coca-Cola's Shocking History

What about soda? In Dr. Neil Barnard's book, *Breaking the Food Seduction*, he states that Coke was initially introduced in 1886. When it first came on the market *it actually contained cocaine* (*YIKES!*), which was soon replaced by caffeine. We love our Coke, as evidenced by the fact that we guzzle 50 million cans every day![9] You already understand the horrible (deadly) side effects of Nutrasweet, so I won't go there again regarding diet sodas. But let's address regular sodas, which also have many bad side effects.

Drinking five 12-ounce (or three 20-ounce) sodas puts *one pound of sugar in your system!* If this isn't bad enough news for you (after reading about sugar and its immune-suppressing and other negative effects), I will give you even more bad news: Sodas are extremely acidic. Remember, an acidic state is the perfect environment for disease to flourish. To effectively dilute the acid in one glass of soda, you would need to mix it with *32 glasses of water!*

In addition, an ionization process begins when you drink soda which robs your body of enormous quantities of oxygen. There is a simple way to prove this to yourself. A friend in Florida used this method to convince her teenager, who was also an athlete, to give up soda. She told him to time himself when he ran around the block one day. The next day, she had him drink a soda shortly before he ran, then had him time himself again. The results were obvious and dramatic: He could hardly make it around the block, his body was so starved of oxygen and gasping for air. Hopefully, Nutrasweet, sugar, acid, and oxygen problems should be sufficient to at least cause you to pause before having your next carbonated beverage, or at the very least to cut back your consumption.

Fruit and Vegetable Juices – Are Some Better Than Others?

Then there are fruit juices. What's the difference between juice drinks and juice? Juice drinks are a blend of water, sugar, and perhaps 10 percent real juice. Fruit juices are all real juice, either unsweetened or sweetened. Read the label carefully and select the unsweetened ones, choosing bottled over canned. Unsweetened frozen juice concentrates are also good choices. However, even real juices are refined foods because they have been extracted from the whole fruits. This removes the dietary fiber and concentrates the sugar, even though it is natural sugar. This doesn't mean you have to stop drinking them, but I would dilute them 50-50 or more with water, and not necessarily serve them daily.

Fresh fruit and vegetable juices are in a class by themselves because none of the enzymes or other nutrients have been destroyed. The enzymes die within about thirty minutes after the fruit/vegetable has been juiced, so drink it right when you make it. Fresh juices can be very beneficial in cleansing the system during a short fast of up to three days. But, again, the immediate rush of sugar (even natural sugar) is not particularly desirable as it is usually followed by a quick crash.

Kool-Aid is mainly artificial flavoring and food coloring. I have to confess that it is one of my husband's favorite drinks. While I could not convince him to give it up, I was able to get him to switch to honey or stevia as a sweetener, making it slightly less harmful and slightly more beneficial.

Another note regarding drinking beverages: Most nutritionists tell us not to drink water with meals because it dilutes the digestive juices in the stomach needed to digest food properly. Drink as much as you want thirty minutes before and thirty minutes after a meal, but do your best to drink very little with the meal, sipping instead of gulping or sloshing down your food with it.

The principle underlying our drink decisions is one of stewardship.
Whose body is it (see 1 Corinthians 6:19 if you aren't sure) and are we going to care for it properly?

Speaking of water, Americans love to drink almost everything but water—but it is making a comeback, thankfully. However, even the "simple" subject of water isn't so simple. Let's dive in and see what we need to learn about this important, life-giving fluid.

END NOTES

1.   K. Yano, "Coffee, Alcohol and Risk of Coronary Heart Disease Among Japanese Men Living in Hawaii," New England Journal of Medicine, 297 (1977):405, ed. Ted Broer, Maximum Energy (Lake Mary, Florida: Creation House, 1999), p. 212

2. Ted Broer, Maximum Energy (Lake Mary, Florida: Creation House, 1999), p.212

3. Ibid., p. 211

4. Emilie Barnes & Sue Gregg, The 15 Minute Meal Planner (Eugene, Oregon: Harvest House Publishers, 1994), p. 169

5. Ted Broer, Maximum Energy (Lake Mary, FL: Creation House, 1999), p. 188

6. Pamela M. Smith, Food for Life (Lake Mary, FL: Creation House, 1994), p. 188; ed Ted Broer, Maximum Energy (Lake Mary, FL: Creation House, 1999), p. 189

7. Ted Broer, Maximum Energy, (Lake Mary, FL: Creation House, 1999), p. 190

8. J. Milton, "Response of Fibrocystic Disease to Caffeine Withdrawal and Correlation of Cyclic Nucleotides with Breast Disease," *American Journal of Obstetrics and Gynecology*, 135 (1979): 157; ed Ted Broer, <u>Maximum Energy</u>, (Lake Mary, FL: Creation House, 1999), p. 190

9. Emilie Barnes, <u>The 15 Minute Meal Planner</u> (Eugene, Oregon: Harvest House Publishers), p. 169

Chapter 26

Water, Water Everywhere...
But Which One Should We Drink?

God's Health Potion

The subject of water seems like it should be the simplest one of all when researching nutrition. Surprise! The variables involved in choosing the right water are numerous, complex, and critically important when it comes to health. Pure water comes closer to being a genuine health potion than any other substance on our planet. Water transports oxygen to your body's cells, helps your body to digest and absorb nutrients, and gets rid of toxins and solid wastes. It lubricates your joints, keeps your skin moist and your organs from sticking together, and maintains proper balance inside and outside your cells.

It is a top priority to provide your body with an abundance of the purest water possible. Most health experts agree we should consume half our body weight in ounces of pure water every day. For example, if you weigh 150 pounds, you should drink at least 75 ounces of water daily. This is more than a half gallon and may seem like the impossible dream if you have not developed the habit of drinking water throughout the day. I had never been a water drinker until I became more conscious of my health and the choices of what I was putting into my body every day. I "taught" myself how to consume this much water on a daily basis by drinking 12 ounces of water as soon as I got up in the morning, then filling a half gallon container with pure water and leaving it on the kitchen counter (or taking it to work), knowing I had to finish that jug before the day was over.

Be forewarned: If you have not been drinking this amount of water and begin to consume what you should, you will be making a *lot* of trips to the bathroom in the beginning. This will change in short order, however, as your bladder begins to expand its capacity. Your trips to the bathroom will become less frequent and your body will begin to experience several improved conditions due to the extra water consumption, such as less stiffness in your joints and better, softer skin and hair to name just a couple.

Sixty-five percent of your body is composed of water; your muscles are 75 percent water. You can go without eating for weeks, but every cell of your body depends on water, and without it you would die in a matter of days. Not drinking enough water and/or drinking poisoned water causes premature aging and disease. Contaminated water contaminates the cells in the body, and they cannot reproduce in a healthy way. When the water supply is depleted of minerals (which it is), the food we eat is deficient in vitamin and mineral content.

Pure, clean, great-tasting water as God made it at the time of creation is a wonderful and essential part of good health – both for drinking and bathing. To find such water today would require traveling to distant lands and civilizations that are almost untouched by modern man and his accompanying pollutants. The question is: Is pure water available to the American consumer?

Our choices of water are many: Tap water from the municipal treatment plant, spring water, reverse-osmosis, and distilled. They all claim to be "pure." Should you buy water at the local grocery store, buy a device to purify water at home, or pay a water service to bring it to your home? Let's take a closer look.

Tap Water

Even though tap water has been treated, our present methods consist of filtering out only dangerous waste from *known sources* of contaminants. We have created more than 4 million chemical compounds in the last century, and our water treatment plants cannot recognize or get rid of any of them. For example, a survey of tap water reserves conducted in 954 U.S. cities revealed that 30 percent were contaminated with 17 kinds of very dangerous pesticides.[1]

Here's a point to ponder: The world's water supply today contains the same amount of water it contained at creation. The volume doesn't change; it simply recycles. This puts a tremendous burden of responsibility on "We, the People" to govern ourselves and our choices, both personally and corporately, in what we are dumping into our waterways. It is calculated that the chemical industry in America produces 60,000 highly toxic compounds that end up in the water supply. The government claims to enforce laws that prohibit the production of many of these substances. Sadly, it is well known that some small chemical plants are not effectively monitored and that some of the industry giants falsify reports and bribe federal agencies. When threatened, some of these companies cover their tracks by criminally disposing of the contaminants into rivers, sewer systems, lakes, and oceans. They manage to avoid sanctions, fines, etc., but at what cost to mankind? Water pollution is the environmental problem that plagues us the most.[2]

Industry giants are not the only problem to safe water. Large livestock farms are also polluting streams and creating public health risks. Incidents of storing uncovered piles of manure, stacked higher than a basketball hoop on outdoor cement slabs, with rainwater washing some of that waste into nearby rivers, have been documented. Water tests found ammonia levels downstream were four times greater than upstream.[3] Megafarms are also the reason the Illinois River in Oklahoma is turning bright green![4] YUCK!

And what about fluoride? Over half the U.S. population is drinking fluoridated water, believing it reduces cavities. If people really knew the effect fluoride has on the body, not one parent would want their children to brush their teeth with fluoridated toothpaste or drink water that contains fluoride. While touted to reduce tooth decay, the truth is that fluoride has been shown to reduce cavities by only one-half cavity per person, per lifetime. However, there is also irrefutable evidence linking fluoride to arthritis, cancer, heart disease, brittle bones, and hip fractures,[5] as well as deregulating our immune system.[6] So why in the world is it in so much of our drinking water? Lack of knowledge (on the part of consumers), irresponsibility or laziness (on the part of knowing consumers), and greed/profit on the part of the aluminum industry, which produced a true "toxic coup."

Historically, fluoride was the aluminum industry's most devastating pollutant. By 1938, hundreds of fluoride-damage suits were filed against the aluminum, iron, and steel manufacturers for poisoning crops, livestock, and humans. In 1939, Andrew Mellon, founder and major stockholder of Alcoa (Aluminum Company of America), hired scientist Gerald J. Cox to find a use for this dangerous yet plentiful byproduct. Cox fluoridated lab rats, concluded that fluoride reduced cavities, and declared flatly: "The case should be regarded as proved." So the first public proposal that America should fluoridate its water supplies was made, not by a doctor or dentist, but by an industry scientist working for a company threatened by fluoride-damage claims and looking for a place to unload tons of unwanted industrial waste.[7]

> My people are destroyed [die needlessly] for a lack of knowledge.
>
> Hosea 4:6 NKJV

God does not want us to be ignorant or "helpless victims" in any area of our lives. Christians have separated themselves from the environmental movement largely due to its liberal underpinnings. Rather than running from environmentalists, Christians need to *become environmental stewards!* Much like the alternative medical practices, it is time to wake up and smell the fluoride!

According to the Environmental Protection Agency (EPA), fluoride emissions into lakes, rivers, and oceans have been estimated to be as high as 500,000 tons a year,[8] in addition to the "legal" fluoridation of half our cities' water systems. Let's get educated and take dominion back. God made us stewards over this planet and our children. We need to learn the truth and stand up for it, regardless of what strange bedfellows we may find ourselves temporarily aligned with. We are allowing ourselves and our children to be poisoned by our lack of involvement. If neither common sense nor conscience is alive in the industrial world, it's time for the general public to hold them accountable with enforceable laws and fines for violations.

The principle is both stewardship of our property – the earth – and the power of unity – working with others to achieve what is right.

Then there are the issues of lead and parasites. Lead is no longer used in our water pipes, but it still bleeds into the water supply from old, outdated water mains. Waterborne parasites carry various diseases, including one that produces flu-like symptoms. In 1993 the water supply in Milwaukee, Wisconsin, became contaminated with a particular parasite (cryptosporidum), resulting in illness for tens of thousands of people, and 100 fatalities![9]

Additionally, our tap water is treated with chlorine to kill living organisms so we no longer have typhoid epidemics or disease outbreaks from our drinking water. The problem is that we forget that *we are a live organism* as well, and the chlorine, therefore, destroys our cells and friendly bacteria – our bodily defenses against disease - just as it does other organisms. Chlorine was used during World War II to gas people to death!

If chlorine is necessary to protect us from disease organisms (and it is), then what are we to do? We must *remove it* from our water before drinking or bathing. A simple carbon-based filter will accomplish this chlorine removal.

A whole house system is needed since it is not just the drinking water we are concerned with, but our bathing water as well. *Your body will absorb as many toxins in one hot shower as if you drank eight glasses of contaminated water![10]* This is why soaking in unfiltered, chlorinated hot tubs is a bad idea for anybody, and a horrible risk for people with heart problems![11] (Pool or hot tub water filters are available. I'll be discussing them shortly.) While a carbon-based filter will take care of chlorine, the most offensive and most common problem in tap water, it will *not* remove the *thousands* of chemicals dumped into the aquifer, nor does it touch the problem of fluoride.

I would venture a guess that by now, you have [wisely] eliminated the possibility of drinking or bathing in "treated" city tap water, as a potential "healthy choice." What about the other possibilities?

Spring Water

Spring water is probably the most popular of bottled waters partly due to the many brand names and varieties. One kind, "natural sparkling water," can contain carbon dioxide or "gas" which imparts a bubbly or sparkly texture. (Tonic, seltzer, and soda water are not classified as bottled water at all since their carbonated fizz is manmade.) Artesian water is collected from naturally occurring underground springs. Mineral water contains no less than 250 parts per million of total dissolved solids and can be either spring or artesian.

The spring water industry caught significant criticism in 1999 when the Natural Resources Defense Council, a well-known and respected environmental group, released a four-year study concluding that bottled water was not necessarily cleaner than what flows from our municipal pipes. They reported, "An estimated 25% or more of bottled water is really just tap water in a bottle – sometimes further treated, sometimes not."[12] Another study released in August 2001, commissioned by the World Wildlife Fund, found little difference in quality between tap and bottled water.[13]

Reverse Osmosis or Distilled

Reverse osmosis and distilled water are both good options, although caution is still warranted. If you buy distilled water from a store, it invariably comes in a plastic container. You will probably even be able to taste the plastic. This is because the water will absorb the plastic molecules, adding the "benefits" of plastic to your distilled water. It is probably possible to find a local supplier who will deliver steam-distilled water in glass containers.

Reverse osmosis, and to a lesser degree distillation, vitalizes the water. The process is similar to what happens in the atmosphere with the interaction of electrostatic charges and high oxygen content. In the wild, animals would rather drink moving, oxygenated water, even if it is muddy water in a ditch. In reverse osmosis, we are trying to emulate God's method of sending rain through the atmosphere.

Oxygen is what gives water its taste; minerals provide the aftertaste. The reverse osmosis process removes minerals from the water.

Interestingly, the minerals removed by the reverse osmosis process are needed by your body; however, they are generally too large for your cells to assimilate properly. Dr. T.C. McDaniel of The Golden Years Society, Inc., has found a solution to this dilemma. He has formulated an electrolyte solution that can be easily and inexpensively added to reverse osmosis water, thereby reintroducing the necessary minerals in the proper balance and in an absorbable form. His recipe is very effective in helping to achieve the proper acid/alkaline balance in your body as well as assisting with good blood circulation. For more information you can call his office at 513-761-3307.

Bottled distilled and reverse osmosis water sometimes has small amounts of chlorine added as an additional sanitizer or to extend the shelf life. Once again, be a wise consumer and do your homework. Investigate name brands of bottled water before you become a regular customer of any of them. The International Bottled Water Association (IBWA) has a contact list of many companies and a list of frequently asked questions on its website at www.bottledwater. org.

The "Best of the Best" Option

By now you understand that you have the choice to either "be a filter or buy a filter" for your water. My personal recommendation for the best tasting and safest water system is Essential Water & Air, a company that produces state-of-the-art air and water purification systems with the best cleansing features I've seen on the market today. Their four-stage reverse osmosis appliances effectively reduce metals, salts, fluoride, and large organic molecules, in addition to chlorine and other odor causing compounds. Even trace chemicals are removed, making this an ideal choice for well water, most of which contains farm chemicals (fertilizers, herbicides, and pesticides).

In addition, they offer pool (or hot tub) filters, shower filters, counter units, or a whole house system that removes or reduces chlorine, pesticides, herbicides, insecticides, and lead. This system includes new technology utilizing magnets, ultraviolet filtration, and four other media to *naturally soften* the water without adding salt. Saltwater softeners have significant drawbacks when it comes to your health. The salt used in salt softeners is absorbed through your skin, particularly when showering or bathing with hot water. The human body treats salt in this form as a toxin, unlike the sodium found naturally in fruits and vegetables.[14]

There are no known health detriments, only benefits, to Essential Water & Air filtration systems. For more information on these products, you can go online to www.ewater.com or call 800-964-4303. All of their products are backed by a six-month, unconditional, money-back guarantee.

One of the "side effects" of buying a good water system is a great increase in water consumption simply because it tastes so good. Do yourself and your family a favor and don't settle for anything less than the best when it comes to water. It is truly one of the best "prescriptions" you can give yourself and your loved ones. Water is God's elixir of life, the most basic need of every living person. Drink it pure and drink it often.

Environmental Stewardship

As stated earlier in this chapter, many are the woes and contaminants we face today in our environment. How can we begin to clean up this mess? When the evidence is investigated carefully it shows that free-market principles and private ownership of natural resources provide better stewardship of the environment than government controls ever have or ever could.

Many voices, conservative and liberal, have argued on behalf of the state as an environmental steward and created the expensive, expansive, and exasperating government department known as the Environmental Protection Agency (EPA). Their assumption is that the government will do the job better and more efficiently than the private sector. However, the federal government has proven itself to be demonstrably inferior to the private sector in many other areas, largely because it separates authority from responsibility. In other words, the incentives that drive the behavior of politicians and government officials are very different from those that operate in the sphere of private enterprise. The free-market system allocates costs directly to those making the choices while government decision-makers are largely immunized from the financial, managerial, and other negative consequences of their decisions. Why should we think stewardship of our natural resources would be any different? A few stories and a history lesson will clarify the merits of government versus private management of resources.

You may remember the disaster at Love Canal, the toxic waste dumping site in upstate New York that contaminated a large residential area. The Hooker Electrochemical Company began dumping waste into this abandoned canal in the early 1940s, *after carefully lining the canal with impermeable clay to ensure the chemicals never leaked out.* When the canal was filled it was sealed with a waterproof clay cap to prevent rainwater from washing the chemicals out. In the early 1950s, however, the local school board forced Hooker to sell the site to construct a new school.

In spite of Hooker's warnings of the dangers of the buried waste, including details of the chemical hazards that Hooker insisted be included in the transfer papers, the school board proceeded to build the school, scraping away part of the clay cap in the process to use as dirt for other construction sites. The government's wanton irresponsibility continued when, in the late 1950s and early 1960s, the city built a sewer line right through the property that punctured both the walls and cover of the waste container. As if this was not horrific enough, still later the state built an expressway through the site, creating even more punctures. As a final and ultimately deadly decision, the school board sold the southern part of the site – the area where most of the waste was concentrated—*for residential development!* Over and over the local and state government acted reprehensibly, ignoring repeated warnings from Hooker Electrochemical. Despite this, it was Hooker that received the blame when toxic contamination of residential water supplies forced entire neighborhoods to be evacuated in the late 1970s. The question is: Who was a better steward of this environmental problem – private owners or government? The answer is obvious and the outcome was lethal.

The Love Canal story is one of hundreds like it. Even with such instances of gross governmental incompetence in environmental issues, the notion persists that environmental regulation is a necessary evil. After all, we are told that water and air are not subject to the constraints of private ownership. Since we have no incentive to safeguard that which we do not own, regulation is needed to enforce a conservation ethic. This is not necessarily the case! There are free-market alternatives worth considering, the most compelling of which is to extend private property rights to air and water. Sound crazy? Consider a history lesson...

Up until around 1830 the courts had based decisions in "nuisance cases" – which we would today call environmental litigation – on a reasonably close approximation to a free enterprise legal system with effective liability laws. If a farmer could show that a railroad engine was spewing forth sparks and setting his haystacks on fire, he could collect damages. If the housekeeper complained that factory fumes were dirtying the clean laundry she hung on her clothesline, she would typically be granted a "cease and desist" order. Injunctions were invariably granted to downstream users victimized by upstream waste dumping. But in the 1850s and thereafter, a new philosophy began to infiltrate and permeate the legal fraternity. It was determined that the "public good" required economic progress. In the view of this new thinking order of judges, this could only be attained by supporting manufacturing. Property rights of the next victim of pollution gave way to the "greater good for the greater number," and market-oriented environmental incentives came to a halt.

Ironically, in our day the pendulum of legal opinion has swept to the other extreme with the "greater good" now being construed as a healthy environment which is partially defined as saving endangered species (including bugs) to the dismissal of property rights of large corporations and small landowners alike. Both extremes are lacking in wisdom and are counter-productive to individuals and society.

But how can the private sector possibly protect animals and habitats they know and care little about? Federally owned national parks, wildlife refuges, and wilderness areas abound. Are they not better equipped to manage such areas? Such thinking has produced not only a vast and expensive bureaucratic web, but also given us the Endangered Species Act, under which creatures ranging from the majestic whooping crane to inconsequential insects, minnows, and fairy shrimp now enjoy federal protection. It has also brought severe restrictions on private landowners who happen to harbor an endangered plant or animal on their property. These restrictions can range from government-created fire hazards, denial of access to, use of, or even confiscation of an individual's privately owned property. This is silly at its best and thievery at its worst.

The first major instance in the United States of an endangered species being rescued from extinction is, in fact, a saga of private initiative, not governmental intervention. In the 1870s, when the senseless slaughter of buffalo on public lands was taking place, six men – James McKay, Charles Alloway, Charles Goodnight, Walking Coyote, Frederic Dupree, and Charles Jones – began capturing and breeding buffalo. Nearly all plains buffalo today are descended from the private herds of these men, and it is estimated that roughly 90 percent of the 250,000 buffalo surviving today are in private herds.[15]

The Roney Ranch in central California is another excellent example. This is a commercial ranch located in a unique habitat dotted with "vernal pools," temporary ponds and puddles that support a unique array of flowers, grasses, and aquatic life (including several kinds of fairy shrimp). The Roneys use careful grazing practices to maintain the fragile environment while simultaneously running a successful, profitable, private ranching business.

There is also Deseret Land and Livestock, a private, for-profit corporation owned by the Mormon Church, located in northeastern Utah. The cattle on the ranch are moved frequently from one pasture to another, keeping overgrazing to a minimum. Large herds of elk and deer coexist with the cattle and are managed by controlled hunting. Cattle are kept off the best fawning areas during the appropriate season. As a result, the elk population has grown to the point that elk from the ranch have been transferred to public lands to replenish herds elsewhere.

Contrast this to a property owner in New Mexico who is being paid $2.5 million *not* to develop a 4,000-acre parcel of land as part of a government program to preserve natural areas and allow elk and other wildlife to roam freely.[16] You decide: Which is better stewardship of land and money?

*The principle of stewardship is one of **personal** responsibility to properly manage and care for **privately** owned property. It is not within the federal government's jurisdiction.*

Examples abound of private individuals and organizations who have taken steps to protect privately owned habitats. This is not to say that most landowners will set aside their land from development or create nature preserves, but one of the conditions of freedom is tolerance for differing priorities, preferences, and goals. While one man may be inclined to protect a tract of woodland for hunting or hiking, another may prefer to harvest all or part of the lumber and sell the land to a developer. Indeed, within the definition of property is seen both inherent rights and responsibilities:

property – The exclusive right of possessing, enjoying and disposing of a thing; ownership. In the beginning of the world, the Creator gave to man dominion over the earth, over the fish of the sea and the fowls of the air, and over every living thing. This is the foundation of man's *property* in the earth *and in all its productions.* Prior occupancy of land by wild animals gives to the possessor the *property* of them. (*Webster's 1828*)

With this understanding of property, there is no contradiction between free-market principles and protection of the environment. God gave dominion of the earth to man to *replenish it, not destroy it.*

...and God said to them, "Be fruitful and multiply and replenish the earth..."

Genesis 1:28 KJV

replenish – to fill; to stock with numbers or abundance.

If you own land, it is your responsibility to properly care for it and all the plants and animals thereon – to *replenish* it. You cannot replenish something you are abusing. Within the responsibility of replenishing is the privilege of using that property as the owner sees fit, not as the government allows. The evidence confirms that the incentives offered by private ownership are far more favorable to the health of the environment than are state controls. As is so often the case with human affairs, freedom is the best solution when we are willing to give it a chance.

END NOTES

1. Francisco Contreras, Health in the 21ˢᵗ Century, Will Doctors Survive? (Chula Vista, CA, Interpacific Press, 1997), p. 62-63.
2. Ibid., p.63-64
3. Mike Wagner, "Get big or Get out – Family farms are giving way to factory farms," Springfield News Sun, 1 December 02, sec. A, pp. 1 & 9.
4. Ibid.
5. Tonita d'Raye, What's the Big Deal about Water? (Keizer, Oregon: Awieca Inc., 1995), p. 9
6. Gary Young, "Essentially Yours," Young Living Essential News, September 2002, p. 2.
7. Joel Griffith, "Fluoride: Industry's Toxic Coup," Covert Action Quarterly, Fall, 1992
8. Ibid.
9. Tonita d'Raye, What's the Big Deal about Water? (Keizer, Oregon: Awieca Inc., 1995), p. 11
10. Fred Van Liew (interviewed by Ted Broer), "Water: Why you absorb as many toxins in one hot shower as if you had drunk 8 glasses of contaminated water," no. 8, tape in a series – "Forever Fit at 20, 30, 40 & Beyond, 1993.
11. Ibid.
12. Andrew Nelson, "Clearing the Waters - How to Pick a Bottled Water," Alternative Medicine, Issue 45, January 2002, p. 86.
13. Ibid.

14. Ted Broer, <u>Maximum Energy</u> (Lake Mary, Florida: Creation House, 1999), p. 29
15. Steve Bonta, "Environmental Stewardship," <u>The New American,</u> 25 September 2000, accessed on website <u>www. thenewamerican.com/tna/2000/09-25-2000/vol6no20_ environment.htm</u>, on 4/18/05.
16. David Wallechinsky, "Are Your Tax Dollars Being Wasted?" <u>Parade</u>, 6 November 2005, p. 5

PART SEVEN

HELP! I'M OVERWHELMED!

A Few Recommendations -
"The longest journey begins with a single step."

I call heaven and earth as witnesses today against you, that I have set before you life and death, blessing and cursing; therefore CHOOSE LIFE, that both you and your descendants may live. Deuteronomy 30:19

Chapter 27

Where Do I Begin?

Wow! You have read *so much* information, and for many of you it is probably overwhelming. It's all sound data, but where in the world do you start? First and foremost, *do not be discouraged*. Everyone has need for improvement in their lifestyle and habits. Life is a journey, not a destination; it is about continuously improving yourself. The most important thing is to *begin*. Take a step, a baby step. If you try to implement it all, you will burn out and probably give up. So begin slowly, but *do* begin.

> ...be doers of the word, and not hearers only, deceiving yourselves.
>
> James 1:22 NKJV

> ...he who is a doer...this one will be blessed in what he does.
>
> James 1:25 NKJV

I've heard that the definition of insanity is doing the same thing the same way and expecting different results. (This isn't *Webster's 1828*, but it sounds good!) If we want to improve ourselves and our family's health and well-being we must strive for the best. Average is the best of the worst and the worst of the best. Average is as close to the bottom as it is to the top. It is mediocre. We need to strive for the best, not settle for the mediocre.

If you keep doing things the same way, you will never get different results. Begin by doing something new.

To be "user friendly" I am going to list my personal recommendations by category:

- Shopping
- Dietary and personal habits
- Reading list

Please keep in mind that the most important recommendation is for *you* to research and make your own *personal* priority change list. The following recommendations are based on my research, my priorities, and my choices. Yours may vary. The important thing is to start.

Shopping Recommendations - Food

I've already mentioned the importance of buying organic, or at least fresh, produce. If you can't grow your own, a local farmer's market or roadside vendor is your next best choice. Even if the farmer's market and roadside stand are not selling organic produce, it is fresh and vine-ripened. Also, health food stores are no longer the only source of organic produce. Most grocery stores are now carrying a good selection of organically grown fruits and vegetables as well.

For meat and eggs, buy organic if you can, but since the cost is often prohibitive, seek out a local farmer or butcher shop. Though not organic, their eggs and meat will most likely be "free-range" and more likely to be hormone and antibiotic free. If a local farmer is not possible, keep after your local supermarket and butcher shop managers to stock these products. We *must* support the small farmer once again if we expect to "clean up" our meat supply, which would also be a big step toward cleaning up our water and air supply (due to methane levels and manure runoff into streams from the "factory farms").

Shopping Recommendations – Personal Care

Though not previously mentioned in this book, it is also very important to use personal hygiene items – shampoos, deodorants, toothpaste, lotions, soaps – that are chemical free. In hair products, two of the single most offensive ingredients to avoid are propylene glycol and sodium laurel sulfate. (Read the labels!) One is an engine degreaser, the other a main ingredient in antifreeze! Both are extremely potent chemicals that you don't want touching your skin, a porous organ these chemicals will pass right through, entering your body and over time creating all sorts of havoc. In toothpaste, look for one without fluoride, for reasons stated in Chapter 26 on water. Avoid antiperspirants, if at all possible. Sweating is cleansing and is a necessary body function. Deodorants should be free of any aluminum products as aluminum products have been linked to Alzheimer's disease (see Chapter 12 on vaccinations). *Read the labels!* You will probably have to buy these items from a health food store or buyer's co-op, but be sure to *read the labels* even there, as many of the products in these stores will not necessarily be free of the above ingredients. *Read the label!* Be a wise consumer.

Another excellent option for shopping is a health food co-op that delivers to your area. They are usually structured around a monthly group order of both grocery and personal hygiene items. By ordering in bulk from a co-op, your prices will probably be lower than a health food store, and you will have a greater variety to choose from since you are ordering from a catalog and warehouse instead of a store with limited shelf space. Co-ops are also a great source for experimentation with new healthy foods for you and your family. One that I am familiar with is www.naturalfarms.org. They have a huge selection. I am sure there are others. Go online to find one that delivers to your area.

Dietary and Personal Habit Changes

This list is long and, as stated previously, they are *my* choices and *my* priorities. Make this a personal challenge with *your* priorities and *your* choices. You know yourself and you know your family. Don't try to do it all in a day, but don't avoid it either. Pick out something and do it *today* and continue until it's a habit. Then pick another and another—become a new person from the inside out!

- Start drinking and bathing in purified water (www.ewater.com or 800-964-4303 for all contaminant removal)
- Start taking Juice Plus+® - a simple, sensible way to consume added nutrition from 17 different fruits, vegetables and grains - your best degenerative disease protection is *prevention* (www.juiceplus.com)
- Begin an exercise program, alternating aerobic one day, resistance training the next (www.healthmasters.com or 800-726-1834 or www.winsorpilates.com)
- Begin a personal detoxification program (for *deep* colon cleansing, call 800-877-0414 or go to www.DrNatura.com or go to www.NaturalHealingToday.com for reviews of top 10 colon cleansing products.
- Find and join a health food co-op (www.naturalfarms.org)
- Eat something living (raw fruits and/or vegetables) with every meal or snack
- Try a new fruit or vegetable once a week
- Use only canola or olive oil (cold pressed, extra virgin)
- Use butter or make "Better Butter" (see Chapter 20) – *stop* using margarine, white shortening, or other butter substitutes.
- Reduce refined sugar use
- Start using natural sweeteners – honey, Sucanat, agave, stevia, etc.
- *Stop eating/drinking anything with Nutrasweet and other artificial sweeteners!*
- Drink mainly purified water, some herbal teas, fruit and vegetable juices; reduce or eliminate soda, coffee, and black tea.
- Reduce or eliminate cow's milk; replace with soy, rice, or almond milk; reduce other dairy products.
- *Stop* (or greatly reduce) *eating sea scavengers* – lobster, clams, shrimp, scallops, oysters, etc.
- Eat free-range beef, chicken, and eggs (or organic)
- Reduce or eliminate pork products and processed meats

- Make a new, healthy recipe once a week
- Buy a grain mill to begin making your own whole grain products (ourdailybread@mcg.net))
- Consider replacing non-prescription drugs with essential oils (www.youngliving.com))
- *Continue your education* – read some of the books on "Suggested Reading List" (for detox, cooking, nutritional and environmental research, etc.), and others also.
- *Get involved in the political process with Christian stewardship principles to clean up the air and water.*
- Tell others what you know about vaccinations, drugs, etc.
- Work for insurance coverage on non-allopathic treatments.
- Recommend *this* book to others.

Recommended Reading List

This is by no means an exhaustive list but includes many of my favorite resources to give a well-rounded foundation for *total health* - in spiritual roots, detoxification, natural healing, meal preparation (with shopping and nutrition tips as well), and general nutrition and healthy environmental information:

Spiritual Roots	*An Integrated Approach to Biblical Healing Ministry*, by Chester and Betsy Kylstra (A guide to receiving healing and deliverance from past sins, hurts, ungodly mindsets, and demonic oppression.)
	A More Excellent Way – Be in Health, by Henry W. Wright (Spiritual roots of disease and pathways to wholeness explained.)
Detoxification	*Toxic Relief*, by Don Colbert, M.D. (Very reader friendly resource for "do-it-yourself" cleansing.)
	Fasting Can Save Your Life, by Herbert M. Shelton ("Nuts and bolts" of fasting plus individual case studies.)

Cleansing Made Simple, by Cheryl Townsley (Various modalities explained for various organs)

Tissue Cleansing Through Bowel Management, by Bernard Jensen (This one is a real eye opener and motivator for personal detox!) www.TrueNorthHealth.com (*Fantastic for the best fast possible.*) www.naturalhygienesociety.org (*List of health professionals who assist in fasting.*)

Ted Broer's Colon Detox Plan – www.healthmasters.com

Natural Healing   Website for functional medicine – www.functionalmedicine.org

Essential Oils Desk Reference, compiled by Essential Science Publishing - www.essentialscience.net (First choice and absolute necessity if you are going to begin using essential oils. A literal encyclopedia with everything you need to know to begin!)

Young Living website – www.young-living.com

Prescription for Nutritional Healing, by James S. and Phyllis Balch (Extensive use of various vitamins and minerals as treatments)

Cooking & Nutrition *The 15 Minute Meal Planner*, by Emilie Barnes (Fantastic, quick resource for nutritional information, as well as some great recipe and meal ideas.)

From the Kitchen of Two Sisters, by Danielle and Lindsay Voeller

(Personal favorite for variety, especially for *raw* recipe and salad ideas, in addition to snacks – written by a homeschool family!) *Visit their website – www.thetwosisters.com*

Maximum Energy Cookbook, by Sharon Broer (Shopping tips in addition to recipes.... excellent and user friendly)

Cooking for Life, by Gordon and Laura Tessler (Good general info as well as specific recipes.)

The Breadman's Healthy Bread Book, by George Burnett (Only buy this one if you plan to buy a flour mill....yummy!)

Website for mill information – www. ourdailybread.mcg.net

Natural food co-op www.naturalfarms. org

Concentrated whole food website – www. juiceplus.com

General Nutrition & Environment

From Here to Longevity, by Mitra Ray

Health in the 21st Century – Will Doctors Survive? by Francisco Contreras

Maximum Energy – Top Ten Foods Never to Eat; Top Ten Health   Strategies to Feel Great – by Ted Broer

The Genesis Diet, by Gordon S. Tessler

Lazy Person's Guide to Better Nutrition, by Gordon S. Tessler

Health Begins in Him, by Terry Dorian

Sugar Blues, by William Dufty

Purified water – www.ewater.com

A Biblical and Scientific Encouragement

Change begins in your mind. Consider the following encouragements from both scripture and the scientific world:

...put off, concerning your former conduct, the old man which grows corrupt according to the deceitful lusts, and *be renewed in the spirit of your mind.*

Ephesians 4:22-23 NKJV (emphasis added)

Whether you eat or drink or whatever you do, do all to the glory of God.

1 Corinthians 10:31NKJV

"We can't solve problems by using the same kind of thinking we used when we created them."

—Albert Einstein

Begin your changes today, and you will be a better, healthier person every day hereafter. The battle begins in your mind. You *can* make healthy changes. You *can* create a better tomorrow for yourself, your children, and your grandchildren. You *can*...but you must begin.

Chapter 28

Back to the Seven Principles

My Vision

You've read a lot and hopefully learned a lot. Don't let it end there. It's time to apply it!

> But be doers of the word, and not hearers only...
>
> James 1:14 NKJV

It excites me *greatly* to think about some of the changes that can take place in individuals' lives, their families, and even potentially this nation as you begin to put these principles into action, *because I have a vision!*

My vision is for men, women, and children – entire families – to learn the seven principles that lead to Christian liberty. My vision is that these individuals will learn how to apply these principles in every area of their lives. My vision is that their lives will so stand out in the crowd as to draw others to the principles as well. My vision is that individuals' personal changes will lead to corporate changes as they impact those around them

> Where there is no vision, the people perish, but he that keeps the law, happy is he.
>
> Proverbs 29:18 KJV

> Blessed is the man who walks not in the counsel of the
> ungodly, nor stands in the path of sinners, not sits in the seat
> of the scornful; but **his delight** is in the law of the Lord...
>
> Psalm 1:1-2 NKJV

We've looked at many commandments, laws, and statutes in our search of Scripture concerning food, health, and the environment. Don't ever let anyone accuse you of "legalism" because you desire to adhere to God's Word in regards to food or any other area of your life. According to the above passages (and others), keeping God's law brings happiness and blessing. We are to delight in the law, not call each other names for keeping it.

At this time, I would like to place my vision before you in the hopes that it will be contagious. Let's envision what acting out these principles will look like:

We began with Scripture and seven principles. Let's end there as well.

1 - SOVEREIGNTY

Everything about God is absolute, including His love and care for us. It is within the framework of that love that He told us what to eat and what *not* to eat. As you begin obeying His dietary laws, your health *will* improve. Fixing healthy meals and snacks for your family will do the same for them. Improved health translates into more energy to *do* that which God has called you to do—walking out your destiny!

The key thought for sovereignty is:

God's Word is the final authority on what to eat, not your
taste buds!

2 - INDIVIDUALITY

God created you as a distinct, unique individual in every way, including the destiny He planned for you. He wants what is good for you. He wants you to live a long, healthy life so that you can accomplish your calling and go home to Him victoriously, having *finished the race He set before you*, not having to drop out of that race prematurely because of illness and early death. To walk fully in your talents and abilities, you must be healthy. This requires proper care of the body He entrusted to you, including eating, drinking, and exercising. As we begin walking out our individual callings, the *church* will be blessed because the *body of Christ* will begin to become a *healthy body*, with more of us actively *doing* the role to which God called us.

The key thought for individuality is:

Eat to live – don't live to eat

3 - GOVERNMENT

Government begins with self and then extends to family, church, and community. As more members of the body of Christ begin to walk in and work out their individual callings, these works will spill over into our communities, creating wonderful transformations. One example: "Smart Lunches" was born because of nutrition-conscious parents. A high school in Appleton, Wisconsin, traded in their soda vending machines for ones with juice, water, and energy drinks. The cafeteria contract was awarded to Natural Ovens and Bakery, a local company who offered fresh fruits, vegetables, whole grain breads, and entrees free of additives and chemicals. The outcome was astounding. Discipline statistics plummeted: zero weapons, zero expulsions, zero premature deaths or suicides, zero drugs or alcohol, and students concentrating for longer periods in the class-room.[1] When such changes occur, others are being affected positively by your obedience.

The key thought for government is:

Good self-government leads to improved civil government.
Get involved!

4 - PROPERTY (STEWARDSHIP)

Ultimately, your body belongs to God, who gave you steward-ship over it. When that stewardship involves wise choices regarding food and exercise, health and energy are natural byproducts. Less time and money spent in the doctor's office and hospital allows more time and money to be spent on family, church, and community. Wise choices in nutrition translate to *prevention*, much better than treatment or even early detection! Approximately one-seventh of the U.S. economy - **$1.4 trillion!** – is devoted to sickness.[2] As more and more individuals focus on prevention, some of these medical dollars will be freed to go to better places in our economy. Our positive, individual, healthy actions can begin to penetrate and permeate society.

The key thought for stewardship or property is:

Nothing tastes as good as healthy feels.

5 - CHRISTIAN CHARACTER

Part of the definition of character is "peculiar qualities or habits which distinguish one from another." Eating properly will truly be seen today as "peculiar" in many places, including the church fellowship hall! Without being legalistic, you can be "peculiar," and others will begin to notice what food you bring to share, what you put on your plate, and what you don't put on your plate. Opportunities will arise to share how your improved health enables you to do more for God and your family.

Reality dictates there will be times when you mess up or make wrong choices. Don't beat up on yourself for mistakes, past or current! Remember, God is looking for *diligent [steady application] obedience, not perfection.* You don't have to eat right 100 percent of the time. Your new habits are not meant to be a dietary prison; they are intended to set you free to serve others. Indulging in an *occasional* hot fudge sundae or other treat is not a problem. Dr. Pam Popper, nutritionist and author, has a 90/10 rule. If you eat right 90 percent of the time, you are able to sustain any damages that will come from the other 10 percent.

The key thought for Christian character is:

Your character is the trait that will enable you to start over again, even when you mess up.

6 – SOWING AND REAPING (EDUCATION)

The fields of health, nutrition, clean air and water, exercise, and alternative medicine are all areas of information that are bursting at the seams with new discoveries daily. It is imperative that you continue to educate yourself and stay informed for your benefit, your family's, and those around you. New findings need to be investigated and held up to the biblical principles you have learned in this book. Time and circumstances may change, but principles are timeless and therefore are your best measuring rod for discerning what is good or not in any and all arenas. Encourage your children's natural curiosity while simultaneously teaching them to learn to discern and make wise choices. No one can escape reaping what they sow in any field – environment, diet, or lifestyle. Your decision today does effect future generations.

The key thought for sowing and reaping is:

Remember the Pottenger cat study and sow to the future generations!

7 - UNITY AND UNION (COVENANT)

This principle truly is the capstone of them all and the one that excites me the most. It is where societies begin to change. "No man is an island." As you make personal changes, others' lives are impacted for better or worse depending on those changes. The principle and strength of unity are described in Scripture:

Though one may be overpowered by another, two can withstand him. And a threefold cord is not quickly broken.
Ecclesiastes 4:12 NKJV

As we walk out these principles, we can begin to effect changes in ourselves, our children, our churches, our schools, and even our civil government. We need unity and union, a *group* effort, to clean up our water and air, to end mandatory vaccinations, to abolish legislation that limits our choices in medical care and insurance coverage, to name just a few. Armed with truth and principles, you can join forces with like-minded individuals and begin to take on the

"Goliath" of your choosing to make this world a healthier place for your children and grandchildren.

God is our most important covenant partner. David took out Goliath with God's help, but even after Goliath was dead, there remained a Philistine army. David also needed to be backed up by (*in unity with*) his own army of like-minded warriors in order to continue in the battle after the giant was dead. The cost of liberty is eternal vigilance!

The key thought for unity and union (covenant) is:

There are many "Goliaths" to be conquered in this nation regarding health and environment, and there is strength in numbers! "We the people" do have the power when we are united behind a purpose.

Final Admonition and Encouragement

God is our covenant partner in all good things. As we internalize and practice the principles of nutrition and a healthy lifestyle, we will indeed enter into the blessings of the union of our mind, will, affections, and interests being one with His. With this unity comes power from above to execute whatever we are called to do, individually or corporately. God loves you! Actively seek to work out your destiny. Enter into covenant agreement with Him. You *and* future generations will be blessed.

> I call heaven and earth as witnesses today against you, that I have set before you life and death, blessing and cursing; therefore *choose life*, that both you and your descendants may live.
>
> Deuteronomy 30:19 (emphasis added)

Many people view this verse as God giving us a choice to follow His ways or not. I don't see it that way. He clearly has set two paths before us, but He has also clearly *commanded* us as to which road we are to take – CHOOSE LIFE!

God's warning and admonition to choose life includes a *generational blessing or curse*. We have the power to break the curse of premature death by disease by *choosing life* – as God commands in the above passage. We must do this both individually—with proper lifestyle choices—and corporately, by working diligently with others on important health issues of this nation. Obedience to the above verse includes a *generational blessing*. Truly, the best gift you can give to your children is health – yours and theirs. Begin today!

> "...I know what I have planned for you," says the Lord. "I have good plans for you. I don't plan to hurt you. I plan to give you hope and a good future."
>
> Jeremiah 29:11 NCV

END NOTES

1. Smart Lunches? – Students Behave Better with Healthy Lunches," ABCNEWS.com, 22 January 2003
2. Paul Zane Pilzer, The Next Trillion (VideoPlus, Inc., 2001)

****

To invite Ricki Pepin to hold a health seminar at your church or town you may contact her at:

Ricki Pepin
2000 S. Tecumseh Road
Springfield, Ohio 45502
937-290-6573
ricki@pepin.com

Printed in the United States
208484BV00002B/100-1176/P

9 781602 666986